# THE PLAINTIFF'S PERSONAL INJURY CASE: ITS PREPARATION, TRIAL AND SETTLEMENT

# THE PLAINTIFF'S PERSONAL INJURY CASE: ITS PREPARATION, TRIAL AND SETTLEMENT

John A. DeMay

PRENTICE-HALL, INC.

ENGLEWOOD CLIFFS, NEW JERSEY

Prentice-Hall International, Inc., *London*
Prentice-Hall of Australia, Pty. Ltd., *Sydney*
Prentice-Hall of Canada, Ltd., *Toronto*
Prentice-Hall of India Private Ltd., *New Delhi*
Prentice-Hall of Japan, Inc., *Tokyo*
Prentice-Hall of Southeast Asia Pte. Ltd., *Singapore*
Whitehall Books, Ltd., *Wellington, New Zealand*

Fourth Printing . . . . . December, 1980

"This publication is designed to provide accurate and authoritative information in regard to the subject matter covered. It is sold with the understanding that the publisher is not engaged in rendering legal, accounting, or other professional service. If legal advice or other expert assistance is required, the services of a competent professional person should be sought."

—From the Declaration of Principles jointly adopted by a Committee of the American Bar Association and a Committee of Publishers and Associations.

Library of Congress Cataloging in Publication Data

DeMay, John
    The plaintiff's personal injury case.

    Includes index.
    1.  Trial practice--United States.  2.  Personal injuries--United States.  I.  Title.
KF8925.P4D44                346'.73'032                76-54347
ISBN 0-13-679357-6

Printed in the United States of America

# A Word from the Author

This book is directed to every attorney who represents a plaintiff in a personal injury action.

For the practitioner who only occasionally gets such a case there is a great deal of essential information relating to the details associated with the preparation of a case, some suggestions regarding the trial of that lawsuit, and of great importance, how to properly settle the cases he has or will get as a result of successful trials. It is my hope that this will be a standard desk reference for the lawyer handling a personal injury claim.

For the experienced plaintiff's lawyer there is much that can be relearned by way of review. Such review is always needed. For example, just a few years ago a very great trial lawyer somehow managed to sue the wrong defendant in a multi-car collision and then compounded the error by letting the Statute of Limitations expire as to the correct defendant. As he often wryly commented, "It took a hell of a lot of skill to make those kinds of mistakes." Actually he had simply violated some fundamental rules of preparation—rules that he properly demanded everyone else comply with. A similar incident occurred in a medical malpractice case filed against one of the leading orthopedic surgeons in Western Pennsylvania. He had examined a woman for a few minutes, diagnosed a herniated lumbar disc, operated without the benefit of a myelogram and, to his chagrin and financial embarrassment, found that there was no herniated disc. She did have problems but he had missed the diagnosis entirely! The lady went to another doctor—a neurosurgeon—who eventually corrected the condition; and I asked him how in the world the orthopedist, with all of his magnificent skill, could have made such a mistake. His succinct answer: "The ignorance of experience."

There is such a thing as knowing too much. We become careless, we cut corners; in truth, we get lazy. This book will clear out the cobwebs

5

and help the experienced practitioner remember, remember, remember—
and should induce him to recheck his procedures and practices to insure
that his cases are being properly processed.

The book contains three major sections dealing with preparation,
trial and settlement. Trial preparation is hard work, immediately
unrewarding, colorless, and necessary. Many lawyers yearn to skip this step
and to leap immediately into trial. Yet, there is no contest, at least no good
contest, unless the plaintiff's lawyer has first gone through the interviewing
of the client at length, directed the investigation, decided on the
photographs he wants, taken the depositions, ordered the hospital records,
collected the bills, talked to the doctors and done all of the key things that
go into the preparation of a case for trial. It is hard, laborious work
requiring both stamina and imagination. And so, in Part I there are several
chapters dealing, step-by-step, with each of the tasks mentioned above.
Remember that you can win a case on the basis of a deposition, and lose a
case if you neglect to talk to your witnesses before trial.

The trial of a lawsuit is pure art and every expert in this field has
his own unique and inimitable way of proceeding. For one, cross-
examination is the key to success; to another, the closing address; but in
every case, each person must go through the task of immediate pretrial
preparation, must make an opening statement, present one's case-in-chief,
cross-examine defense witnesses, and make a closing address. My own
views, observations and recommendations on handling each of these phases
of a trial are set out in separate chapters. In addition, I have felt it appropriate to include a chapter dealing with Trial Memoranda, Briefs on
anticipated evidentiary or substantive law problems and Points for
Charge.

Finally, a considerable portion of this book is devoted to Settlement. The sad fact is that most lawyers are very poor at settlement and
pay little attention to the details involved in effecting a good settlement.
They either use the "seat of the pants" approach, make an exorbitant
demand, and thus close the door to settlement or they adopt the attitude of
"take what I can get" and settle too low. Comparatively very little has been
written on the subject. This is a surprise and a shame, for, after
preparation, settlement should be the most time-consuming part of the
plaintiff-lawyer's practice and certainly should be the most pleasant part of
his work. It's normal for every lawyer to love a trial—especially if vic-
torious. Trial brings glory; settlement pays the bills. It behooves us,
therefore, to give considerable time and attention to the subject. Separate
chapters discuss the various problems relating to the insurance company
one deals with, the necessity of knowing the members of the claim
department, gathering and submitting pertinent data, how to handle your

client (perhaps the hardest job of all), arriving at the proper "area of settlement" (*Note:* I did *not* say "the proper figure"), when a case should be settled and how to negotiate the settlement. Each is a worthy subject for discussion. Essentially, it is your understanding of your case, the personalities of the people you deal with, and your negotiating acumen that can lead you and your client happily to the bank.

This is a book, then, whose goal is to help you prepare a case thoroughly, to suggest scores of tested and reliable ideas about the manner in which your case should be tried, and which will go into detail about the manner in which you can arrive at a settlement that will be a source of pride to you and a source of satisfaction to your client.

*John A. DeMay*

# ABOUT THE AUTHOR

John A. DeMay is in private practice as a trial lawyer in Pittsburgh, Pennsylvania. Since 1957, he has devoted himself exclusively to representing the Plaintiff's case, particularly in personal injury actions. A graduate of the University of Pittsburgh Law School, Order of the Coif, he was admitted to the Bar in 1953. He is a former Assistant United States Attorney for the Western District of Pennsylvania and is admitted to practice before the U.S. Supreme Court, the U.S. Court of Appeals, 2nd & 3rd Circuits, the U.S. District Court, Western Pennsylvania, and all Pennsylvania State Courts. He is a member of the American Bar Association, Pennsylvania Bar Association, Allegheny County Bar Association, the Association of Trial Lawyers of America, the American Judicature Society, the Pittsburgh Institute of Legal Medicine, and the Academy of Trial Lawyers of Allegheny County.

# CONTENTS

# PART I
# Preparation of the Case

# CHAPTER 1

# The First Meeting with the Client

It is surprising how little attention most attorneys give to the initial interview with the client. They are anxious to impress him with their personality and their competence, but far too often they listen only briefly to the client's story and the notes they make are the bare minimum needed to enable them to begin to work on the case. There is no good reason for this attitude. The client is entitled to an appointment that will give him sufficient time to acquaint the attorney with all of the facts he knows.

## TAKE THE TIME TO LISTEN

When the client comes into your office he or she has a story to tell. Often it won't be told in the short, direct, concise manner that you would like—the client will ramble, he will talk about Uncle Joe and Cousin Jane who have nothing to do with the case, he will confuse street names and forget dates. He doesn't know medical terms and talks too much about his pain and inconvenience. Be patient and let him talk. Leave your pencil on the desk—you can take notes later. This is your opportunity to listen to his story told in his way and to appraise him as a person. Watch the way he is dressed and the way he talks. Peculiar mannerisms become apparent and they may have to be dealt with at a later date. As you are watching him don't forget that he is appraising you. He is looking for sympathy, understanding and an analysis of what he thinks to be a legitimate claim. Listen to the man—that's why he came to you.

It is at this point that you have the duty to analyze the facts that he has given you and to express an opinion about the merits of his case. If he doesn't have a case, tell him now, but be pleasant and gentle about it. Explain the law to him and point out wherein his case is deficient. With a bit of wit and good humor you can point out that the Law, as fine as it is, simply doesn't have the solution to all of mankind's problems. It never will. Try to see to it that if the client must leave disappointed, let him not leave antagonistic to you or the "System."

## THE CLIENT DOESN'T KNOW ALL THE FACTS

It should come as a surprise to no one that frequently a client does not know all of the facts of a matter. This can be due to shock, ignorance or forgetfulness. Keep this in mind at all times. Aren't we all familiar with the psychology class that is rudely interrupted by two men rushing into the classroom, shouting, cursing and fighting and then rushing back out of the room? The students are shocked and upset—some may rush to assist one of the men, others leave the room for safety or to seek help. When the excitement is over and the class has settled down, the teacher asks each student to write a report on what he saw, heard and did. If there are thirty students in the class he gets thirty different reports! The same thing applies to your client. If he was involved in an automobile accident, he may have been in such a state of shock that he can't tell you how far back from the intersection a "stop sign" was located, or whether the car approaching him was dark blue or black. If his is a medical malpractice case, he may have been unconscious when the negligence occurred or, even if conscious, he won't know the medication he was given or why certain tests were ordered. If the incident involved an expert such as a contractor, architect or mechanic then, almost by definition, your client doesn't know what went wrong and why. Don't forget this as you listen to his tale of woe. This is why you have investigators and experts of your own.

## COMPLETE A DETAILED QUESTIONNAIRE

After you have heard your client's story in detail and have questioned him to the extent appropriate, it is time to start writing. At this point I suggest that you not try to write everything down in narrative fashion. To begin with that will lead to sloppy workmanship. You will have the phone number on page two of your notes, the date of birth somewhere else, and the list of attending physicians interspersed with the width of the street, weather conditions or the names of witnesses. Every time I have a case referred to me I groan because never, never does the referring attorney use a detailed questionnaire. I get scribbles and notes on envelopes or legal pads (both long and short) and the writing itself is often undecipherable. I'm lucky if a telephone number is included so that I can call the client to come to my office. Do yourself a favor. In the name of simplicity, orderliness and detail prepare a good questionnaire, make plenty of copies on your duplicating machine and use it! Such a questionnaire, which has served me well for years, is illustrated by Exhibit 1-1. It's not perfect, but it's adequate. Look at it for a moment. The first section contains biographical data concerning the client. It contains a place for a photograph in the event you want to refresh your memory after not having seen your client for a long period of time—especially if you have many clients. The second section deals with his employment record. Section three relates to his medical history. Miscellaneous expenses are separately listed. Then come two pages dealing with the accident; the first addresses itself to necessary data and the second allows for a brief narrative statement and a sketch. After you have listened to your client's story so that you know what is relevant and what is not, you should be able to fill out this questionnaire in twenty to thirty minutes. Believe me, that is time well spent. In one simple document you have all of the significant facts that you will be referring to time and again until it is ragged from use. Keep it in the front of your file so that it is always accessible.

## AN ALTERNATIVE: TAPE-RECORD THE INTERVIEW

Some attorneys have begun the practice of tape-recording the initial interview. This is a good idea as you will have a permanent record of precisely what the client told you. You can go into more detail while talking than you usually will by writing, and it is an easier technique. The only drawback is the fact that some clients tend to become suspicious and to "tighten-up" in the presence of a tape recorder and the conversation becomes a little formal. In addition, if there are two or more people with you there is the danger of several people speaking at once which may make the tape unintelligible. However, you can control that with a few "stage directions." After the interview the conversation can be transcribed and sent to the client for any additions or corrections he deems necessary.

This is a good technique and the only criterion for its use is whether it fits in with your way of doing things. Certainly the cost is minimal.

# CASE
# QUESTIONNAIRE

| Atty Assigned | THE CLIENT | Type of Case |
|---|---|---|

| | |
|---|---|
| 1. Name | |
| 2. Address | |
| 3. City — State | |
| 4. Phone Area Code: | 5. 2nd Phone Area Code: |
| 6. Age | 7. Birthdate | 8. Birthplace |
| 9. Parents | |

**ATTACH PHOTO of CLIENT**

| 10. Marital Status | ☐ Married | ☐ Divorced ☐ Separated | ☐ Widow ☐ Widower | 11. If Single Give Name-Address of Nearest Relative ☐ Single |
|---|---|---|---|---|

12. Spouse and Dependents (Names-Ages-Birthdates)

### EMPLOYMENT

| 13. Present Employer (Name-Address-Division) | | |
|---|---|---|
| 14. Date Hired (Month-Year) | 15. Job Classification | 16. Salary (Basic-Monthly or Yearly) |
| 17. Previous Year's Earnings | 18. Average Annual Earnings past 4 Years | |

18. Average Annual Earnings past 4 Years
1.)19 _____ Am't _____    3.)19 _____ Am't. _____
2.)19 _____ Am't. _____   4.)19 _____ Am't. _____

| 19. Dates Absence From Work | 20. Absence Continuing ☐ Yes ☐ No | 21. Total Wage Loss to Date |
|---|---|---|

22. Previous Employment

| Employer | Address | Duties | Rate of Pay |
|---|---|---|---|

**EXHIBIT 1-1**

## MEDICAL

**23. Injuries (General Description)**

**24. Is Disability Continuing (Describe)**

**25. Hospitals**

| Name | Address | Dates of Confinement | Bill |
|---|---|---|---|
| | | | |
| | | | |
| | | | |

**26. Doctors**

| Name | Address | Dates Treated | Bill |
|---|---|---|---|
| | | | |
| | | | |
| | | | |
| | | | |

**27. Previous Injuries (Include Dates)**

**28. Previous Hospitalizations (Include Dates)**

| 29. Previous Litigation | 30. Reason | 31. Attorney |
|---|---|---|
| | | |

## EXPENSES

**32. Property Damage (Description-Amount)**

**33. Out-of-Pocket Expenses (Does Not Include Doc.-Hosp.)**

| ITEM | BILL |
|---|---|
| | |
| | |
| | |
| | |

**34. Are Expenses Continuing**

☐ Yes    ☐ No

Total Exps. to Date: _____

**EXHIBIT 1-1 (continued)**

THE ACCIDENT

| 35. Date—Time | 36. Day | 37. Location (List Boro, Township, City, County, State) | | |
|---|---|---|---|---|
| 38. Weather | | | | |
| 39. Police | 40. Police at Scene ☐ Yes ☐ No | 41. Did Police Make Report ☐ Yes ☐ No | 42. Favorable To Client ☐ Yes ☐ No | |
| 43. Clients Vehicle | | | 44. Photos of Client's Veh. ☐ Yes ☐ No | |

45. Other Vehicles (Also Identify Operators)

46. Names of All Passengers

| Name | Address | Vehicle |
|---|---|---|
| | | |
| | | |
| | | |
| | | |
| | | |

47. Witnesses

| Name | Address |
|---|---|
| | |
| | |
| | |
| | |
| | |

| 48. Client's Insurance Carrier | 49. Any Claims Filed Against Client (Inc. Police) ☐ Yes ☐ No   By Whom: |
|---|---|

THE DEFENDANT

| 50. Name | 51. Address |
|---|---|
| 52. Vehicle | |
| 53. Occupation | 54. Employer |
| 55. Insured ☐ Yes ☐ No | 56. Insurance Carrier |

57. Other Significant Facts

**EXHIBIT 1-1 ( continued)**

### THE ACCIDENT (cont'd.)

58. Client's Description of Accident

59. Draw Brief Sketch

This Case Referred By:

### RECOMMENDATIONS

60. Should Counsel Commence Immediate Investigation

☐ Yes  ☐ No

61. Type of Investigation

☐ Exhaustive ☐ Routine ☐ Limited ☐ Discuss with Inv.

62. Reasons For Above Recommendations

63. This Case Questionnaire Prepared By

Name:                    Date:              Where:

**EXHIBIT 1-1 ( continued)**

## HAVE NECESSARY FORMS SIGNED NOW

Don't let your client leave without signing all of the forms that you will need in the processing of his case. These forms should include a Power of Attorney, authorizations to secure doctors' reports, hospital records, employment records and tax returns. An example of each is shown in Exhibits 1-2 through Exhibits 1-6. You will note that on the Power of Attorney there is a short paragraph about the costs of the case. Many attorneys do not like it and do not use it. They feel that it stirs up needless concern in a client about how much these costs will amount to and how they are going to be paid. My opinion is that this is the ideal moment to discuss those very problems. The client has a right to know that he is going to have to pay the costs and is entitled to a reasonable estimate from you of the amount of those costs. Sooner or later you are going to have to face the problem and I think it might as well be done at the beginning of this new attorney-client relationship. In this way hard feelings and cries that "You never told me"—and "You should not have allowed the costs to get so high" are easily avoided.

Returning to the authorization forms, you should have some of them notarized. Hospitals nearly always demand it as do some employers. Ordinarily doctors do not require it nor does the Internal Revenue Service. Local practice and custom will control here.

Finally, be certain to have extra copies of each form signed by the client. It is both time-consuming and annoying to run out of these forms and have to mail off more of them for signature. This is just one more area in which a little advance planning can save a few pennies in time and effort.

## EXHIBIT 1-2

### POWER OF ATTORNEY

KNOW ALL MEN BY THESE PRESENTS, That

do hereby appoint JOHN A. DeMay, to be　　　　Attorney to represent　　in a claim for damages　　have against

resulting from personal injuries sustained by　　on or about the　　day of　　, 19

And as his fee in this matter,　　hereby agree that the said JOHN A. DeMAY, shall retain　　percent of the sum collected by settlement or verdict of Court.

I understand that the expenses of litigation, such as Court costs not payable by the Defendant, expert witness fees, photographs, hospital and medical records, and investigation are my responsibility and I agree to make payment of these expenses promptly or in the alternative, I agree to reimburse JOHN A. DeMAY, for any expenses of litigation advanced by him as a matter of convenience.

IN WITNESS WHEREOF,　　have hereunto set hand (s) and seal (s) this　　day of 19

　　　　　　　　　　　　　　　　　　　　　(SEAL)

Witness

　　　　　　　　　　　　　　　　　　　　　(SEAL)

Witness

## EXHIBIT 1-3

### AUTHORIZATION FOR EXAMINATION OF DOCTOR'S RECORDS

To:

This is your authorization to permit JOHN A. DeMAY, ATTORNEY, or his designated representative, to examine and make copies of your records in connection with the treatment of

WITNESS:

Date:

## EXHIBIT 1-4

### AUTHORIZATION FOR EXAMINATION OF
### HOSPITAL RECORDS

TO:

(Hospital)

(Address)

Authority is hereby given to the bearer, a representative of JOHN A. DeMAY, ESQ., to examine and make copies, or have copies furnished of all records and charts including x-rays, in connection with the confinement and/or treatment of
who was a patient in your hospital between                    and


WITNESS:

(Date)

## EXHIBIT 1-5

### AUTHORIZATION FOR EXAMINATION OF
### EMPLOYMENT RECORDS.

TO:

THIS is your authority to permit, JOHN A. DeMAY, Esquire, or his representative to see my employment records, to make copies thereof, and to give him any information in regard to my employment which he may desire.

Witness

Date


COMMONWEALTH OF PENNSYLVANIA :

                                       : ss:

    COUNTY OF ALLEGHENY    :

personally subscribed and acknowledged before me this
day of                    , 19         , to be the true and correct signature of the above named party.


Notary Public

My Commission Expires:

FORM **4506**
(12-68)

DEPARTMENT OF THE TREASURY - INTERNAL REVENUE SERVICE

## REQUEST FOR COPY OF TAX RETURN

*(Prepare a separate form for each request)*

NAME AND ADDRESS OF TAXPAYER(S) AS SHOWN ON RETURN:

| SOCIAL SECURITY OR EMPLOYER IDENTIFICATION NUMBER | DOCUMENT LOCATOR NUMBER *(If known)* |
| --- | --- |
| KIND OF TAX *(Income, Estate, Excise, Gift, etc.)* | TAX PERIOD |
| TAX FORM NUMBER | INTERNAL REVENUE OFFICE WHERE RETURN WAS FILED |
| PHOTOCOPIES *(Number Desired)* | CERTIFICATIONS *(Number Desired)* |

MAIL PHOTOCOPIES TO:

THE INTERNAL REVENUE SERVICE WILL ENCLOSE A BILL WITH THE ITEM(S) SENT TO YOU.

I agree to pay the Internal Revenue Service for the reproductions noted above, at the following rates:

● The basic rate for reproduction of a tax return or other document is $1 per page. The cost per page increases in multiples of 50¢ for pages substantially larger than an 8½" X 11" tax return.

● The cost of certification (confirmation that the reproduction is a true and correct copy) is $1.

_____
*Signature of Taxpayer (or requester)*

_____
*Date*

Please enclose a certified copy of your authorization to receive this material if you are not the taxpayer.

GPO : 1969 O - 108-123

FORM **4506** (12-68)

## EXHIBIT 1-6

## DISCUSS THE APPLICABLE LAW WITH THE CLIENT

It is very appropriate at this stage to tell your client about the law that applies to his claim. The chances are that he is quite ignorant of the law and he should be apprised, in a general sense, of the rules that will determine success or failure in his case. Isn't this a part of the "Informed Consent" doctrine and aren't attorneys bound by that doctrine as much as doctors? Be sure to discuss questions of negligence, contributory negligence or assumption of risk, evidentiary rules, problems of proof, and whether the case should be filed with a demand for a jury trial or whether it should be heard by a judge alone. These are the things the client is interested in learning and which he should know so that he can help you make some of the decisions in the case—and by all means let him help to make some of those decisions. It is his case not yours and, therefore, he ought to be consulted about some of the basic policies that you think ought to be adopted. For example, you might be able to file the lawsuit in one of several localities, in state court or federal court. Since the client pays the bills, either now or at the end of the case, he ought to be consulted about that matter. The choice of forum might make quite a difference in the expenses involved. In like manner if you think the case ought to be filed non-jury, tell your client about the whys and wherefores of the matter and let him help make the decision. Incidentally, given the average client's desire for a jury trial, if you and he decide to proceed before a judge alone, make sure you get a written authorization from him to go ahead in this manner. This will avoid some nasty recriminations later should the result be an unhappy one.

This is also a good time to discuss the question of settlement—not in terms of a definite sum because you cannot accurately appraise a case at this point—but in terms of its desirability and likelihood. If a client is reluctant to go to court, and some are, he should know about the possibility of effecting a good settlement.'

Finally, tell the client what you are going to be doing on his case. Tell him about your work in preparing a complaint, invoking discovery procedures, retaining an investigator, having photographs taken and utilizing the help of an expert. He will be interested and appreciative. Above all, he will have some idea of why he is paying you a substantial fee.

## DISCUSS THE FEE ARRANGEMENT

A frank discussion of the fee is certainly one of the most onerous tasks we face. Difficult it may be, embarrassing it sometimes is, but it must be done. There are three ways to charge for your services:

A.  A contingent fee in which the client pays the attorney a percentage of the recovery.

B.  A single fixed fee.

C.  An hourly fee.

Each of these has its advantages but in determining how you will charge you must keep in mind the client, the case, and your own needs. Let us look at each:

### A.   The Contingent Fee

This is undoubtedly the most common method by which a plaintiff's attorney is paid. It has been vehemently criticized by the insurance companies and many defendants and routinely upheld by the courts. The reason is simple enough—the average client simply cannot pay good lawyers any other way for the months of time and effort that go into a case. A contingent fee arrangement permits plain John Doe to retain a good attorney, pay nothing while the work is being done, and then, at the end of the case, give the attorney a substantial part of the recovery. All of the risk is on the lawyer. If he fails, then 40 percent of zero is still zero. From the lawyer's point of view he is either going to earn a quite substantial fee or nothing, depending on his skill in appraising his chances of success initially and in handling the case thereafter. The amount of the contingent fee seems to vary from 33-1/3 percent to 50 percent. The standard is pretty well established in your community and you should abide by that standard. In my community the standard is 40 percent except in death cases and those involving minors where the court has set the fee at not more than 33-1/3 percent. One thing should be made clear to the client—that the fee will not vary according to some arbitrary determination of the stage of the proceeding. I have seen contingent fees of 25 percent if the case is settled before it is filed, 33-1/3 percent if settled prior to trial and 40 percent if settled at trial. This arrangement is a headache and leads to arguments— avoid it! The vast majority of your cases will not settle prior to filing, so why mention it? As far as settlement "prior to trial" is concerned a reduction in fee is not justified since all of the hard work—the preparatory work—is done before trial. If you ever deserve a 40 percent fee, it is when you have settled the case after careful, laborious and extensive preparation. It is best to tell the client that your fee is 40 percent of the recovery whenever, and however, that recovery is achieved.

If you are going to take a case on a contingent fee basis, make sure that the case warrants it. There is nothing worse then ending up with a poor result and a low fee, or nothing, after having spent a lot of time at work on a case. If you decide that the case is a poor one, but your client insists that he wants to proceed, then charge him in a different manner.

### B. The Single, Fixed Fee

This system is very good in the case just previously mentioned— where the case is not good enough to justify a contingent fee, but your client wants you to proceed. To ascertain the amount of the fee you must make a very careful analysis of the amount of time and effort that will be involved. If you make a mistake—you'll regret it. In addition you may have to tailor your charge to your client's pocketbook. There is no point in charging $1,500.00 if the client can pay no more than $500.00. Try to work out some accommodation with the client. Having done so, you can proceed with the certainty of being paid for your work and the client can then proceed to make the necessary arrangements for payment of the fee. Both of you know that there will be no further charge.

### C. The Hourly Charge

This is clearly the best arrangement if the client can afford it. It provides the attorney with a stable, easily computed income and the assurance that he will be paid irrespective of the outcome of the case. The hourly rate can vary from $35.00 per hour to $100.00 per hour and once again community standards tend to fix the rate. Most attorneys charge in this manner when their client is a corporation, and these organizations seem to prefer such an arrangement. Billings are made monthly, accompanied by an itemized statement of the charges. Unfortunately most plaintiffs' attorneys represent individuals, not corporations, so that the opportunity to utilize this fee arrangement does not occur very often.

Whatever the fee—and however it is to be paid—it is of great benefit to have a clear understanding with the client at this time. Remember to put it in writing! In that way there can be no arguments or recriminations at a later date.

## SHOULD THE CLIENT ADVANCE MONEY FOR COSTS?

This is another knotty problem that has to be worked out. Traditionally the plaintiff's attorney has paid the costs as they occur and has made the appropriate charge to the client at the end of the case. Ethically, this is acceptable. From a practical point of view, however, it should be avoided where possible. The attorney is tying up his own money for a substantial period of time and at the end of the case when he presents his bill to the client he may be met with many questions about the necessity and propriety of items in the bill. Perhaps it comes down to the question whether the client has the financial means either to advance money for the costs or to pay for them as they are incurred. This matter calls for frank discussion with the client and a decision made on the basis of his ability to pay.

There are certain cases in which I insist on an advance of costs—those instances in which a substantial amount of work must be done to determine if there is a legitimate claim. Medical malpractice cases are in this category as are cases involving the crash of an airplane. As a rule of thumb I demand an advance of estimated costs in any case in which an expert is needed to tell me whether there is a valid basis for a lawsuit. If you do not do this, you will find that you will go broke just getting the facts to tell your clients they have no case! A minimum advance in cases like this should be $500.00.

In any event, all matters concerning costs should be reviewed in detail with your client. His clear understanding of this matter will lead to a pleasant relationship with you throughout the case.

## THE NUISANCE CLAIM

A point or two should be made about your handling this type of case. Unfortunately we use words so carelessly that the phrase "nuisance claim" can have a variety of meanings. It can refer to the case of clear liability with small damages or a doubtful case of liability irrespective of the damages. The insurance companies commonly use the word to apply to any claim in which their administrative costs and legal fees are high in relation to the amount of money involved. They are very unhappy with this type of case. From the point of view of the Plaintiff, however, if his cause is just he is entitled to a recovery despite the fact that the amount involved is small. Accordingly, I recommend that such cases be accepted, that they be handled diligently, and that the goal be a prompt settlement on as favorable terms as possible. The trial of such cases should be avoided since their numbers do tend to clog up the judicial machinery, the award, whether from a jury or an arbitration panel, may not be much higher than your settlement offer and the time and effort involved cannot be compensated for by the client. I also suggest that you charge no fee in these cases. Since they are small cases your client will not have much left if you charge more than a nominal fee. If you adopt this approach, you will be performing a valuable service to the public and will gain a good deal of gratitude from your client.

There is one type of nuisance case that should not be accepted—the case that has no merit and is filed solely to force the defendant to pay something. The thought here is that the defendant will pay in settlement something less than the sum he will expend in defending the case successfully. I view this as legal blackmail and will have nothing to do with it. To handle a case in which either liability, injury or damages will be difficult to prove is one thing; to handle a case in which these elements are substantially non-existent borders on the unethical, is immoral and wrong. No attorney has to stoop so low as to get involved with cases like this. It is demeaning to you, a poor reflection on the legal profession, and a perversion of the cause of justice to try to force a defendant to pay a few pennies rather than to spend money to defend himself. Almost every lawyer has done this a few times in his lifetime—"to err is human"—but the situation should be avoided like the proverbial plague.

Your client is a human being with a problem. When he first comes to your office give him plenty of time. Listen to his story, fill out a detailed questionnaire, have him sign the needed authorizations and explain the law and your plans for future action. He deserves kind attention and will appreciate it.

# CHAPTER 2

# Investigation

There is simply no doubt that a good investigation is essential to the preparation of every case. If there is a witness to be seen, a picture to be taken, or a measurement to be made, you need a trained investigator.

A good investigator, almost by definition, is a reasonably intelligent, pleasant-appearing, well dressed and articulate person. He is gregarious and affable—the kind of person who can put one at ease quickly and can then proceed to get the information he is after—hopefully, a written, signed statement. He must be able to have coffee in the morning with a university professor and to drink beer in the evening with a bulldozer operator and get both of them to tell him what he wants to know. In short, he has to mix easily and well. His basic tools are a smile, a handshake, an open ear and a keen eye. Such an individual can be invaluable to you.

## DON'T DO IT YOURSELF

There is nothing magic about investigation and if you want to do it yourself go ahead. You will soon learn that:

1. Witnesses are not waiting at home for you to appear.

2. Witnesses are not garrulous persons who are anxious to tell you all they know.

3. It takes a lot of time to write out a statement correctly.

4. The witness will not voluntarily sign the statement.

5. You do not have the necessary tools and equipment to do a good job.

6. You do not know where to go to find the records, reports, and regulations that you need or which just might lead you to other data.

Investigation is a specialized vocation and it takes a certain type of personality and several years of training and experience before one becomes competent in this type of work. The average attorney lacks both the time and the experience to get involved in it. From the standpoint of pure economics, how often can you go to the home of a witness only to be told that "Joe had to drive our son to a Little League baseball game" and then to find that Joe decided to stay for the game? This, after he had solemnly promised to meet you at an appointed hour. How often do you care to go out at 11:30 P.M. to meet a witness coming off the 3-11 P.M. shift and find that he wants to stop for a few drinks before going home? Not only will he expect you to pay for the drinks, but his capacity may be a great deal more than yours. As far as public offices and records are concerned the trained investigator knows exactly where to go and when he walks into an office he can call everyone by his first name, get what he wants and be gone while you are still standing in the doorway asking a quizzical secretary if you can see the Administrator for a few moments. It simply doesn't work to try to do it yourself.

## DIRECT THE INVESTIGATION

When you decide (wisely) that you will not do the investigation, then at the same time make up your mind that you are going to direct the investigation. Don't be timid about this! You tell the investigator exactly what you want done, establish a time limitation and discuss the cost. To do otherwise would be to permit him to go on a frolic of his own which definitely will be expensive and will result in a less than satisfactory job. You be the boss—controlling, directing and supervising the work.

The investigator has to be told definitely the ideas you have with regard to the work on your case. There are four items you must go over:

1. The facts that you know from your interview with your client;

2. Your theory of the case;

3. The applicable law; and

4. The facts you need to establish a case.

Explain these thoroughly so that the investigator is well aware of the kind of information to look for. If you have a good rapport with him, this is a good time for a lively exchange of views. There may be one or two other possible theories of liability that he should be aware of because when he gets to work the facts may be different from what you anticipated and he, aware now of other possible approaches, can switch to a different theory and proceed to develop the case. This is going to happen fairly often because at this point, when developing a theory of liability, you must rely on the facts your client gives you and, as has been previously stated, the client is frequently wrong. Thus, when the investigator finds out that the facts will not support your theory, he has to have enough background of the case, and understanding of the law, to be able to develop the case on an alternative theory that the two of you have discussed.

In addition, go over with him in detail the various items that you want covered in the investigation. It stands to reason that you will want statements from witnesses, photographs and measurements. Tell him specifically what else you want but at the same time remember that he must have reasonable latitude to exercise some judgment in these matters. For example, he will have a chance to look over the scene of the accident and decide whether it is suitable and appropriate that good aerial photographs should be taken.

Sometimes a newspaper or television station has prepared a news story of the incident and he should be advised whether he should talk with those people and try to secure data or leads from them. On other occasions you may want him to look up an expert from the area in which the accident occurred and take the expert to the scene, give him some background information and get him started on tests, examinations, or experiments before you get involved. This is especially true where a bridge has collapsed, a building been damaged, or a machine has malfunctioned and caused injury. If a government inspector was somehow involved the investigator must decide whether to try to get his report, or interview him, if this entails long-distance traveling and consequent expenditure of time and money.

These are all "iffy" matters but they should be discussed so that the investigator knows that "if" a certain situation exists he has the authority to take certain action. In like manner if you are dealing with a simple matter such as a rear-end collision to which there are half-a-dozen witnesses be sure to tell him to limit his investigation to only two or three persons. There is such a thing as over-doing an investigation and spending your money foolishly. The important thing is that the investigator has a clear understanding of what he is after and the authority to proceed in a different manner from his express instructions if the situation warrants it. You might remind him that there is always a telephone nearby and that you are to be contacted if he is thinking about doing some work that will substantially increase your costs.

### Whom Should You Get—Where to Find Them—What Should You Pay?

If you do not know a trained investigator turn at once to the Yellow Pages of your local telephone company and look under "Investigators." Most of the individual and corporate listings will be primarily concerned with plant or building security but you will find some that specialize in private investigations for lawsuits. Interview two or three of these men and select the one who seems to have the best qualifications and who suits your own temperament. This latter is important because you will be working closely with the man and you might as well select one who tends to think and act as you do. There is an association of investigators known as the National Association of Legal Investigators who might be contacted, especially if you have no trained men locally or you have work to be done in some distant area. Unfortunately the mailing address of this organization is that of the current President and this changes year by year. One of the founders is Fred C. Koerner, Director, KBI Force, Frick Building, Pittsburgh, Pennsylvania 15219, and that organization does act as an informal clearing house for all inquiries directed to the national organization. In addition, there are the well-known nationwide organizations such as Pinkerton, Burns, Wackenhut and Allied Security. Finally, there is a Society of Former Special Agents of the FBI, Inc., with offices in the Statler-Hilton Hotel, Suite 118-A, 33rd Street and 7th Avenue, New York, New York 10001. They maintain a list of about 3,000 members and should be contacted to secure the identity of a person in your vicinity who might be interested in working for you.

### What Will It Cost?

The average investigator in my area will charge $10.00 to $15.00 per hour, 20c per mile, and expenses. Naturally, the cost will vary by geographic area and will fluctuate with economic conditions generally. If the investigation is going to require a considerable amount of driving and a large amount of work at the destination it is frequently better to work out a flat fee on a daily or job basis.

There continues to be much debate whether it is better to have an investigator as part of your staff or to "farm out" the work to an independent man. Your case load will heavily influence this decision. If you have a large number of cases it might be best to hire an investigator, buy him a car, camera, recorder, and the rest of his equipment and keep him going on your cases. At least you know that you always have a trained man available for investigation and court appearances. On the other hand, the cost is going to be substantial and continuous. It is a matter of balancing the convenience of having your own investigator against the lower cost of retaining a private investigator who may not be readily available when you want him. My strong suggestion is to retain the investigator on an "as needed" basis. This eliminates a serious overhead and administrative problem since you need not worry about the constant demand of salary, taxes, car payments, and the like.

## HOW CAN THE INVESTIGATOR HELP YOU?

Essentially you are hiring this man to do for you those necessary things that require a specialist or which are too expensive to do yourself. The first order of business is to review again the facts that you know, your theory of the case, and all of the data you are going to need to prove your case. Then prepare a list of those items upon which you want the investigator to concentrate—always bearing in mind that he must have the authority to vary from this list as circumstances warrant. Let's consider some of these items:

### 1   Signed Statements from Witnesses

Absolutely imperative! Not only signed, but notarized as well. Certainly the investigator must see all of the persons who witnessed an accident, but should not forget other types of witnesses. He should visit persons who know nothing of the accident but may know a great deal about a condition—"notice" witnesses. These are the persons who smelled gas in the neighborhood hours before an explosion and who reported it to the gas company; the ones who forbade their children to play around a crumbling building and reported the condition to the police weeks before the building collapsed; the ones who arrived at the accident scene after it happened but can testify about the position of the vehicles, the presence of skid marks, or the anguish of the injured plaintiff. Their testimony is priceless but they may be hard to find. Your man may have to knock on the door of every house within a block or two of the accident site to find them.

You should expect that the investigator, in his report, would begin with a short description of the accident, provide you with a summary of the statement of the witness, and express his opinion of the type of person the witness is. This latter is important so that you have some idea, from the observations of a trained person, what kind of an individual you are dealing with. This may influence you to a very great extent when it comes time to choose your witnesses later on. An illustration of this type of report is the following:

INVESTIGATION REPORT

Plaintiff: James D. Moore                    Commenced: May 2
                                             Completed: May 25

THE ACCIDENT:

This accident occurred on Thursday, April 18th at approximately 11:00 A.M. on Camp Horne Road, in front of the Hastings Garden Center, 532 Camp Horne Road, Pine Township, Allegheney County, Pennsylvania 15202.

Involved in this accident was a 1975 Ford Sedan, operated by Betty Smith, traveling in a southwesterly direction on Camp Horne Road, turning left to a southerly direction, toward the Hastings Garden Center, colliding with the left side of a 1975 Honda motorcycle, operated by James D. Moore, traveling in a northeasterly direction on Camp Horne Road.

Although there are no known witnesses to the impact, the investigation will reveal the operator of the 1975 Ford Sedan, Betty Smith, was entirely responsible for the accident. The statement of Keith Mesmer will be of particular interest. He was first to observe the vehicles, immediately subsequent to the accident, and gives a detailed description of his observations.

In beginning this investigation I first interviewed:

William L. Brown
123 Camp Horne Road
Pine Township
Allegheny County, Pennsylvania
May 2        10:45 A.M.
Telephone: 123-4557

who was reluctant to cooperate but signed the enclosed, notarized (2) page statement.

Mr. Brown, owner of the Brown Gas station, stated he did not become aware of the accident until he observed from the front window of his business establishment, a crowd gathering on Camp Horne Road. He gave a vague description of his observations, and obviously was not relating all his detailed knowledge of the accident.

OPINION:

This witness, age 45, makes a fair appearance, is of average intelligence, and extremely nervous of the possibility he may become involved in a trial. It is this possibility which made him reluctant to give detailed information. Mr. Brown will be of little help regarding the liability aspects of this case, but if forced to testify, I believe he will be able to give more detailed information on the events which took place subsequent to the accident.

I next interviewed:

> Keith Mesmer
> 10 Switch Avenue
> Pittsburgh, Pennsylvania   15123
> May 24      10:00 A.M.
> Telephone:   891-1234

who was very cooperative and signed the enclosed, notarized (6) page statement.

This witness was at the scene, heard the crash, but did not see the actual impact. He observed the motorcycle while it was still in motion, and the exact position of the defendant vehicle immediately subsequent to the impact. He gives an excellent description of the position of the vehicles, the condition of the plaintiff, and the pain he suffered as the result of this accident. He also talked to the defendant driver, who admitted to him she was responsible for the accident. He also relates in his statement information which indicates the plaintiff could not possibly have been speeding at the time of the accident. This witness is the owner of a motorcycle, and is very familiar with their operation. This familiarity, and the fact that he observed the plaintiff at a service station just prior to the accident, helps to establish that the plaintiff could not have been speeding.

OPINION:

This witness, age 40, is very friendly, makes an excellent appearance, and undoubtedly will be your best witness. He stated he was questioned by the defendant's insurance carrier, on the telephone shortly after the accident, but did not relate the detailed information given in this statement. He is most anxious and willing to testify on behalf of the plaintiff.

## 2.  Photographs

One picture is still worth a thousand words. You will want lots of pictures—of vehicles, scene, machinery, and persons. Colored pictures are best and photographs should be taken from different angles and various distances. Is this a case for an aerial photograph? Is the subject such that an expert photographer should be brought in? These are decisions the investigator must frequently make based on your prior discussion with him and confirmed by a telephone call. Incidently, make sure your man has a good camera whose pictures can be easily enlarged. Also, he must prepare a Photo Data Sheet identifying the subject, date, place, direction of camera, and range to the subject.

### 3. Measurements

Most people are very poor at estimating distances. Therefore, in order to have any kind of intelligent discussion with them, you, at least, must have accurate knowledge of the exact location of things. As with photographs, your investigator cannot make too many measurements. Consider for a moment that in an intersection collision you may want the distance from the corner of the street back to a stop sign, from the stop sign back to a curve, the width of each street at the intersection, the width of each lane of traffic, the width of sidewalks, the distance from the sidewalk to a certain bush or shrub that may block one's view. This is one occasion where the investigator might as well take all the time in the world—measure, measure, and measure again. You will be surprised at how important all of these measurements will be when you get your witnesses together to discuss the case.

### 4. Weather Reports

If rain, snow, fog, or ice, and early sunrise or an eclipse of the moon are involved in a case, a weather report is almost mandatory. It's true that your secretary could write for a weather report but they are a little tricky to interpret. If the weather condition at a particular time is really important, it is best to let the investigator get the report and then discuss it with one of the personnel at the Weather Bureau. In this manner he will get all of the information you need because in a few minutes' conversation he will always get details and explanations that are missing in a written report.

### 5. Prior Accidents

If a machine has malfunctioned and caused injury or a train has gone off the tracks at a curve or a large pothole has caused a driver to lose control of his car, your investigator is going to begin to think about prior similar accidents occurring at the same place. This is the best possible evidence of a negligent condition permitted to exist for a long period of time. It's certainly difficult for a defendant to deny that a condition was negligently maintained and that he knew it was defective when you are able to prove that one or two prior accidents occurred because of the condition. This is a good objective for any investigator.

## 6. Public Records and Technical Data

This is surely one of the most important aspects of investigation. A competent investigator will instinctively suspect violation of some statute or governmental regulation and will spend a good part of his time tracking it down. This is where his personal contacts come into play—friends he can call who work in the Department of Labor and Industry, inspectors for the Bureau of Mines or the Federal Aviation Authority, a chemist with the Environmental Protection Agency or a nurse at the Health Department. If he is successful—if he can find a specific regulation the defendant has violated, your case becomes as solid as the proverbial Rock of Gibraltar. I can illustrate the importance of this with three specific instances:

(a) A teen-age boy was stopped at the door of a drugstore by an acquaintance. He had one hand on the door ready to push it open. As he paused to talk he was bumped by another patron of the store. Pushed forward, his hand went through the glass. He sustained grievous injury to his hand. The investigator arrived weeks after the accident when the glass had been replaced. He noted that the replacement glass was plain plate glass. With his charm he got to look at the old order sheet and invoice for the glass involved in the accident. He went to the retailer who advised him that the original was plate glass. Suspicious, he went to a friend in the Department of Labor and Industry and found a specific regulation requiring safety glass in a public building such as this. From that moment the case was won.

(b) A huge automatic milling machine was installed in a factory. To set the controls the operator had to stand on a gently sloping metal shelf—always covered with oil. As might be expected, he slipped and fell, sustaining a serious back injury. Suit was brought against the manufacturer. The case was successfully concluded only after a trained investigator became suspicious about that oily metal shelf—did some extensive snooping and found a regulation that specifically required that such an area be "roughed" up to provide traction or be covered with a special abrasive substance so that men could walk on it with greater safety.

(c) A public swimming pool had only 6-1/2 feet of water under a one-meter diving board. While diving, a young man broke his neck. An inquisitive investigator found borough regulations, a state statute, and recommendations of the

Swimming Pool Institute were all violated. What could the defendant say to this?

This is merely illustrative of the importance of public records and the way in which a good investigator becomes, literally, the attorney's strong right arm. This is time-consuming work and depends often on knowing whom to contact. Just remember that you are paying for your investigator's experience and contacts as well as his time.

### 7.   Police Reports

This is another area in which friendship can make a lot of difference. Your secretary can order the police report—that is no problem. It's much better though to send an investigator to the police department, pick up a copy of the report, and then stop and chat with the Chief, meet the reporting officer, and pick up a dozen and one little things that aren't in the report. He will learn, for example, that the description of the accident came solely from the defendant—your plaintiff having been taken from the scene in an ambulance, or that there were two or three other witnesses that the officer knows of and didn't list because he was in a hurry or ran out of space on the reporting form.

Let's take just a moment to talk about this business of ordering a report rather than sending an investigator out to get it and to talk to the men who prepared it. The former method is substantially cheaper but you take a chance on missing so very much. The investigator can read the report, analyze it in view of the other facts that he knows and then interview the reporting officer with regard to:

(a) Facts not in the report; and
(b) Interpretations of the information on the report.

Do you recall the last time you filled out a report? I'm sure it was done hurriedly—such things usually are—and then the space provided for an answer or the printed responses which require a check-mark are never quite adequate to describe what you want to say. "Was it daylight or dark?" (Actually, it wasn't quite either—sort of late dusk.) "What was the posted speed limit?" (Well, it was 35 m.p.h. but weather conditions were so foul no sane driver should have gone over 15).

Unfortunately, this is the kind of answer you can't put on a form. The only thing you can do is to fill out the form and then later, if anyone comes around to talk to you, make a more adequate explanation of what you really meant.

That is why an investigator should go out to get reports.

### 8.  Newspaper Reports

Many accidents are newsworthy and when they are the newspaper reporters, photographers and TV cameramen are there quickly. Their records are very valuable and are probably the earliest reports you will find. An added bonus is the fact that these people are also trained observers. They will nearly always cooperate with you in permitting you to make copies of their films and records. The visit of your investigator will enable you to secure specifically what you are after, but will also establish a nice rapport with someone at the newspaper or television station. You may need those people for witnesses.

### 9.  Securing Physical Evidence

Paint scrapings on a bridge—left by a car before it swerved into the next lane.

A tire from a wrecked car.

A piece of wire used to bale papers—identical to the one that snapped and pierced a man's eye.

Nails from the box that didn't stay together.

A small slab of concrete—typical of that which crumbled under a load.

A tireless investigator roaming the scene of an accident, looking and thinking, will pick up each of these items—label them as to date, time, exact location, and relationship to other objects. They are priceless— absolutely priceless. When placed in the hands of an engineer or metallurgist—a good expert—they tell a story of their own. When that story is known to you, your case may suddenly assume a value and importance that it completely lacked before.

Once again I must state that this is another illustration why you cannot place absolute credence in what your client tells you. He simply does not know all of the things that you can find out—matters which literally spell the difference between success and failure in a lawsuit.

### 10.  Locating an Expert Witness

The choice of an expert has to be the function of the attorney, but the preliminary legwork of meeting with several men and deciding which kind of expert should be used and who, in this specialized field, would be willing to assist and cooperate is surely a chore that the investigator can do. When he reaches the point that he thinks an expert is needed, then he already has such a good knowledge of the case that he can interview several men and decide which one or ones you should take the time to see. Remember that he can help you find that person who not only knows what he is talking about but can also express that knowledge forcefully and clearly. The men you select must be both experts and good witnesses. Your investigator can help with this problem.

### 11. Your Investigator as a Witness

When you come to choose an investigator don't forget that he also must be an expert and witness! There are going to be numerous times when he is going to be called upon to testify. Sometimes he will be used in your Case-in Chief to tell what he saw, did, measured, photographed, or heard. At other times, he will be called in rebuttal to testify, in contradiction to a defense witness, that he took a true statement from the witness that is at odds with what the witness said on the stand. Therefore, you had better think about how good an impression your investigator will make. Is he sure of himself? Does he present a good appearance? Is he articulate? A colleague who specializes in criminal law as a defense attorney once told me he thought it was almost unconstitutionally prejudicial for an FBI agent to take the witness stand. They are invariably so handsome, well-dressed, self-confident, and knowledgeable that no jury can ever disbelieve them! His point, while slightly exaggerated, is well-taken. Think of this when you retain an investigator.

CHAPTER **3**

# Collecting the Data

There is a substantial amount of information you will have to secure relating to your client's injuries and losses. This data will take a lot of time to accumulate initially and, thereafter, will have to be reviewed on some kind of periodic basis. Certainly it need not be kept current in the sense that you know the amount of particular bill on a month-to-month basis. It is sufficient if you take a look at the bills and reports in each file about every four months and are sure that they are brought up-to-date. Let us take a look at some of the basic records your file must contain:

## HOSPITAL RECORDS

Whether your client has received X-ray examinations as an out-patient, emergency room treatment, or in-patient treatment you must get a copy of the hospital records. Since these records will be detailed and thorough, this is the best way to learn about the injuries and the nature of the treatment given to the plaintiff. However, most of the time you do not need the whole record. That may become necessary at a later date but you will not want the entire record initially. These records are expensive—sometimes costing $1.00 per page—and they often run 50 to 75 pages just for a relatively short hospitalization.

Nearly all hospital records contain the following:

1. Cover Sheet;

2. History and Initial Physical Examination;

3.  Physicians' Orders;

4.  Medication Records;

5.  Operation Records;

6.  Anesthesia Records;

7.  Reports of Consultations;

8.  Temperature Chart;

9.  Progress Notes;

10. Nurses' Notes;

11. X-ray Reports;

12. Laboratory Data;

13. Physical Therapy Reports; and

14. Discharge Summary.

In your ordinary case, and as an initial document in unusual cases, you should order items 1, 2, 5, 7, 11, and 14. At a cost of about only $10.00 to $15.00 you can get a good general idea of what happened to your client during his stay at the hospital. The cover sheet gives you biographical data; the history will tell you how and why your client was admitted; and the initial physical will outline his condition on arrival; the operation record will explain that procedure in detail; the consultation reports will help explain miscellaneous problems that the attending physician could not handle; X-ray reports will discuss skeletal problems and some disease processes; and the discharge summary will very nicely tie-up all the loose ends. These documents will provide you with a good basic record.

Then, after reviewing these, you can decide whether to order additional portions of the record. Was your client in a lot of pain? Order the nurses' notes, the medication record or the doctors' orders. Was traction utilized or special therapy given? Get the doctors' orders and the physical therapy records. Was there some problem with infection? Get the laboratory reports. The determination of what you want to order will depend on the nature of your client's problems and what you have to prove in court.

## THE HOSPITAL BILL

If your client was an in-patient, you can secure either an itemized bill from the hospital or a simple statement showing the dates of admission and discharge and the total amount of the bill. The latter bill is best for the simple reason that it will be on one sheet and be uncomplicated. When you receive an itemized bill it will frequently consist of several sheets and there will always be some silly miscellaneous charge listed that will open a Pandora's Box for a picayune, but inquisitive, defense attorney. Save yourself that trouble. Get a simple statement of the total charges.

Be sure to notify the Accounting Department or Business Office of the hospital to give you a bill that contains no notation of payment from a collateral source. You should always conclude your request for a bill with the statement "total bill, irrespective whether any part of it has been paid, and showing no notation of payment thereon." Undoubtedly the bill has been paid by Blue Cross, some private insurance of the client's, or perhaps by the employer. If there is a reference to this fact on the bill you will either have to delete it before the jury sees it or you will have to explain the Collateral Source Rule to them. Believe me, most jurors do not understand that rule. It will save you a lot of trouble to have a simple bill to offer into evidence, with no notation of payment.

If your client was in the hospital because of injuries received in an accident but, while there, he also received treatment for an unrelated condition, you will have to get an itemized bill. Then you will have to get together with the attending physician and delete those charges relating to the treatment for that other, non-related, problem. Thereafter, it would be best to show the modified bill to the defense attorney and secure his consent to substituting a new bill from the hospital showing only the adjusted amount.

## PHYSICAL THERAPY

Physical therapy is frequently given at a hospital on an out-patient basis. Sometimes it is given at a private clinic or in the office of a physiatrist. When the therapy has been given at a hospital you have no choice but to order whatever records the hospital has, and these are often inadequate. They will report the dates of treatment and the cost but will be very brief—sometimes using only one or two words—in describing the nature of the treatment and, usually, there will be no comments about the results of that treatment. You will have to fill in the gaps through the testimony of your client and the attending doctor as best you can and, oftentimes, they will not have a clear recollection.

If the therapy was given at a private clinic, you stand a much better chance of getting a complete report. You will want to know:

1.    The dates of treatment;

2.    The nature or type of therapy given;

3.    A discussion of the progress of your client;

4.    The total bill.

Don't forget that quite often therapy is given for a period of time, is interrupted, and then renewed at a later date. You will have to be alert to secure a later report if your client tells you he has to go back for more treatment, or when the necessity for more treatment is mentioned in the initial report of the therapist. As soon as you know that more treatment will be needed you should "diary ahead" to make sure a later report is ordered.

## THE MEDICAL REPORT

There are four things that you want from any treating doctor:

1.    His diagnosis;

2.    The nature of his treatment;

3.    His prognosis; and

4.    His bill.

On rare occasions you will need an expression of opinion from him whether the accident caused the condition he was treating. These instances are infrequent because, usually, the cause and effect relationship is so obvious.

Nearly every doctor knows what you need—the problem is that he wants to say it in as few words as possible. We can all sympathize with the large amount of paper work that confronts every doctor, but we can not accept a single-paragraph, four-sentence, "bare bones" type of report. If you let them, some doctors will write:

1.    Simple fracture—rt. fibula

2.    Closed reduction

3.    Good

4.    $75.00

This, for a patient who was in a lot of pain at the time of treatment and required some powerful medication, who wore a cast for four weeks and couldn't work for some time after the cast was removed, and who had to take "whirlpool" treatment for two weeks. The report is accurate as far as it goes but it's very incomplete. The doctor knows this—he knows what you want—he is simply too busy (lazy?) to give it to you. It is always best to talk with the doctor before he writes the report to make certain that he understands what you need. Otherwise, upon receipt of a report such as I have just outlined, you will have to write again asking for more details.

Since your client will be seeing the doctor on a fairly regular basis—i.e., once every ten days, twice a month, etc.—you are going to have to get follow-up reports. These requests should be sent out not more than every four months and in some instances once in six months would be enough where the treatment is routine. If you write more often than this, you are really burdening the doctor for no good reason.

Be certain that you do request an up-to-date bill in your follow-up letter and, once again, tell the doctor you only want the total charge "irrespective whether all or any part of it has been paid and with no notation of payment."

All doctors will charge for these reports and so long as the charge is reasonable you must pay it. I would suggest that $35.00 to $50.00 is reasonable. Where the charge begins to go substantially above that point, and if the doctor is uncooperative, you might advise him that he is simply forcing you to subpoena him to your office for a deposition. The mere threat of this is usually enough to cause him to write a report. However, if he persists in his obstinacy, you will have to take his deposition. When you do so, be prepared for an argument about his giving a diagnosis and prognosis. He must give you facts—dates of visits, type of treatment, his charges—but he may argue that diagnosis and prognosis are opinions which he need not state. You can meet this by pointing out that his diagnosis is the fact upon which his treatment is predicated. If he still refuses to discuss it ask for, and make copies of, his office records. The diagnosis will be there. You can also ask him to describe the nature of the injury and most of the time he will inadvertently give you his diagnosis.

Most lawyers feel that subpoenaing a doctor will antagonize him. This is true, but the fact that this procedure is necessary in the first place establishes that the doctor is already antagonistic and uncooperative. Why pretend that it is otherwise? If he won't cooperate with you regarding a simple report, you can hardly expect a sudden change of personality at the time of trial. If he is going to be angry because you subpoena him for a deposition, so be it. If you need help on medical causation, you had better plan now to get another doctor for that purpose. There is no point, however, in letting a doctor bully or blackmail you simply because he is the attending physician.

## BILLS FOR DRUGS, MEDICATIONS, AND APPLIANCES

Most of these products are purchased at a drug store. Nearly all of them are modest in price and are purchased frequently—refills of a prescription, as an example. Therefore, unless you're careful, you will have a host of small, individual bills—often just a torn-off cash register type. Your secretary will go crazy trying to keep together all of these little slips of paper—for certainly you are not going to do it. There isn't much you can do about the bills incurred before you were retained, but from that point on change your client's bookkeeping system. Advise him to go to the neighborhood pharmacy and arrange a charge account which he is to use solely for the purpose of drugs, medicines and appliances that the doctor has prescribed for injuries relating to his accident. Be certain that he understands that that account is not be be used for any other purpose—not for buying aspirin for his wife, a tranquilizer for his daughter, or shaving lotion for himself. Then, at the end of each month, he should receive a statement showing the date of purchase, the prescription number, and the charge for all medicines ordered that month. Actually, you could probably arrange with the pharmacist to submit these statements quarterly. In this manner you have all the information you need on a single sheet or a relatively few sheets of paper. When your client pays the bill it is best that he pay it by check so that you will have a record of the payment. This is a neat, sensible way to keep a record of medicine bills.

## GETTING THE WAGE RECORD

With one simple letter you can get all of the data you want from almost any employer. They may charge a nominal fee for the work but they have the information and you need it. Any insurance company you will deal with is going to want this information to substantiate your claim for lost wages.

In writing to the employer you will have to give your plaintiff's Social Security number and usually a badge number, plant number, or some other identifying symbol. They also want you to tell them specifically what information you want. Ordinarily you should ask for the following things:

1.    The job title or classification;

2.    The initial date of employment;

3.    The basic hourly rate or monthly salary;

4. The amount of any differential pay due to overtime, incentive, bonus or otherwise;

5. The length of time your plaintiff was off work due to the accident—i.e., the beginning and ending dates;

6. The amount of his yearly earnings in the year of the accident and two prior years; and

7. His earnings by month in the year of the accident.

This will give you an accurate basis for computing his loss of earnings.

There are problems on occasion. The client may have been injured during a busy season when he could have earned differential pay in substantial amounts. He may have lost a chance for a bonus, a promotion, or some other increment to his base pay. When this happens it may be difficult to compute the loss of earnings. One way to do this would be to ask the employer to give you data concerning the monthly or yearly earnings for the men who are next junior and next senior to your client on the seniority list. Usually this is a simple, and fruitful, way of computing your client's loss and one that is generally acceptable both in court and in your settlement negotiations with the insurance company.

Sometimes the employer hesitates to divulge information about co-employees even if their names are not disclosed. This can best be resolved by having your client speak to these men, whom he surely knows, and getting them to sign an authorization that will permit the employer to give you the requested facts.

## TAX RETURNS AND SOCIAL SECURITY INFORMATION

These are the two types of Federal documents that you will normally require.

The tax returns are needed when your plaintiff is self-employed, when he holds a variety of jobs, and in a few other unusual circumstances. Tax returns are frequently requested by insurance companies (I often suspect they are looking for evidence of cheating) and you might as well order them as a matter of convenience to yourself. They are needed in the case of a self-employed person to help establish his claim for lost earnings. They are also required when your plaintiff works for many different employers. These are usually men who work out of a union hiring hall. In Pennsylvania, ironworkers would be a good example. These men go from job to job—now for six weeks, again for two months—and they may work for ten employers in a year. Rather than write each employer for information it is much easier to use the plaintiff's tax return.

The Social Security information is normally needed when your plaintiff is receiving a disability pension. You will want to know the date he qualified for the pension, the amount he receives, and the reason he is eligible. This can be used to establish the permanency of a disability. The extent to which you will use the information will depend upon the particular circumstances of your case. It is difficult to generalize how, or whether, you would want to use it in a trial, for example. However, in any event, it is information you ought to know and should be requested.

A special authorization available at any Internal Revenue or Social Security Office is required for these documents. It is a simple matter to pick one up, fill it out, and send it off.

## PUBLIC RECORDS

There are very few public records that you will need. Of those that you might want—mortgages, deeds, judgments, recorded Separation Agreements, assessed valuations of real estate, weather reports—you can either get the defense attorney to stipulate to them, ask the court to take judicial notice of them, or, if necessary, secure properly certified copies to introduce into evidence. They should pose no problem except in remembering to order them.

## BILLS FOR REPAIRS

It is obvious that when a car or a house has been damaged you are going to need a bill to prove the cost of repairs. That bill has to be itemized and should list every repair made that was caused by the accident. That latter phrase "caused by the accident" is important. It is embarrassing to have your client on the witness stand testifying about the damage done to the front and right side of his car and then to submit a repair bill that includes a charge for replacement of the left, rear fender. It is more than embarrassing. If the jury gets the notion that your plaintiff is cheating— whether on a repair bill, drug bill, or some other matter—they may well decide that his whole claim is "tainted" and return a defense verdict or a very low verdict. Jurors begin a case by being a little skeptical of the average plaintiff and you simply prove that their skepticism is justified when you offer a bill that has non-related charges on it. Don't let this happen. Your client will try to get away with it.

I get the impression that every American feels that he has a right to get all necessary repairs done to his car, or home, when part of it has been damaged in an accident and to try to get the insurance company to pay for it. Insurance personnel and defense attorneys know this too (they probably do it themselves) and are alert to it. Therefore, go over these repair bills carefully, verify them with the mechanic, carpenter, electrician, or whomever, and make sure they contain charges only for damage caused by the accident.

The bill should be itemized and signed by the person who did the work or the owner of the business who knows that the work was done and that the bill is accurate.

If you will show such a bill to the defense attorney in advance, he will nearly always stipulate to it and spare you the trouble of calling a witness to prove it. However, if you must call a witness, beware of the owner of the business or a billing clerk. Very often they do not know why certain work was done or even, for certain, that the items listed on the bill were actually repaired. It is much better to call the repairman who actually did the work.

In many small businesses there is a good deal of movement on the part of the mechanics. They seem to change jobs with great frequency. Since you will be receiving the repair bill many months prior to trial, it is a good idea to put the name of the mechanic on the bill together with his home address and telephone number.

## ESTIMATES REGARDING LOSS OF PERSONAL PROPERTY

The cases that you will handle involving substantial loss or damage to personal property are usually going to be those where a house or building has been damaged by blasting, fire or water. The property that has been affected will vary from furniture, rugs, drapes, valuable paintings, up to heavy machinery. It is difficult to try to get an evaluation of the loss since one is dealing with purchase value, length and type of usage, replacement value, and other variables. The best, most acceptable, and frequently, the only, way to get an estimate is to retain a professional appraisal company. Every city has them and they are listed in the "Yellow Pages" of the telephone directory.

You must meet with the appraiser to outline exactly what you want done, to discuss his fee and costs, and to explain to him what you want his report to include. It is helpful if you go with him to the house or building— at least to acquaint yourself with the damage—and to show him in more detail the items you are interested in. There is no point in his going to the scene and charging you for time spent in looking around trying to determine what has to be done.

Many of these appraisers take photographs, but if your man is one who does not have a camera make certain that he either gets one or takes a photographer with him. Photographs are an excellent way to show the extent of damage and are essential in preparation of the case. Time dims memory and after the damaged goods are repaired or disposed of, you, your client and the appraiser will have a hard time recalling the damage done to a particular item. That is where the photograph becomes invaluable. You need not necessarily use them in court but you will use them in the office and they are available if you need or want them at the trial.

## RENTAL CHARGES

In some instances your client may have to rent a car, a house, or stay at a motel while repairs are being made or as an emergency measure. There is no problem in getting these bills—and your client can testify to their necessity—but you must remember to order them. They are in the category of things that are easy to forget until, at the last moment, you suddenly find you need them and don't have them.

## USE YOUR SECRETARY

Most of the routine, but essential, documents that you need involve work that ought to be done by your secretary. You should have a form letter requesting hospital records and medical reports and she should be able to type a simple request for bills to car rental agencies, druggists and the like. Beyond these things, the matter of follow-up should be a responsibility of hers if she is properly trained. Doctors are notorious for requiring two or three letters before they send a report. Your secretary should know this and routinely check to see if the initial letter was answered and, if not, send out a reminder note. Likewise, she should know to write to the doctor for current reports every four or six months, and to do the same with some of the "on-going" bills such as the druggist's bills. These things should be a matter of routine in your office. Unfortunately, most lawyers have not taken the time to sit down with their secretaries and establish a set of guidelines for handling them. If you have not, this would be a good time to do so. It will save you time and avoid a great deal of trouble.

CHAPTER 4

# Filing the Lawsuit —
# the Formal Case Begins

Filing the lawsuit represents the second climatic step in the handling of a case. It is the time when you must formalize, and, of necessity, publicize your allegations against the defendant. It begins that period in which you had better know what you are doing and where you are going, because from this point to the conclusion of the case other people are going to be looking over your shoulder and searching for your mistakes—the defendant and his attorney, for certain, and, perhaps, the Court. At the same time it opens the door to all kinds of interesting and, hopefully, fruitful opportunities—to meet the defendant and question him in a deposition, to gather information from the files of a business corporation or hospital, or the chance to ask a whole series of searching questions through the use of interrogatories. In short, from the time the lawsuit is filed you should be busily about the very essence of those activities which principally engage the time and attention of the plaintiff's lawyer.

## WHEN SHOULD YOU COMMENCE THE ACTION?

Now! What are you waiting for? Your investigation is complete, you have a report from your expert, you know your case, —what's the delay? It's amazing how many lawyers almost have to be forced into filing their lawsuits. The reason for this, I believe, is a human, and professional, reluctance to commit one's self, in writing, to a definite position in a matter. Forget it. A complaint is a pleading, not a Magna Carta. It can be amended if you make a mistake. Like the kick-off in a football game its purpose is to get the lawsuit underway by apprising the defendant of what he has done that has injured the plaintiff.

One very important consideration is the fact that the principal cause of malpractice actions against lawyers is having allowed the Statute of Limitations to run on a case. Filing your lawsuit promptly is an excellent way to alleviate any worries in this line.

Another reason for delay—frequently cited by the uncertain lawyer—is the pious hope that the case can be settled without suit. Not likely! If the case has problems (and most cases do) you're going to have to work hard for a settlement. You're going to have to convince the insurance company that they *must* pay you and, normally, this can only be done after discovery—and discovery can only be called into play after the case is filed. In addition, claims personnel are very busy people. They are overworked most of the time. If your case is not filed, they can put it at the bottom of that pile of papers commanding their attention. If it is filed, they know that Rules of Court, and of Procedure, now come into play and that there are time limitations for various actions that they, and you, must comply with. Thus the case is constantly coming across their desk, drawing their attention to it. Even the language is different: Unfiled, it is a claim; filed, it is a lawsuit.

In summary, then, there are four good reasons for filing suit promptly:

1. It protects you with regard to the Statute of Limitations.

2. The defendant is forced to recognize your case as a serious claim. Bound by Rules of Procedure he knows that time limitations must be complied with, that the case must be attended to, and that final decisions must be made.

3. It is the only way in which to invoke necessary discovery techniques.

4. It enables you to engage in settlement negotiations, at the appropriate time, without imposing delay in terms of getting the case to trial.

## WHAT FORM SHOULD IT TAKE?

In general there are three ways in which one may begin a lawsuit— one's local rules will govern here—

1. A Praecipe for a Writ of Summons;

2. By a notice complaint such as the Federal Rules permit and some states' rules permit;

3. A detailed complaint which many states' rules require.

If there is a choice in the matter we can make several observations.

### When the Praecipe Is Recommended

The Praecipe should be utilized only when the client rushes in at 3:00 P.M. on the day that the Statute of Limitations is due to expire. An example follows:

### EXHIBIT NO. 4-1

IN THE COURT OF COMMON PLEAS OF ALLEGHENY
COUNTY, PENNSYLVANIA.

CIVIL DIVISION.

| | | |
|---|---|---|
| SAM COOK, | : | |
| Plaintiff, | : | |
| | : | |
| v. | : | No. 75 - 2107 |
| | : | IN TRESPASS. |
| ROBERT SMITH, | : | |
| Defendant. | | |

PRAECIPE FOR WRIT OF SUMMONS

TO:    JAMES BROWN, CLERK

Please issue Writ of Summons in Trespass in an amount in excess of TEN THOUSAND ($10,000.00) DOLLARS, exclusive of interest and costs (or "in the amount of $          " if permitted by local rules).

John A. DeMay,
Attorney for Plaintiff.

Then have your secretary (or you, if you're a sprinter) run, not walk, to the Clerk's Office to file it.

This will protect you, but rest assured that defense counsel will shortly be demanding that you follow through with a complaint.

The only other time a Praecipe should be used would be on those rare occasions when you have few facts, are uncertain how to proceed, and are hoping to utilize discovery to get the facts so you can file a complaint. Be prepared to follow the filing of the praecipe with interrogatories and notices of depositions. There could be an argument on the matter since defense counsel may demand a complaint before you invoke discovery. However, a reasonable judge will usually understand what you are doing and go along with it.

### Use of the Notice and Detailed Complaint

The notice complaint, permitted by the Federal Rules, is certainly the best of all. You are not committed to very much, the right to amend is freely granted, and you have great flexibility. Happy the man who lives in a state which has adopted the Federal Rules. The complaint should be a five-paragraph pleading, setting forth:

1. The identity of the plaintiff, his address, and state of citizenship;

2. The identity of the defendant, his address, and state of citizenship;

3. The basis of the jurisdiction of the Court;

4. The date and place of the incident; and

5. A brief statement of the incident.

Of course, it concludes with a demand for relief.

Here are two complaints which comply with the Rules—one in which jurisdiction is based on diversity of citizenship and a claim exceeding ten thousand dollars in value, the other is based on a federal statute—in this case, the Federal Employers Liability Acts. These sample complaints would, naturally, comply with the rules of any state which has adopted the Federal Rules.

### EXHIBIT 4-2

IN THE UNITED STATES DISTRICT COURT FOR
THE WESTERN DISTRICT OF PENNSYLVANIA.

| | | |
|---|---|---|
| DAVID RAMSEY,<br>　　　　Plaintiff, | : | |
| | : | |
| 　　v. | : | |
| PENN LIGHT COMPANY, | : | CIVIL ACTION NO. 75-173 |
| a Pennsylvania<br>corporation, | : | |
| | : | |
| 　　　　Defendant | : | |

## COMPLAINT

AND NOW comes the plaintiff above named by his attorney, JOHN A. DeMAY, and for his cause of action against the defendant sets forth as follows:

1. The plaintiff is DAVID RAMSEY, who resides at 123 James Street, New York, New York 10038 and who is a citizen of the State of New York and of the United States of America.

2. The defendant, PENN LIGHT COMPANY, is a Pennsylvania corporation, which maintains its principal office and place of business at 386 Ninth Street, Pittsburgh, Allegheny County, Pennsylvania 15219.

3. Jurisdiction is conferred upon this Court by virtue of the diversity of the citizenship of the parties and by reason of the fact that the amount in controversy exceeds TEN THOUSAND ($10,000.00) DOLLARS, exclusive of interest and costs.

4. The accident here involved occurred on August 23, 1974, at approximately 3:30 P.M. at the defendant's South Hills substation outside of Sewickley, Pennsylvania.

5. At the aforesaid time and place the plaintiff was working as a painter for the Allen Painting Company, which had a contract to paint various towers for the defendant. While the plaintiff was painting a tower, he sustained severe electrical burns by virtue of the negligence of the defendant and was thrown from the tower to the ground.

WHEREFORE, judgment is demanded against the defendant in an amount in excess of TEN THOUSAND ($10,000.00) DOLLARS, exclusive of interest and costs.

A JURY TRIAL IS DEMANDED.

Respectfully submitted,

John A. DeMay,
Attorney for Plaintiff

## EXHIBIT 4-3

### IN THE UNITED STATES DISTRICT COURT FOR THE WESTERN DISTRICT OF PENNSYLVANIA.

SAMUEL J. GEORGE,
    Plaintiff,

    v.

GRANT RAILROAD COMPANY,     CIVIL ACTION NO. 75-869
a corporation,
    Defendant.

COMPLAINT

AND NOW comes the plaintiff above named by his counsel, JOHN A. DeMAY, and for his Complaint does hereby set forth as follows:

  1. The plaintiff is SAMUEL J. GEORGE, who resides at 124 Lane Street, Pittsburgh, Allegheny County, Pennsylvania 15239, and who at all pertinent times was employed by the defendant as a car repairman.

  2. The defendant is a railroad company which engages in the interstate transportation of freight for hire and which has an office and place of doing business in Pittsburgh, Pennsylvania.

  3. At all pertinent times, both the plaintiff and the defendant were engaged in interstate commerce or in activities which substantially affect interstate commerce.

  4. Jurisdiction is conferred upon this Court under and by virtue of the provisions of the Federal Employers Liability Acts of Congress.

  5. On or about April 7, 1975, at approximately 10 P.M., and in the vicinity of Track No. 3, at defendant's station in Pittsburgh, Pennsylvania, the plaintiff sustained serious injuries by virtue of the negligence of the defendant.

  WHEREFORE, judgment is demanded of the defendant.

John A. DeMay,<br>Attorney for Plaintiff.

As you can see, these are very simple, basic documents. They inform the defendant of the fact that he is being sued, and why, yet neither document gets bogged down in details. Even in an emergency situation a complaint such as one of these can be quickly prepared.

The third form of complaint is that which requires a detailed statement of the facts, explicit allegations regarding the defendant's negligent acts, and an itemized statement of the plaintiff's injuries and losses. This can be sticky. To begin with, you had better know your case very well. If by virtue of the circumstances there are unknown or uncertain facts, you must either plead evasively or alternatively, leaving sufficient leeway so that you can later squeeze the facts into the language of your allegations. It's unfortunate that you must do this, or adopt such an attitude, but there is no choice if you are required to be very specific at the beginning of the lawsuit. Really, this is an excellent argument against those rules which require specificity. It is amusing that those same rules always provide for discovery, but it is only through discovery that one gets the facts which permit him to be specific. To require a detailed complaint before discovery is to put the cart before the horse. Nonetheless, we all must work with what we have and if the rules require it they must be complied with. Let's take a look at three such complaints for a moment—one involves damage to a building, the second a medical malpractice case, and the third an automobile accident. First, the "building" case:

## EXHIBIT 4-4

### IN THE COURT OF COMMON PLEAS OF ALLEGHENY COUNTY, PENNSYLVANIA.
### CIVIL DIVISION

| | |
|---|---|
| FIRST HOLY CHURCH OF BROOKLINE, Plaintiff, v. BROWN TELEPHONE COMPANY OF PENNSYLVANIA; JAMES J. FULTON COMPANY, INC.,; NICKOLAS PILE COMPANY; and J.A. McCANN and R.E. McCANN, trading and doing business as McCANN DRILLING COMPANY, Defendants. | APPEARANCE DOCKET NO. 75-1970 IN TRESPASS |

## COMPLAINT

AND NOW, comes the plaintiff, FIRST HOLY CHURCH OF BROOKLINE, by its Attorney, JOHN A. DeMAY, and files the following Complaint against the defendants, averring the following:

1. Plaintiff is the FIRST HOLY CHURCH OF BROOKLINE, a non-profit corporation, created and existing under the laws of the Commonwealth of Pennsylvania, with its principal office at Bell Avenue, Pittsburgh, Pennsylvania.

2. One of the defendants, BROWN TELEPHONE COMPANY, is a business corporation, having its principal place of business at 561 Jones Street, Pittsburgh, Pennsylvania.

3. One of the defendants, JAMES J. FULTON COMPANY, INC., is a business corporation, having a place of business at 6 Fulton Center, Pittsburgh, Pennsylvania.

4. One of the defendants, NICKOLAS PILE COMPANY, is a business corporation, having a place of business at Creeks Run Road, Ambridge, Pennsylvania.

5. One of the defendants, McCANN DRILLING COMPANY, is a business corporation, having a place of business at Route 33, Pennswood, Pennsylvania.

6. Plaintiff is, and at all times relevant hereto was, the owner of a tract of land located in the Fourth Ward of the City of Pittsburgh at the intersection of Bell Avenue and Toll Way, on which it erected a church.

7. Defendant, BROWN TELEPHONE COMPANY OF PENNSYLVANIA, is, and at all times relevant hereto, was the owner of a tract of land in the Fourth Ward of the City of Pittsburgh fronting on Bell Avenue and adjacent to the property of plaintiff described in the foregoing paragraph.

8. Beginning on or about January, 1975, the defendant, BROWN TELEPHONE COMPANY OF PENNSYLVANIA, through its contractors and/or subcontractors, being the defendants named in Paragraphs 3, 4, and 5, began erecting an office building on the property described in Paragraph 7 hereof.

9. In erecting the aforesaid office building, the defendants performed construction operations, other engineering activities, and removed earth and other supporting subjacent and adjacent strata so close to the property of the plaintiff as to destroy the lateral and vertical support thereof.

10. In removing the earth and other supporting subjacent and adjacent strata, the defendants were negligent and careless and their negligence and carelessness was the proximate cause of plantiff's damage in the following respects.:

(a) In failing to properly test the soil that was to be excavated.

(b) In failing to advise the plaintiff of the results of the tests that they conducted.

(c) In failing to give to the plaintiff timely and sufficient notice of the extent of the excavation and of the nature of the soil to be excavated.

(d) In failing to provide support by shoring of sufficient strength and by acceptable methods and procedures.

(e) In maintaining the excavation for such a length of time as to cause unreasonable risk of harm to the property and church of plaintiff.

(f) In failing to consider the effects of exposure to rain, frost and weather when determining the amount of shoring necessary.

(g) In failing to adjust the method and procedure of shoring in accordance with changes in weather conditions and soil conditions caused by weather.

(h) In failing to make proper studies as to the effects of the excavation and the stress release on the property and church of the plaintiff.

(i) In failing to advise the plaintiff concerning the unstable condition of the land and soil.

(j) In using improper procedures, tools and equipment in excavating the land.

(k) In failing to take adequate precautions to support the land of the plaintiff.

(l) In making the excavation when defendants knew or should have known that harm would come to the plaintiff's land and church as a result of the excavation.

(m) In violating Ordinances of the City of Pittsburgh and the Statutes of the Commonwealth of Pennsylvania and rules and regulations of the Department of Labor and Industry.

(n) In performing other engineering activities relative to the foundation of the structures in a negligent manner.

(o) In being otherwise negligent under the circumstances.

11. By reason of the aforesaid negligence and carelessness of the defendants, constituting the proximate cause, the plaintiff's property and church were damaged in that portions thereof subsided causing extensive structural damage and damage to the interior design and construction.

12. By reason of the negligence and carelessness of the defendants, the plaintiff has been, and will be in the future, put to considerable expense and costs in rectifying the aforesaid damage caused by the defendants.

WHEREFORE, plaintiff demands judgment against the defendants in a sum in excess of TEN THOUSAND ($10,000.00) DOLLARS, exclusive of interest and costs.

John A. DeMay,
Attorney for Plaintiff.

In analyzing this Complaint you will find that the first eight paragraphs simply identify the parties, set forth the fact of ownership of the land, and state that defendants were constructing a building. Paragraph 9 is important because it contains five key words: "... construction operations, other engineering activities ...". This is sufficiently definite that the defendants know which of its activities are involved but sufficiently evasive that later—when plaintiff's counsel knows precisely what went wrong—the facts will match the allegations. Similarly, in Paragraph 10, the defendants are reasonably apprised of the manner in which they were in error but certain subparagraphs were deliberately inserted to provide a degree of flexibility. These are:

\* \* \* \* \*

"(j) In using improper procedures, ...
"(k) In failing to take adequate precautions ...
"(l) In making the excavation ...

\* \* \* \* \*

"(n) In performing other engineering activities ..."

These allegations are broad enough that no matter what facts discovery might uncover, they can be conformed to the allegations. I think it significant that with numerous defense counsel involved the complaint was not challenged and after-discovered facts did fit within the framework of the negligent acts alleged.

The second complaint concerns a medical malpractice action. The plaintiff had been "mugged" and taken to the hospital where he was treated for a broken nose and a fractured pelvis. These healed nicely. When he was permitted to sit up in bed he began to complain about neck pains. He was treated with a cervical collar, traction, and physical therapy to no avail. A psychiatrist was called in for consultation. Eventually, at his insistence, he was transferred to another hospital at which he was soon diagnosed as having a broken neck—fracture of the odontoid process—and a cervical fusion had to be performed resulting in partial permanent disability. The poor man cannot turn his head to the left or right very well. Here the hospital records were carefully reviewed (they were priceless, especially the nurses' notes and comments from the physical therapy department) and an interview was had with the operating surgeon at the second hospital before filing the Complaint. Thus, I was able to be fairly definite in my allegations of negligence. Nonetheless, perhaps out of an excess of caution, I deliberately inserted some language that would protect me should unexpected facts later develop.

## EXHIBIT NO. 4-5

IN THE COURT OF COMMON PLEAS OF ALLEGHENY
COUNTY, PENNSYLVANIA.
CIVIL DIVISION.

| | |
|---|---|
| JOHN F. CARSON,<br>        Plaintiff,<br><br>   v.<br><br>MARTIN H. ANDREWS, M.D.,<br>THOMAS A. HENDERSON, M.D.,<br>WILLIAM SMITH, M.D., and<br>SOUTH GENERAL HOSPITAL,<br>a Pennsylvania corporation,<br><br>        Defendants. | No. 75 - 303.<br>IN TRESPASS |

COMPLAINT IN EXCESS OF
$10,000.00.

AND NOW, comes the plaintiff above named by his Attorney, JOHN A. DeMAY, and for his cause of action against the Defendants, sets forth as follows:

1. The Plaintiff is JOHN F. CARSON, who resides at 123 East 23rd Street, Homestead, Allegheny County, Pennsylvania 15120.

2. The Defendant, MARTIN H. ANDREWS, M.D., is a physician who resides in Allegheny County, Pennsylvania, and engages in the practice of medicine at 1718 Seventh Avenue, Pittsburgh, Pennsylvania 15213.

3. The Defendant, THOMAS A. HENDERSON, M.D., is a physician who resides in Allegheny County, Pennsylvania, and who engages in the practice of psychiatric medicine at the South General Hospital, 1235 East Street, Homestead, Pennsylvania 15120.

4. The Defendant, WILLIAM SMITH, M.D., is a physician who resides in Allegheny County, Pennsylvania, and engages in the practice of medicine at 3688 Thomas Street, Pittsburgh, Pennsylvania 15208.

5. The Defendant, SOUTH GENERAL HOSPITAL, is a Pennsylvania corporation, with its principal place of business at 1235 East Street, Homestead, Pennsylvania 15120.

6. Between April 21, 1975, and June 12, 1975, the Plaintiff was a patient at the South General Hospital under the care of Martin

H. Andrews, M.D.; William Smith, M.D., was the Radiologist who attended Plaintiff; and Thomas A. Henderson, M.D., is a psychiatrist who was called in for consultation.

7. With regard to Dr. William Smith, it is alleged that at all pertinent times he was the agent, servant and employee of the Defendant Hospital acting under the direction, supervision and control of that Hospital and he was on or about the business of the Hospital.

8. While a patient in the South General Hospital, the Plaintiff complained extensively of pain in his neck. Some physical therapy treatment was given to the neck which included traction at 50 lbs weight for ten (10) minutes interval over a period of several days. Other forms of traction were applied. Plaintiff complained most bitterly about the pain from this treatment.

9. The Plaintiff finally insisted on being transferred to St. Sebastian's Hospital. The transfer occurred by ambulance and he was admitted to St. Sebastian's Hospital on June 12, 1975, where a diagnosis of a fracture of the cervical spine was promptly made and Plaintiff had to undergo a cervical fusion operation from the occiput to the C-2 level. The Ondontoid process was fractured.

10. The Plaintiff was negligently treated by the Defendants and the Defendants were negligent in the following respects:

a. As to Dr. Martin H. Andrews:

(1) In failing to order additional numbers of X-rays;

(2) In failing to order additional X-rays from different positions;

(3) In having ordered the cervical traction in the Physical Therapy Department;

(4) In having continued the traction in the face of complaints of severe pain from the Plaintiff;

(5) In having made a faulty diagnosis;

(6) In failing to give proper attention to the Plaintiff's complaints;

(7) In failing to adopt diagnostic techniques that were available to him;

(8) In ignoring the Radiologist's statement that additional X-rays should be taken;

(9) In failing to immobilize the Plaintiff in a halo traction or other suitable device;

(10) In failing to properly analyze and discuss the reports coming from the Physical Therapy Department

with regard to the plaintiff's complaints and the severe pain occasioned by the traction process;

(11) In failing to adequately review and analyze the patient's hospital records;

(12) In failing to call for an orthopedic consultation;

(13) In disbelieving the Plaintiff and the records to the point of calling for a psychiatric consultation;

(14) In failing to call for a neurological consultation;

(15) In failing to refer the Plaintiff to an Orthopedist; and

(16) In being otherwise negligent under the circumstances.

**b. As to Dr. Thomas A. Henderson:**

(1) In misdiagnosing the Plaintiff's condition;

(2) In failing to adequately study the chart;

(3) In failing to call for an orthopedic consultation;

(4) In failing to order additional X-ray studies or other diagnostic techniques;

(5) In failing to pay attention to the complaints of the Plaintiff; and

(6) In being otherwise negligent under the circumstances.

**c. As to Dr. William Smith:**

(1) In failing to take the proper number of X-rays from differing positions either at the time the X-rays were first taken or after the Plaintiff's symptoms of cervical pain became persistent and demanding;

(2) In failing to review the chart and to take affirmative action with regard to the Plaintiff's complaints;

(3) In failing to follow up the care and condition of the Plaintiff and to take additional X-rays to determine the cause of Plaintiff's complaints;

(4) In failing to take an "open mouth" X-ray of the Plaintiff upon admission or at a later date;

(5) In failing to follow through on his statement to Dr. Andrews for additional cervical X-rays;

(6) In failing to properly read the X-rays; and

(7) In being otherwise negligent under the circumstances.

d. As to South General Hospital:

(1) The allegations set forth as to Dr. William Smith are incorporated herein

(2) In having an incompetent Radiologist;

(3) In failing to properly supervise and direct the work of Dr. William Smith; and

(4) In being otherwise negligent under the circumstances.

11. As a result of the negligence of some or all of the Defendants, Plaintiff has sustained the following losses and injuries:

a. Plaintiff has undergone considerable pain, suffering and inconvenience;

b. Plaintiff has incurred numerous hospital, medical nursing home care and other associated bills and expenses;

c. Plaintiff has had to undergo a cervical fusion operation and to undergo extensive hospitalization at St. Sebastian's Hospital and then in the Woodmont Residence, Inc.;

d. Plaintiff has incurred a loss of earnings;

e. Plaintiff has incurred a partial permanent disability;

f. He has had to seek employment as a handicapped person and cannot return to his former employment as a machinist;

g. His life was placed in serious jeopardy by the actions of the Defendants; and

h. Some or all of the foregoing may be permanent in nature.

WHEREFORE, judgment is demanded against the Defendants in an amount in excess of TEN THOUSAND ($10,000.00) DOLLARS, exclusive of interest and costs.

John A. DeMay,
Attorney for Plaintiff.

There is a certain degree of vagueness in some of these allegations. Look at Paragraph 10a, subparagraphs

(6) "In failing to give proper attention....";

(7) "In failing to adopt diagnostic techniques....";

(10) "In failing to properly analyze and discuss....."; and

(11) "In failing to adequately review and analyze....".

Similar language is used as to the other Defendants. Look at Paragraph 10c, subparagraphs

> (2) In failing to review the chart and to take affirmative action....''; and

> (3) In failing to follow up the care and condition of the Plaintiff....''.

The vagueness is necessary at the beginning of the action when you just can't be sure what did happen. Incidently, don't be fooled by the argument that after discovery you can easily amend the Complaint. If the Statute of Limitations expires before discovery and at a deposition, for example, you learn important new facts, and then you try to amend—you will have a real fight on your hands which you just might lose. Avoid this headache! The men who wrote the Rules hoped that you would get the right to amend the Complaint, but where are they when a Judge insists that you're changing your cause of action and refuses your Motion? They're not in the Courtroom with you—that's for sure. All you have to show for your efforts are the remains of your case and an irate client. It is far the safer course to include a multiple of allegations, based on "information and belief"—or strong suspicion—then, after discovery, you can pick and choose the theory on which the case is going to be tried. If your state has adopted the Federal rules, this sort of problem will not even arise.

Finally, let us look at a simple automobile accident in which a boulder rolled down a steep hill, owned by the City of Pittsburgh, and hit a taxicab proceeding up a roadway. In this case, alternative allegations were used, i.e., "in permitting the condition to exist..."; "in failing to correct the condition ...''; "in failing to erect a fence or warning system ...''; and "in failing to give notice ...''. This seemed to include nearly every circumstance that I could think of that seemed likely to develop in discovery.

### EXHIBIT 4-6

IN THE COURT OF COMMON PLEAS OF ALLEGHENY
COUNTY, PENNSYLVANIA.
CIVIL DIVISION.

| FRANK T. JAMES, | : | |
| Plaintiff, | : | |
| v. | : | APPEARANCE DOCKET |
| CITY OF PITTSBURGH, | : | No. 75-4503 |
| a Municipal Corporation | : | IN TRESPASS |
| | : | |
| Defendant. | : | |

## COMPLAINT

AND NOW comes the plaintiff above named by his Attorney, JOHN A. DeMAY, and for his cause of action against the defendant sets forth as follows:

1. The plaintiff is FRANK T. JAMES, who resides at 1530 Jane Street, Pittsburgh, Allegheny County, Pennsylvania.

2. The defendant is the CITY OF PITTSBURGH, a municipal corporation, with its principal place of business at 313 City-County Building, Pittsburgh, Allegheny County, Pennsylvania.

3. The accident here involved occurred on the Franklin Roadway approximately one-half of the distance west of the South Tunnels on April 18, 1975.

4. At the aforesaid time and place the plaintiff was a passenger in a taxicab going up the Franklin Roadway at about 10 A.M. Suddenly a boulder and other debris rolled down the hillside and smashed into the cab, thus causing serious injuries to the plaintiff.

5. The defendant is the owner of the property to the south of the Franklin Roadway in the area where this accident occurred. The defendant was completely aware of the dangerous condition existing on its property, similar occurrences having taken place numberous times in the past few years and in the year 1975.

6. This accident was caused by the negligence of the defendant, and the defendant has been negligent in the following respects:

A. In permitting the condition to exist;

B. In permitting rocks, boulders and other debris to slide onto the Franklin Roadway;

C. In failing to erect a fence, wall or other similar device to stop the debris from falling onto the Roadway;

D. In failing to erect a warning system to warn motorists of the movement of rocks and debris toward the Roadway;

E. In failing to correct the ground condition so that rocks and debris would not roll onto the Roadway;

F. In failing to give notice of the dangerous condition to the traveling public, including the plaintiff;

G. In violating the statutes of the Commonwealth of Pennsylvania; and

H. In being otherwise negligent under the circumstances.

7. As a result of the negligence of the defendant, the plaintiff has sustained the following injuries and losses:

A. He has undergone considerable pain, suffering and inconvenience;

B. He has sustained a loss of earnings and an impairment of earning capacity;

C. He sustained injuries to his neck;

D. He sustained injuries to his upper back;

E. He suffers from nervousness and severe headaches;

F. He has incurred numerous hospital, medical and other similar expenses; and

G. Some or all of the foregoing may be permanent in nature.

WHEREFORE, judgment is demanded against the plaintiff in an amount in excess of TEN THOUSAND ($10,000.00) DOLLARS, excluding interest and costs.

John A. DeMay,
Attorney for Plaintiff.

I would hope that by reviewing these several Complaints you get a better understanding of some of the intricacies involved in preparing this important pleading. Your Complaint should be reasonably definite and specific, but at the same time, as a protective device, you must insert allegations that will be sufficient to protect you should discovery disclose new and unexpected facts.

# CHAPTER 5

# How to Use Discovery—
# the Weapons in Your Armory

## BEGIN DISCOVERY IMMEDIATELY

Just as your complaint should be filed as promptly as possible, so should your Discovery begin as quickly as possible. There is such a thing as "priority of discovery." If you file interrogatories first, you need not answer defendant's interrogatories until he has first answered yours—the same rule applies to depositions. This is a minor tactical advantage but one worth taking advantage of. More important though is the fact that after you have dictated your complaint, you know that file as well as you will ever know it. This is the perfect time to dictate a set of interrogatories, prepare Notice of Depositions, and Motions to Produce. Let your secretary do them all at once and let them sit in your file. You can tell her the order in which you want them filed and set the dates in accordance with your local Rules of Procedure—then it's a purely routine matter for her to go ahead and file them. The important thing is that they are prepared when the facts are fresh in your mind and that they are ready to file on the dates you set.

## INTERROGATORIES—MAKE THE
## DEFENDANT WORK FOR YOU!

Let me ask a candid question: When is the last time you had an opponent completely at your disposal, working for you, and it never cost you a penny? Answer: The last time you served a set of interrogatories. Think of it for a moment—this is a wonderful tool. Interrogatories are best used to establish "static" or "unchangeable" or "non-argumentative" facts such as dates, times or distances. The questions should be of the *who, what* and *where* variety. Save the *how* and *why* questions—which lead to variable answers and invite discussion—for depositions.

### Use Your Imagination

All that is required is that you sit back in your chair and let your imagination go to work. What do you really want the defendant to tell you? The names of witnesses, surely, the make and model of his car, the mileage on it, date of last inspection, and items repaired. Keep going. In a medical malpractice case involving surgery, how many operations did the doctor perform that day? How long did each take? What time did he check out of the hospital the night before? You may well find the poor man checked out at midnight after a long, long day, his first operation was scheduled for 6:00 A.M. the next morning, and your client's operation was his fourth for the day! He was dead on his feet when he got to your client!

### Ask Too Many Questions, Not Too Few

The nice thing about interrogatories is that you can file a set, get the answers, follow up with Supplemental Interrogatories, receive the answers to those, and still file more questions. Within reason there is no end to it since, with your imagination busily at work, each set of Answers calls forth new questions. So long as the questions are relevant and you are not being deliberately annoying, you can't be stopped. So, keep asking. Don't forget—the defendant is working for you. Keep him busy. Ask too many questions, not too few.

### Let's Nail Down the Unchangeable Facts

In every case, there are a host of essential but miscellaneous facts that you would like to have clearly established so that you can concentrate on the central issue of the case. This would include such things as the date and time of an accident, its location, the identity of the vehicles involved, the width of the roadway. Interrogatories are uniquely suited for this purpose. When you get the Answers it becomes a simple matter to read the questions and answers into the record and to the jury so that these facts are beyond dispute and require no proof.

## ILLUSTRATIVE INTERROGATORIES—

## THEIR USE AND EFFECTIVENESS

Let's take a look at some interrogatories to see what can be accomplished with them. The first set involves a case (See Exhibit 4-2) in which a light company hired an independent contractor to paint its high-tension towers. On one tower there were "potheads"—devices to hold the wires passing over the tower—located on the horizontal beams outside of the main body of the tower. The painters were merely warned to "stay away from the potheads." They naturally took this to mean not to touch them. As plaintiff was painting about ten feet off the ground he swung around a vertical beam four feet from a pothead. There was a flash of electricity and he was thrown to the ground and injured. I served two sets of interrogatories in this case. Consider them for a moment.

The first question is a standard one, relating to witnesses, that should always be asked. At least it insures the fact that you have a complete list of witnesses—those known to you and to them.

1. Identify by name and address every person known to the Defendant or its Counsel who has any knowledge concerning the facts and circumstances surrounding: (a) the accident itself, (b) events immediately preceding the accident, (c) events occurring subsequent to the accident.

In the next two questions, I was interested in warnings given to the painters—what they were, who gave them, and when they were given.

2. State what measures, if any, were taken by the Penn Light Company to warn the Plaintiff and his co-employees of any dangers to them in working on the tower here involved.

3. If any verbal warnings were given by any employees of the Penn Light Company concerning dangers to the Plaintiff and others working on this tower, set forth: (a) the name and address of the person giving the warning, (b) as specifically as possible, set forth in detail the nature of the warning or instruction, (c) set forth when the warning or instruction was given.

In Nos. 4 and 5, I was curious about safety regulations the Light Company might have. My plan was to follow through with a Motion to Produce, if necessary, and hope that there would be something in this written material that would be helpful.

4. Set forth whether Penn Light Company has any rules, regulations, instructions or brochures giving instruction to their employees or to outside personnel such as the painters here involved with regard to safety measures to be taken when working on towers such as the one here involved.

5. If the Defendant has such rules, regulations, instructions, or brochures, either identify them specifically or attach hereto a copy of such.

Now, questions 6, 7, 8, and 9 relate to those necessary miscellaneous facts referred to previously that I simply wanted established so that there would be no dispute and I wouldn't have to worry over them.

6. Set forth how long prior to August 23, 1974, employees of the Sunset Painting Company, Inc., were painting towers for Defendant and how many towers had been painted.

7. Set forth whether the tower here involved had what are known as "potheads" attached to one or more of the horizontal beams of the tower.

8. Set forth how many "potheads" were on the tower here involved.

9. Set forth the amount of electricity that was contained in or passed through each of the "potheads" on the tower here involved.

Nos. 10 and 11 are "chancy" types of questions. I hoped for a satisfactory answer but there was nothing lost if defendant replied negatively.

10. Set forth whether Defendant knows that electricity will "arc" or "jump" from a "pothead" to a person even though a person may not touch the "pothead".

11. If the answer to the foregoing question is yes, set forth the distance it may be expected that electricity will "arc" or "jump" from a "pothead" to a person where the "pothead" is such as that on the tower here involved and carrying the amount of electricity such as that which was carried by the "pothead" here involved.

The answers to these questions were:

10. Yes.

11. A minimum safe working distance is at approximately six to eight feet. However, once an "arc" occurs, it

follows an object (or person) it touches and can go any length due to the ionization of air.

That clinched the case. Defendant couldn't prove any more than a general warning to "stay away from the 'potheads'." Nothing was said to the painters about arcing electricity that would actually chase after a man. Needless to say, the case settled—Please Note—it settled *after* the Complaint was filed and *after* the defendant was forced to make this admission in Interrogatories Nos. 10 and 11. I am sure that it would not have settled prior to this time.

However, when dictating the questions I had no idea what the answers might be to Questions 10 and 11, so I moved on:

12. Identify by name and address of the person involved, and the date of any incident within a ten-year period prior to August 23, 1974, when to Defendant's knowledge a person was struck by arcing electricity from a "pothead" while working on a tower of the Defendant.

I knew there might be federal or state safety rules that could apply to this situation, but which ones? Who would know better than the Company at which they were directed? So, question No. 13:

13. Identify specifically those federal or state regulations pertaining to safety measures which are applicable when painters such as the men involved on the day of this accident are working on towers of the Defendant such as the one here involved.

No. 14 was asked because this tower is well inside defendant's property and my investigator could not get a picture of it. It's true I could get a Court Order to get onto the property, but if the defendant had photographs, why bother. In addition I just suspected defendant might have taken photographs the very day of the accident. They had.

14. Does the Defendant have' any photographs of the tower and the scene generally of this accident? If so, set forth where these photographs may be viewed and copied if necessary.

That completed the first set of Interrogatories. After receiving the Answers to these questions, it occurred to me that I might inquire into a few other areas. Why wasn't the electricity shut off? What warning signs, if any, were posted? What physical barriers, if any, were erected to keep men from getting too close to the "potheads."

Incidentally, I knew by talking with an electrical engineer, that:

1.  Safety devices were available commercially;

2.  Physical barriers are frequently constructed; and

3.  The electricity could have been shut off because a "redundant" system should exist in the event the tower was put out of commission by lightning, earthquake, and the like.

So, with this information and some idle musing, I came up with Supplemental Interrogatories Nos. 15 through 25:

> 15. State whether this accident happened at the South Hills Power Station located outside of Sewickley, Pennsylvania.
>
> 16. If the answer to the foregoing Interrogatory is "No," identify precisely where this accident happened.
>
> 17. Identify whether this Power Station services residential or commercial customers or both and if the commercial customers are less than ten (10), identify them.
>
> State whether defendant has in its possession rubber, wooden, porcelain, ceramic, or plastic covers which could have been placed over the "pothead" involved in this accident.
>
> 19. If the Defendant does not possess such covers, state whether Defendant knows whether they are commercially available, and, if so, set forth
>
> > (a) Where they can be purchased; and
> >
> > (b) The price of such products.
>
> 20. State whether any warning signs or other written notice of hazards to persons such as Plaintiff working on this tower were posted on the tower and, if so, identify the warning signs and where precisely they were located.
>
> 21. Identify whether any such warning signs were posted anywhere in the immediate area and, if so, identify the warning signs precisely and set forth the exact distance from the scene of this accident and where they were located with reference to the scene of this accident.
>
> 22. State why the electricity on this tower was not shut off.
>
> 23. State why a ground or other safety device was not affixed to the pothead or the wires going in or leading from it while the men were working on the tower.

24. State whether Defendant has a "redundant" system for transferring electricity to its customers in the event that in an emergency the tower here involved would be shut down or unavailable for the carriage of electricity.

25. On the tower here involved and at the point where this accident happened, state whether there were any physical barriers either wooden, rope, or otherwise, to prevent Plaintiff and his co-employees from stepping beyond the vertical beams of the tower and if none were in use, state why they were not used.

These Interrogatories took some time and effort—not too much, however. But was it worth the effort? Of course, it was—they settled the case. A little time, a little imagination—idle musing as I like to refer to it— and a fine result. The defendant did all the work and it didn't cost me a penny.

Let's examine another set of Interrogatories that resulted in a settlement. The Plaintiff, in a taxicab, was going up a roadway, adjacent to a hillside owned by the City of Pittsburgh. A large boulder rolled down and hit the taxicab, injuring him. The Complaint in this case is set forth as Exhibit No. 4-6. The following questions were asked and answers received:

1. Set forth whether the defendant is the owner of the real estate on the Southerly side of the Franklin Roadway at a point approximately one-half of the distance west of the South Tunnels, and on April 18, 1975.

ANSWER:     Yes.

2. Between January 1, 1966, and the present time set forth the number of times that employees of the defendant were obliged to remove rock slides from the Franklin Roadway and, further, set forth the precise dates on which this work was done.

ANSWER:     Rock slides were removed from Franklin Roadway on the following dates—3/2/66, 3/22/66, 3/23/66, 3/24/66, 3/25/66, 4/28/69, 6/6/71.

3. Identify with particularity those measures taken by the defendant between January 1, 1966, and the present time:

A.     To prevent rock slides.

ANSWER:     Retaining wall approximately six foot high and one foot wide installed to catch any debris or rocks, the rear of which is cleaned out periodically.

B.    To warn automobile drivers of the existence of rock slides.

ANSWER:    None.

C.    To warn automobile drivers of the possibility of rock slides.

ANSWER:    None.

4. Set forth what measures have been taken by defendant by way of inspection or otherwise to ascertain whether a rock slide is likely to occur from the hillside onto the Franklin Roadway.

ANSWER:    Roadway is traveled by 5th Division Supervisor or Foreman each and every day. If anything looks dangerous or if anything is on roadway it is taken care of that day.

The catch basins in back of retaining wall were cleaned April 3, 4, 5, and 10, 1975 by Highways and Sewers—5th Division.

5. Does defendant have any report of a rock slide occurring on April 18, 1975, and state whether defendant cleaned up any rock or rocks from the Franklin Roadway on or shortly after that date?

ANSWER:    According to Mr. Ron Smith, Supervisor of the 5th Division, no report or notice of any rock slide was received nor do records show that they cleaned any rocks from the roadway on or shortly after April 18, 1975.

Question 2 and its answer clearly establish notice to the City. So does the answer to Question 4 since, if the catch-basin had to be cleared within eight days of the accident (April 10, the accident date being April 18), debris was still falling from the hill. With regard to protection of the road, what did the City do? Nothing outside of erecting the retaining wall mentioned in answer to Interrogatory No. 3. My investigator took pictures of the rear of the retaining wall about May 1—two weeks after the accident—and it was packed with rocks, dirt and boulders almost to the top. It took a long time to build up that debris to a six-foot height! Finally, I knew that railroads have erected electric warning fences on hillsides so that when a boulder goes through the fence a red light alerts oncoming trains of the possibility of boulders on the tracks. Such a system was feasible here to warn motorists but didn't exist. Therefore, negligence; therefore, settlement. Once again, however, until the City was forced to put into writing, under oath, that it knew of the danger and did little or nothing to prevent it or warn passing motorists, there was clearly no hope of a settlement.

### Work Closely with an Expert
### in Preparing the Questions

If you have a case that requires an expert, be sure to use him in preparing the Interrogatories. If he is needed in the case, it is obvious that he has much more knowledge than you do about the subject matter. In addition, he will have some ideas of his own about what *he* wants from the defendant. He can help with technical jargon and can advise with regard to various types of books, records and other data that the defendant ought to have. A good example of this type of Interrogatory is shown in Exhibit 5-1. My experts, a Soils Engineer and a Construction Engineer, knew exactly what they wanted and we spent several hours together drawing up these questions. They are rather lengthy but worth the time to review.

## EXHIBIT 5-1

### IN THE COURT OF COMMON PLEAS OF ALLEGHENY
### COUNTY, PENNSYLVANIA.
### CIVIL DIVISION.

| | | |
|---|---|---|
| FIRST HOLY CHURCH OF BROOKLINE, | : | |
| Plaintiff, | : | |
| v. | : | |
| BROWN TELEPHONE COMPANY OF PENNSYLVANIA; | : | APPEARANCE DOCKET |
| JAMES J. FULTON COMPANY, INC.; | : | No. 75 - 1970 |
| NICKOLAS PILE COMPANY; and | : | Issue No. 76383 |
| J.A.McCANN and R.E. McCANN, trading and doing business as McCANN DRILLING COMPANY, | : | |
| Original Defendants, | : | |
| v. | : | |
| CITY OF PITTSBURGH, | : | |
| Additional Defendant. | : | |

INTERROGATORIES.

AND NOW comes the plaintiff, FIRST HOLY CHURCH OF BROOKLINE, by its Attorney, JOHN A. DeMAY, and pursuant to the Rules of Court, demands that the BROWN TELEPHONE COMPANY answer the following Interrogatories under oath within twenty (20) days from the date of service herewith:

1.    Identify by name and address the following persons:

    A.    The Project Manager
    B.    The Project Engineer
    C.    The Job Superintendent

2.    A.    Set forth the column loads that were designed for this structure.

    B.    Set forth the column loads as actually constructed.

3.    Set forth the type of of foundation that was utilized by the defendant—i.e., piles or on caissons.

4.    Was water pumped out of this excavation at any time? If the answer to the foregoing is yes, set forth:

    A.    The date or dates on or during which water was pumped from the excavation.
    B.    The amount of water pumped from the excavation.
    C.    By what manner and means was the water pumped from the excavation?
    D.    Who did this work?

5.    What kind of deflections did the defendant design the temporary retaining walls to contain?

6.    Set forth whether there were any drawings on the sheet-pile retaining walls as built and, if so, set forth:

    A.    In whose possession these drawings may be found?
    B.    Where may they be examined?

7.    As to subsurface work, set forth the following:

    A.    Whether there were any subsurface explorations and, if so, set forth the following:

        (1)    By whom were they made?
        (2)    When were they made:
        (3)    Where may the reports of such explorations presently be found?

    B.    Does this defendant have foundation investigation reports and, if so, set forth:

        (1) In whose possession may these reports be found?
        (2) Where may these reports be examined?

C.    Were test borings made? If so, set forth:
    (1)    Who made the test borings?
    (2)    Where can the records presently be found?
    (3)    In whose possession may the records be found?
    (4)    The date or dates of the test borings.

8.    Set forth whether any blasting was done and, if so, set forth:

A.    The date or dates on which blasting was done.
B.    The location of the blasting.
C.    The total charge per blast.
D.    The number of delays per blast.
E.    The maximum charge per blast.
F.    The charge per blast.

9.    State whether the defendant conducted any monitoring of the church structure and, if so, set forth the following:

A.    Who monitored the church structure?
B.    What means were utilized to monitor the church structure?
C.    Give the dates or periods of time in which the church structure was monitored.
D.    Where may the records concerning the monitoring of the church structure be found:

10.    State whether defendant took photographs of the church structure and, if so, set forth the following:

A.    The date or dates on which photographs were taken.

B.    Who took the photographs?
C.    In whose possession may the photographs be found?

D.    Where are the photographs available for inspection?

11.    Does defendant have construction photographs dealing with all work done with the excavation up to the ground surface and, if so, set forth the following:

A.    During what period of time were the photographs taken?

B.    Who has possession of the photographs?
C.    Where are the photographs available for inspection?

12.    Set forth whether defendant, itself or through the use of any independent organization, performed ground water hydrology studies and, if so, set forth the following:

    A.    Who ordered the studies made?

    B.    When were the studies made?

    C.    In whose possession are the reports of the studies?

    D.    Where are these reports available for inspection?

    13.    State whether subsurface studies of soils were conducted by defendant or on behalf of defendant by any independent organization and, if so, set forth the following.

    A.    What studies were made?

    B.    Who made them?

    C.    When were they made?

    D.    How were they made?

    E.    In whose possession may a copy of these studies be found?

    F.    Where can a copy of these studies be examined?

    14.    As to the retaining walls adjacent to the plaintiff's property, set forth the following:

    A.    What studies were made as to the strength and design of the retaining walls?

    B.    Who made them?

    C.    When were they made?

    D.    In whose possession may a copy of these reports or studies be found?

    E.    Where may they be inspected?

    F.    Where may blueprints concerning the construction of the retaining walls be found?

    G.    State whether there was any change between the design and construction of the retaining walls before construction and during construction. If so, set forth:

    (1)    What changes were made?

    15.    A.    Set forth where the original foundation design drawings may be examined, and in whose possession they are retained.

    B.    Set forth whether there were any revisions to these design drawings and, if so, indicate where the revisions may be inspected.

    C.    Set forth whether the "as built" foundation drawings are the same or different from the original design drawings and, if so, set forth where a copy of the drawings may be inspected in their "as built" condition.

    16.    State whether any heavy loads were brought into the area during the construction period—such loads relating to loads of 100 tons or more and, if so, set forth the following:

    A.    When such loads were brought into the area.

B.    The exact weight of such loads brought into the area.

C.    What were the contents of the loads?

John A. DeMay,
Attorney for Plaintiff.

Look at No. 2. I didn't know anything about column loads—much less that there should be a difference between "design" loads as opposed to "as constructed." The same applies to the "deflections" referred to in Question No. 5, "subsurface explorations" (No. 7A), foundation investigation reports (No. 7B), and the data concerning blasting (No. 8). I not only didn't know about these things, but I would never have ever dreamed of their existence—but my experts did. In addition, they knew what reports the defendants ought to have that we ought to see. So we asked for them in every Interrogatory from No. 9 to No. 15. Then, if necessary, I would file a Motion to Produce to permit us to study and copy them. So, I let them ramble on—writing furiously as they talked. Later, I took my notes, arranged them into a little bit of order and then began to phrase the questions in "legalese." The result was that we secured vital information that helped bring about a good result. Without the experts, I would have been helpless.

Interrogatories are a very valuable tool. They must be specifically designed for each case, they require some time and a lot of imagination. They're worth it. Find yourself a quiet spot, engage in some idle musing about your case, and you'll come up with the questions. And don't ever forget—the defendant has to come up with the answers—free of charge.

## DEPOSITIONS—A PLEASANT CHAT WITH THE DEFENDANT

A deposition is a procedure wherein a witness comes to your office (either voluntarily or by subpoena) and is there questioned by you in the presence of a court reporter and the defense attorney. Interrogatories deal with static facts, depositions deal with variables. The preparation of interrogatories demands a certain solitude, depositions are all action. In a sense a deposition is a quiet chat with the defendant—but with serious intent—you're trying to win a lawsuit right there.

The deposition can be arranged simply by the filing of a Notice of Deposition with service of a copy upon opposing counsel. Illustrative of such a Notice is the following:

## EXHIBIT 5-2

### IN THE COURT OF COMMON PLEAS OF ALLEGHENY COUNTY, PENNSYLVANIA. CIVIL DIVISION.

| | | |
|---|---|---|
| ROGER A. GRAYSTONE, | : | |
| Plaintiff, | : | |
| | : | APPEARANCE DOCKET |
| v. | : | |
| | : | NO. 25 April Term, 1976 |
| HAROLD G. BROWN, | : | |
| | : | IN TRESPASS. |
| Defendant. | : | |

### NOTICE OF DEPOSITION.

TO:     WILBUR J. WOODS, ESQUIRE
2351 Jones Law Building
Pittsburgh, Pennsylvania     15219

TAKE NOTICE that the deposition of HAROLD G. BROWN, Defendant herein, will be taken for the purpose of discovery and for use at trial pursuant to the Rules of Civil Procedure, before a person authorized by law to administer oaths, on the 9th day of November, 1975, at 10:30 o'clock, A.M., at the offices of JOHN A. DeMAY, 3320 Grant Building, Pittsburgh. Pennsylvania, at which time and place you are invited to appear and take such part as shall be fitting and proper. The scope and purpose of the deposition is to inquire into all the facts surrounding the happening of the accident of which the Deponent has knowledge.

John A. DeMay,
Attorney for Plaintiff

The Federal Rules require substantially the same type of Notice. Generally the rules of every state and the Federal Rules state that the party to a lawsuit need not be subpoenaed; however, any other person to be deposed must be subpoenaed.

### This Is a Devastating Weapon

It is at a deposition that you learn at first hand the nature of your defendant—and how you're going to handle him. This is your chance to observe his demeanor, dress, manner of speaking, the degree of his self-confidence, the accuracy of his recollection, the extent to which he can be pushed. Then, too, you force him to commit himself—under oath. There are two good reasons for taking a deposition:

1. To try to get the witness to make a damaging admission that will end the case right then and there; and

2. To commit the witness in detail to a story—any story—so long as he cannot vary from it.

Since you control the questioning, and can inquire into any relevant matter, a deposition can be a devastating weapon. Skillfully utilized, even with an evasive witness, it can bring the walls crashing around his head. Since you are in control of the proceeding there is no need to get agitated, but a certain degree of pointed and persistent questioning is appropriate.

An illustration of this involves a medical malpractice case in which I sued several doctors who worked together. The patient had sustained a broken ankle which was casted. The cast was too tight, an ulceration developed under the cast, infection set in, and eventually the patient developed osteomyelitis. The nurses' notes were filled with comments about the frequency and bitterness of the patient's complaints that the cast was too tight, observations of swelling and discoloration of the toes, and later, evidence of drainage. Red lights were flashing all through the notes. I deposed one of the attending physicians. Initially I began with a colloquy about a discrepancy which appeared in the records. The June hospital records called the diagnosis a "bimalleolar" fracture, the September hospital records called it a "trimalleolar" fracture. Actually the difference was insignificant so far as I was concerned but one diagnosis was clearly in error and I felt the doctor might be put on the defensive right at the beginning of the deposition in trying to explain it. The deposition went like this:

Q. Doctor, did Mrs. Jones suffer from a bimalleolar fracture of the left ankle or trimalleolar fracture?

A. Bimalleolar fracture.

Q. Will you tell me what that is?

A. That means both medial and lateral malleoli are fractured.

Q. Where are the malleoli in your ankle?

A. They are the two bones on either side of your ankle joint.

Q. That protrude?

A. Yes.

> MR. DeMAY: Okay.
> I would like to have this marked as Exhibit 2.
> (Exhibit No. 2 marked for identification.)

BY MR. DeMAY:

Q. This is the September hospitalization?

A. Yes.

Q. Doctor, I show you what has been marked as Exhibit No. 2 being the hospital records for the admission of September.

> Would you be kind enough to look at those.
> What is the date there, September 2?

A. Yes.

Q. September 2nd?

A. Yes.

Q. And on the second page is writing in your handwriting?

A. Yes.

Q. Does it not say near the top there "trimalleolar fracture"?

A. Yes.

Q. Why did you write that?

A. I made a mistake.

Q. How can you explain the mistake, Doctor, in view of the fact that this woman had been hospitalized in June and she had been seen by you three times prior to the hospitalization in September?

A. I can't explain it.

Q. Is there such a thing as a trimalleolar fracture?

A. Yes.

Q. When you made this handwritten note of "trimalleolar fracture" where did you obtain that information?

A. In the discharge summary.

Q. In the discharge summary, does it say "trimalleolar fracture"?

A. Yes.

Q. Now, going to the original operative diagnosis as contained in your office records and in the hospital records, what does it refer to?

A. Compound bimalleolar fracture of the left ankle.

BY MR. DeMAY:

Q. Referring to the June hospitalization, in the handwriting it says "compound bimalleolar fracture" and in the typing on the discharge summary it says: "Compound bimalleolar fracture"; yet in the September sheet, the second page in handwriting, it says "trimalleolar fracture."

Now, Doctor, did you read the discharge summary of the June hospitalization?

A. Apparently not.

So, the stage was set. Now it was time to get serious and to turn the doctor's attention to those vital nurses' notes.

BY MR. DeMAY:

Q. Doctor, you have indicated that when you make rounds there are always two of you; is that right?

A. Usually, unless someone is out of town.

Q. Now, does that appear—does the identity of the two of you who are making rounds, does that appear anywhere in the hospital records?

A. It may appear in the nurse's notes.

Q. And in the nursing notes only one is mentioned, one of you.

A. It doesn't mean anything.

Q. Why not?

A. At South Hospital our entire surgical services are considered Dr. Adams' services.

Q. Are you saying that the entry in the nursing notes would always contain the name of Dr. Adams?

A. I can't say that.

Q. I see.

A. If he and I were there, they might put my name. They might put both names; or his name down. It depends.

Q. Doctor, would it affect your testimony at all were I to tell you—
and you can review these records if you like—that there is not a
single entry any place identifying two doctors as seeing Mrs.
Jones.

A. I would say that I am not surprised at all.

Q. When you go to the hospital—and let's take this special case,
Mrs. Jones' case—do you review the nurse's notes?

A. Not every time.

Q. Why not?

A. If there is a problem and the nurses are making rounds with us
and there are any problems, the problems will be brought up by
her and discussed.

Q. Do I understand your testimony to be then that you do not
necessarily review the nurse's notes as to a particular patient
before you go in to see that patient, but it depends upon the
nurse verbally telling you something or other about that
patient?

A. Unless there is a problem.

Q. How are you going to know there is a problem unless you—

A. The patient will complain.

Q. When the patient complains, what do you do?

A. Then we usually go over the chart.

Q. Is the chart not prepared for your benefit?

A. Yes.

Q. Are not the nurse's notes prepared for the purpose of advising
you of the patient's condition when you are not at the hospital?

A. We make rounds very early in the morning. Many times the
nurse's notes have not been written yet when we see the patient.

The nurses are often at report and the charts are completed
after rounds are made.

I would say that by and large we depend more upon verbal
reports than what has been written on the charts.

Q. Are you saying that if you make rounds at 7:00 or 8:00 o'clock
in the morning, the nurses who work from 12:00 to 7:00 may
not have completed their notes?

A. Yes.

Q. But isn't it true that the nurses that work from 3:00 to 11:00 would have completed those notes and they would be available to you?

A. Yes. That is usually true.

Q. All right.

Once again I ask: Are those notes prepared for the purpose of advising you of the patient's condition during the hours that you are not present?

A. Yes.

Q. And despite that, you tell me that you do not habitually and as a matter of normal routine read those nurse's notes?

A. I do not.

Emboldened by the admissions I was getting, I decided straight out to try to get him to connect the osteomyelitis and the infected ulcerations:

Q. Let me show you a hospital record for January 25, a January 25 admission, Doctor.

In going through there, will you tell me when the diagnosis was made and who made it?

A. Apparently it was made by Dr. Adams on the 26th of January.

Q. What is osteomyelitis?

A. It is an infection involving bone.

Q. What causes it?

A. Bacteria.

Q. Could the infection that had been previously present in the ankle of Mrs. Jones have caused the osteomyelitis?

A. They would be directly related, yes.

End case! An expert looked at the deposition and laughed, "You don't need me," he said. As it turned out, I didn't.

## Consider the Deposition a "Mini-Trial"

A trial and a deposition are identical to the extent that each involves the questioning of a witness by an attorney in an effort to find out what happened at a certain time and place. A trial is much longer and more involved, but insofar as possible you should look upon a deposition as a "mini-trial" and proceed with the same serious attitude you take into the courtroom. The testimony you elicit in the deposition should be the same that you will hear in Court. If it's not, the transcript of the deposition in your hands will make the witness sorry it's not the same. Approach a deposition with the same thoroughness that you approach a trial. The results will justify the time.

### KNOW YOUR ENTIRE FILE

No one can take a deposition "cold" and do a good job. Many large defense firms try to do this by sending in a lawyer who has no knowledge of the case but who carries with him a standard set of questions designed for the type of case involved. To my observation the results are pathetic. Not knowing the case the poor man never realizes when he has received an answer which requires further probing and which could lead to a gold mine of information. "Standard questions" are barely permissible for interrogatories but never for depositions.

Take the time to review your file—especially the summary of the plaintiff's statement, the investigation report and the answers to interrogatories. Study any pictures you may have or other documentary evidence. Then, with the whole story in mind, you are ready to proceed. Now you can be flexible in your questioning—probing here and there for pertinent information or testing the truthfulness of the witness. With the whole case in mind you can really engage in a pleasant—and profitable—chat with a defendant.

### KNOW EXACTLY WHAT YOU ARE AFTER AND GET IT!

Now that you have reviewed your file you must have some ideas as to how this witness can help you. Why are you deposing him? What do you want him to say? Sometimes all you want the witness to do is to fill in some blank spaces in your investigation; other times, as with a defendant witness, you're trying to get him to admit that he was negligent in some manner. You may want observations or opinions or merely verification of documents. But you must have some idea of the specifics that you're after. Otherwise, the desposition becomes a vague, meaningless ramble.

Let's look at two simple examples. In a rear-end collision case, I deposed the defendant to find out why he failed to stop—ever worried about the possibility of sudden, unexpected brake failure, physical disability (heart-attack, black-out), or a claim of "sudden stop ahead." This deposition lasted about two minutes:

Q. All right. Now, as you approached the scene of this accident how fast were you going?

A. At the time I believe approximately between 35, 40 miles. I am not sure. I believe it was the high 30's, maybe 40 miles per hour.

Q. Okay. Now, did you see traffic ahead of you?

A. Yes, sir. I then at the time of the accident—well, as I was approaching the scene where this occurred I was turning. I had my eyes turned. I turned to my left and was watching some—at this here nightclub there were about, maybe, I believe, three or four girls walking into a nightclub. I was watching them. My eyes were not in front of me. I was not watching the front, the traffic in front.

By that time I then—my eyes then noticed the traffic ahead of me. I then applied my brakes too fast or not fast enough to cause a chain reaction.

Q. All right. You struck a couple of cars, as I understand it.

A. Yes, sir.

Ogling pretty girls is no defense to a rear-end collision.

In the next case defendant, while driving along a two-lane suburban road, crossed over into the opposing lane and struck plaintiff's car. Why? Did a tire blow out? Was the steering mechanism defective? Or, was he clearly negligent in his driving? Let's see:

Q. Okay, Suppose you tell me what happened.

A. We were proceeding towards South Hills Village, and I was approximately going 30 or 35 going down a road, and I looked at Miss Smith on the other side of the car. When I turned back, I saw two headlights; and the collision occurred.

Q. As you were proceeding you would have been in your own lane of traffic; is that right?

A. Yes, sir.

Q. Did your car cross over into the opposing lane of traffic?

A. Well, what I remember is when I went up around, I saw the two lights. The reaction of my hands made me move the car towards his lane.

Q. And the lights that you saw, were they in his lane, or the other lane?

A. They were in his lane.

Q. You are telling me that you saw lights in the opposing lane of traffic; is that right?

A. Yes, sir.

Q. You then moved your car to the left, which would be in the direction of the opposing lane of traffic.

A. Yes, sir.

Q. Is this before the collision occurred?

A. Yes, sir.

Q. Did the collision occur in the opposing lane of traffic?

A. Well, I think it did.

Women certainly hold a fatal fascination for men.

Let's move on to a more difficult, but common problem. Everyone has had a case like this. A woman was driving along a two-lane highway with the intention of turning into a garden center to purchase some supplies. The Plaintiff was operating his motorcycle in the opposite direction. His position was that she made a sudden left turn, without any sign or warning, and struck his motorcycle. I had tried to settle this case before deposition but was told by defense counsel it would not settle because defendant was adamant that she had stopped, turned when the way was clear, and that Plaintiff suddenly appeared and struck her car. Her story seemed convincing. Thus, it became necessary to depose her. In a deposition I was interested in:

1.  Whether she ever saw the motorcycle before turning and if not, why not.

2.  If she did see it why she turned before letting it pass her.

3.  Whether she struck the motorcycle or it struck her car.

The first thing to do is to establish that defendant knew the road and the area:

Q. Had you traveled Camp Horne Road to this garden center in the past?

A. Yes.

Q. Were you familiar with it?

A. Yes.

Q. Now, as you were traveling down Camp Horne Road, in the general vicinity, oh, let's say within several hundred yards of the Hastings Garden Center, can you tell me what the road surface is like? Two-lane, four-lane?

A. Two-lane.

Q. Two-lane. And is the road surface made out of asphalt or concrete?

A. Asphalt.

Q. Is there a dividing line down the middle of the road?

A. There was not at the time.

Q. What do you mean, there was not at the time?

A. They came by after the accident and put the yellow line on.

Q. Had that road been resurfaced rather recently?

A. I really don't know.

Q. Did I understand you to say earlier that you were familiar with Camp Horne Road?

A. Yes.

Q. On the previous occasions which you had traveled down that road, was there a dividing line there?

A. Other years, yes.

Q. And what kind of a line was it?

A. Double line.

Next, did she see the motorcycle?

Q. As you were proceeding on this occasion down Camp Horne Road, was there any traffic going in your direction ahead of you?

A. No.

Q. Was there any traffic behind you?

A. No.

Q. All right. As you proceeded closer to the Hastings Garden Center, and by that I mean as you got within, let's say, a hundred yards of it, two or three hundred feet, was there any traffic proceeding toward you in the other lane of traffic?

A. A black Volkswagen had pulled into Hastings before I did.

Q. I see. Was there any other traffic proceeding toward you?

A. No, not that I can remember.

Q. All right. Now, as you got down to the entry to the garden center, let's say within 50 yards of it, did you see an oncoming motorcycle?

A. No.

Q. You did not?

A. No.

Q. All right. Tell me, then, what happened in your own words from a point in which you were, let's say, 50 yards back from the entrace to the garden center up to the time the accident happened?

A. Well, I went up the road and stopped, put my left turn signal on. There was nobody coming, and I pulled across to go into the garden center, when I noticed the motorcycle, and I slammed on my brakes and stopped.

Q. How far ahead when you stopped could you see down the road?

A. Before I turned it?

Q. Yes.

A. About 50 yards.

Q. About 150 feet, is that right?

A. Yes.

Q. How wide would you say that Camp Horne Road is?

A. Two car lengths plus maybe a little bit on each side.

Q. So that you say that you stopped and at that time you could see about 150 feet ahead, is that correct?

A. Before I turned in?

Q. Yes.

A. Yes.

Q. Did you see a motorcycle at that time?

A. No.

Q. Now, when you started to make your left hand turn, how fast were you going?

A. About five miles an hour.

Q. How far in to the opposing lane of traffic did you get before you first saw the motorcycle?

A. I was about two feet from the edge of the road.

Q. So that you would estimate, then, if our estimate of the width of the road is correct, that you had traveled about six or seven feet, is that right?

A. Right.

Q. And you say at that time you first saw the motorcycle?

A. Right.

Q. Where was the motorcycle?

A. Coming towards me.

Q. How far away was it?

A. About 25 or 30 feet.

Q. And what did you then do?

A. I slammed on my brakes.


Finally, how did the accident happen—did she hit the motorcycle?


Q. Why did you not continue the additional two or three feet and then onward to the driveway of the Hastings Garden Center?

A. If I would have, he would have hit me broadside.

Q. Can you tell me how fast the motorcycle was going?

A. No, I cannot.

Q. Where was the motorcycle when you first saw it in terms of his position in that lane of traffic?

A. In the middle. I would say in the middle of the lane.

Q. All right. Tell me what happened, then.

A. He swerved. Whenever I slammed on the brakes, he swerved and went up in the gravel and then came back on the road and caught my left front fender, bumper.

Q. Can you describe for me the position of your car across that lane of traffic?

By that I mean was it directly perpendicular to the lane of traffic or was it at an angle of some kind?

A. At an angle.

Q. Well, about what kind of an angle would you say; a five-degree angle, a sixty-degree angle?

A. I don't know.

MR. JACKSON: Would you like her to make a diagram?

MR. DEMAY: Yes.

MR. JACKSON: I am making an exhibit and I am going to put a dotted line to represent the imaginary center line so that she can place her car.

MR. DEMAY: All right. Just put an entrance or a driveway there of some kind.
That's it. All right. Now just draw on there the position of your car as your remember it when you came to a stop.

Q. What portion of the motorcycle came into contact with what portion of your car?

A. I don't know what part of his motorcycle hit, but he hit me right here.

Q. What part of your car? Can you describe it?

A. The left bumper.

Q. And would that be on the left side of the car or would it be directly to the front of the car?

A. On the left side of the car.

Q. I understand. But if I could just make this as accurate as I can, the contact was made on your car, on the left side of the left front bumper, is that correct?

A. Right.

Q. All right. What happened to the motorcycle and its driver after the impact?

A. He flew off the motorcycle.

The drawing the lady made clearly showed her car perpendicular to the road and completely blocking the oncoming lane. As you can imagine, it was practically impossible for a motorcycle to approach defendant's car from the right, go in front of it, then swing completely around and strike the car on the left side of the left fender. In addition, she was able to see 150 feet ahead when she stopped prior to turning—and nothing was there. Yet within a second or two, when she had traveled six or seven feet across the road the motorcycle showed up only 25 or 30 feet away. Unbelievable. At least the defense attorney didn't believe it—he wouldn't let me out of his office until we had discussed settlement. The insurance company didn't believe it because they paid the policy limits a short time later.

The point to be made is that when you know your case and know what you're after from a witness you can often get it. When you do the case comes to an abrupt halt and the only question from that point on is—how much?

## USE THE DEPOSITION TO "PIN DOWN" A WORRISOME WITNESS

On occasion your investigator will report that a witness is great, but very shaky. Perhaps he is a friend of the defendant and thinks that he is getting his friend into trouble; maybe he is just reluctant to get involved. Sometimes the witness has some tentative plans to move or, while not ill, is quite up in years. In these situations take a deposition. You will be protected as much as is possible by getting his statement, under oath and in detail, with the defense attorney there to examine as much as he pleases. Then, as the trial date draws near, if the witness "doesn't remember because so much time has passed by," or is reluctant or frightened, just let him read the deposition and tell him that you're going to hold him to every word in that transcript. You'll be amused at his sudden change of attitude and how quickly his recollection improves.

### Use It to Get Background Information from Peripheral Witnesses

There are always certain persons who are on the outskirts of a case, but who have something significant to contribute. A nurse, or schoolteacher, perhaps, or a former neighbor or old schoolmate. Sometimes they are reluctant to cooperate and give a statement because of their official position or some other good reason. These people can be deposed to give you background information with the thought in mind that you might use them as "condition" witnesses at trial. Sometimes they can lead you to other witnesses who could be valuable. On "notice" problems—those dealing with the condition of things, the length of time the condition existed, and the defendant's knowledge of the condition—they might be very helpful even though they know nothing of the happening of the accident. Take their depositions and find out what they have to add to your case. The expense is minimal and you may find a pearl in those oysters.

### For Settlement Purposes—
### Depose Some Damage Witnesses

How many times have you run into the situation in which an insurance adjuster says to you: "We agree we're liable in this case but your client is a malingerer—your claim for lost wages is inflated or phony." Or, suppose your client used to do some moonlighting that he can't do anymore and the insurance company won't believe he did all that work. What do you do? You know you could prove it at trial but that is months away. In the meantime you have in your hands a clear-cut liability case and legitimate damages, but the insurance company just stubbornly won't believe the damages are for real. Do yourself a favor—take a deposition—take several depositions.

Get the personnel people in to prove that your man held all those jobs and did all that work. Subpoena them to ring in books and records to prove the loss. Then get in the fellow employees to testify that your client couldn't do the work—that sometimes he tried but couldn't keep up. Let them speak out in sorrowful anger that they had to carry him—do their work and his too. Call in the bosses and supervisors to testify about the change they noticed in plaintiff's attitude, work habits, abilities and the fact that they kept him on for awhile just to give him a break and then had to let him go. This is wonderful testimony. Later, bundle up the transcripts and mail them to the claims manager with a renewal of your demand in the case. When he reads them he may grumble a bit but he can't argue with you. What is there to say? There it is, all spelled out in black and white, under oath. The plaintiff really did hold those jobs, he lost them because he couldn't perform due to his injuries, and the amount of the loss is substantiated by the records. Believe me, your case will settle.

Take a moment to look at excerpts from two such depositions. The plaintiff was a good mechanic. He worked a regular job from 7:00 A.M. to 3:00 P.M. Then, from September to June, he managed a bowling alley in the evenings. From June to September, he "moonlighted" as a mechanic in the evenings. This is how the depositions went. First, from his Boss:

Q. May I have your full name, sir.

A. James A. Roberts.

Q. By whom are you employed?

A. Northern Transportation Company.

Q. For how long have you worked for Northern Transportation Company?

A. Approximately 29 years.

Q. What is your position at the present time, Mr. Roberts?

A. I assist the manager at the Pittsburgh terminal.

Q. Do you know Milton Thompson?

A. Oh, yes.

Q. How long have you known him?

A. Close to 10 years.

Q. How long has Mr. Thompson worked for Northern, approximately?

A. Same amount.

Q. Are you familiar with the fact that he did have an accident in June of 1972?

A. Yes.

Q. Mr. Roberts, can you tell me what kind of work Mr. Thompson did before this accident. What were his duties?

A. He was a mechanic at the shop. We have tractors, and trailers and straight jobs for the city. He repaired them. He did engine overhaul, changed tires on the trailers and tractors, and fueled them, and general mechanical duties.

Q. Did these duties require him to go out of town on breakdown calls?

A. Oh, yes. A truck would break down, and he would be required to go out and repair it—anywhere up to within a radius of sometimes 40 to 50 miles of Pittsburgh—eastbound. Westbound, as far as maybe the Ohio line. Then the terminal at Youngstown would take over from there.

Q. Did these calls to him occur both during the day and the night?

A. Regardless, yes. Day and night regardless. There's no telling when the man can break down.

Q. Was Mr. Thompson always ready, willing and able to go out on these calls?

A. Oh, yes. No problem. I called him and told him where to go— and the truck was broke down and needed lights, or the tires were flat or blown out—he would bring them out a tire. There was no question about it; he was there. Capable, very professional-like mechanic.

Q. I was just about to ask you that. Just how good a man was he as a mechanic?

A. As good a mechanic as you can find today. At that time, not today.

Q. You say not today. We know that he was injured in June and was out of work for a certain period of time. I believe the records show up to around January of '73.

A. I think it's January 2nd of '73 he came back to work.

Q. After he came back to work, did you notice any change at all that you could observe about his working ability?

A. A marked difference. He was slower; he wasn't thinking; he didn't have the strength that he used to have; he was constantly complaining about headaches, or backache or something. It got to the point where we would pass him up in order to get something done on the road, at times, and send another mechanic out. But there was a definite change, definitely.

Q. The conditions that you've just illustrated, how long did they persist?

A. He's still slow. He's still complaining about headaches and taking pills for this. Sometimes I think he's popping pills, but I'm sure he's not. He takes a headache pill about every two hours or so—or backache or something.

And he puts the wrong tire on the wrong frame, and he has to correct it. He neglects to check the tractor out before it leaves the terminal, which is required. It's compulsory, and he should do that. He forgets to fuel tractors up, and subsequently, the driver calls me from 50, 75 miles out. He's out of fuel, and it costs us $85.00 just to bring him fuel. That's happened three times just since he's been back.

Q. Is this like him?

A. No. He's never done that before. He had a system before. The trucks would come in; he fueled them up and put them to the line and checked them out. And we'd hook them up to a trailer going to Chicago, or New York or wherever it's going. He would check the lights, and the brakes and everything; and we don't question him. He signed the paper, and it was fine.

Now I have to remind him: "Did you fuel that tractor up, or did you check them out?" Inasmuch as I'm the close-out man at work, and I'm the last supervisor he has, so to speak, it's my responsibility to see that this equipment is roadworthy when it leaves.

Q. From your observation, have there been very definite changes in Milton Thompson following this accident?

A. Yes, definitely. He's not thinking the way he used to. He's not doing the work he used to do. He don't have the strength he used to.

I then deposed the president of the company at which he worked in the evenings during the summer months:

Q. State your full name, sir.

A. John Jacobs.

Q. What is your position with this company, Mr. Jacobs?

A. I am president.

Q. What is the full name of the corporation?

A. St. Clair Valley Transfer Company, Inc.

Q. All right. Mr. Jacobs, prior to June of 1972 had you ever employed Mr. Milton Thompson?

A. Yes. I believe the last time Mr. Thompson worked for us was either 1967 or 1968.

Q. What would he have been doing for your company?

A. Mechanical work.

Q. As a result of that employment were you familiar with his ability and his qualifications in that line of work?

A. Yes. I knew that man very well. He was a top mechanic for the Northern Motor Lines, which was about a mile away from my location in Braddock. I did know this man's background.

Q. What kind of work would he have done? Could you go into detail? You say mechanical?

A. Yes. Complete overhauling of diesel engines for me. In other words, equipment that was out on the road that came in for Mr. Thompson to tear them down and rings, bearings, pistons, and so forth—heavy mechanical work.

Q. Now, sir, in the early summer of 1972 had you discussed with Mr. Thompson his coming to work for you?

A. Yes, he was to come to work for me, as the letter states, for approximately fourteen weeks until his bowling alley opened up. He could go back to it.

Q. When was he to begin work?

A. I believe June 22nd.

Q. Of 1972?

A. That's right. Yes, it was June 21st or June 22nd.

Q. How much was he to be paid?

A. Five dollars per hour.

Q. Was that to be full-time employment or part-time employment?

A. No, he had a job. He worked for a freight company. I don't remember the name of the company. Milt said he would put in twenty-five hours a week for me.

Q. How many hours a week was he to work?

A. Fourteen.

Q. Why was it set at fourteen hours a week?

A. Yes. It was set for fourteen hours a week. I believe that gave him time to go back down, and the bowling alley was going to open.

This was prime time for me because it is the busiest time of the year in the moving industry.

Q. All right. So these were the terms you established, an hourly rate and the length of time he was to work. Were there to be any set hours?

A. No. He was to work at his own free will. This company loses money because of this problem that Milt had.

We brought equipment in that wasn't functioning properly from other points of the country to be here so that it could be worked on. In other words, we turned down a load for New York out of California because the truck would have to stop in New York or somewhere en route. We knew that some of the equipment had to come home for service, and he was to handle it for me.

Q. Was the equipment here?

A. The equipment was here, and he wasn't.

Q. Was there an injury on the night or early morning of June 21, 1972?

A. Yes.

Q. Now, in 1973 did he work for you at all?

A. No. He thought he might be able to come back to work for me. He came over and we talked, but he just wasn't in shape for that kind of work.

Q. Was there work available for him?

A. Yes.

Q. Could you tell us, sir, what he would have been able to earn, and over what period of time he would have been able to work for your company?

A. As the letter states, somewhere around $2,000.00, I guess, or thereabouts.

Q. What hourly rate would he have been paid?

A. Five dollars per hour.

Q. For how many weeks would he have worked?

A. I imagine the same scope of time—about fourteen or fifteen weeks.

Q. Again, would it be the summer of 1973?

A. Definitely.

Q. I take it that all of his employment or potential employment, would have been summer employment?

A. Yes, that was the only way.

Q. In 1974 did he do any work for you?

A. No, none at all.

Q. Did you discuss with him the possibility of his coming to work for you in 1974?

A. I talked to Milt about the type of work we were talking about. You must understand we have our own mechanics for the minor work here. But when you get into heavier work, you must be physically able to handle that because we are talking about pulling heads and things out of the tractor that weigh like two or three hundred pounds. You are wrestling with drums, wheels, and shoes—things like this. He wasn't in no shape to handle this kind of work.

Now, with the transcript of these depositions in hand who is going to argue with me about my client's physical condition and his loss of earnings? Any reasonable insurance adjuster is simply going to have to accept them as true and adjust his appraisal of the case accordingly.

## USE DEPOSITIONS OFTEN AND WELL

The use of depositions has wide application in every case. As I noted at the beginning of this section, they are a devastating weapon. In a very literal sense they can be the cause of your case coming to an abrupt—and happy—conclusion. Prepare yourself thoroughly and take the deposition carefully. Know what you are after and get it. There is no substitute for a good deposition.

## MOTION TO PRODUCE—WHEN THE DEFENDANT KNOWS AND WON'T TELL

Every person and every corporation in the world is jealous of his, or its, records. It makes no difference who you're dealing with or what you are after. The initial reaction to a request for records is a resounding "No." Governmental agencies, hospitals, universities, "big" business, they're all the same. You could depose their officers by the hour and they don't really mind but just ask for one scrap of paper and they get paranoid. We make jokes about the Federal Government and its propensity to stamp everything "Secret" or "Top Secret," but have you ever tried to get the records of a housing authority, the administrative records of a hospital, or a doctor's office records? How they squeal! On an individual basis it's a matter of suspicion (what am I getting into?); on a corporate basis it's a matter of pride or arrogance (how dare you ask us to give you that). Either way you're stymied. Happily the Law won't let you stay stymied. If the defendant or any other person or organization has information that you need and won't divulge it, file a Motion to Produce. You must have a legitimate reason—which is usually obvious—and the information must be relevant to the case, but if you comply with those requirements you can get anything you want.

Here is a motion I filed against a hospital that was adamant that I shouldn't have the information. No good reason, mind you, but adamant nonetheless. It took the judge only a few minutes to make up his mind and sign the Order.

## EXHIBIT 5-3

IN THE COURT OF COMMON PLEAS OF ALLEGHENY
COUNTY, PENNSYLVANIA.
CIVIL DIVISION.

MARY JONES,          :
      Plaintiff,     :
    v.               :        No. 1234 January Term, 1976
                     :        IN TRESPASS
SOUTH HOSPITAL, a   :
Pennsylvania corporation,  :
      Defendant.    :

### PETITION TO INSPECT
### AND MAKE COPIES OF RECORDS

AND NOW comes the plaintiff above named by her Attorney, JOHN A. DeMAY, and does hereby respectfully submit as follows:

1. That the plaintiff has filed an action In Trespass against the defendant alleging negligence in the care and treatment or lack thereof given to her during her admission to the defendant hospital on January 1, 1975.

2. That in order to properly prepare this case and pursuant to Rule 4009, counsel for plaintiff desires to inspect various books, records, correspondence, etc., at the defendant hospital and to make copies of pertinent portions.

3. That the records desired to be inspected are as follows:

A. Log 1-3- (2 P.M. - 7-4 3 A.M.) ER.

B. OR Log - 5.

C. Minutes or reports of any meeting of the Emergency Room Subcommittee relating to the admission of Mary Jones.

D. Minutes or reports of the meeting of the Emergency Room Subcommittee on the first Friday of January, 1975.

E. Minutes or reports of any meeting of the Utilization Committee relating to Mary Jones.

F. Minutes and reports of the meeting of the Utilization Committee occurring next after January 1, 1975.

G. Minutes or reports of any Medical or Surgical Committee or Subcommittee relating to Mary Jones.

H. Minutes and reports of each and every Medical and/or Surgical Committee or Subcommittee which held a meeting next after January 1, 1975.

I. Copy of Medical Staff By-Laws, Rules and Regulations adopted pursuant to Standard VI of the Standards for Accreditation of Hospitals.

J. House Staff Manual.

K. Any evaluation of the case involving Mary Jones by the Medical Staff organization pursuant to Standard III of the Standards for Accreditation of Hospitals.

L. Minutes and records of those Medical Staff and Departmental meetings held pursuant to Standard V of the Standards for Accreditation of Hospitals held next after January 1, 1975.

M. Records and minutes of any meeting of a Nursing Committee or Subcommittee relating to the matter involving Mary Jones and, in addition, the records and minutes of any Nurses' Committee meeting or Subcommittee meeting held next after January 1, 1975.

4. Counsel for plaintiff believes that an examination and/or copying of these matters are essential to the proper preparation for this case and that defendant will not voluntarily permit him to review the aforesaid items.

WHEREFORE, your Honorable Court is respectfully requested to order the defendant to produce at its offices the aforesaid items for examination and/or copying by counsel for the plaintiff.

Respectfully submitted,

John A. DeMay
Attorney for Plaintiff

COMMONWEALTH OF PENNSYLVANIA :
                      : ss:
COUNTY OF ALLEGHENY :

Before me, the undersigned authority in and for the County and Commonwealth aforesaid, personally appeared JOHN A. DeMAY, Attorney for Plaintiff, who, being duly sworn according to law, deposes and says that the facts set forth in the foregoing Petition are true and correct, to the best of his knowledge, information and belief.

John A. DeMay

SWORN TO AND SUBSCRIBED before me
this     day of     19

Notary Public

## ORDER OF COURT

AND NOW, to wit, this 21st day of May, 1976, upon consideration of the within Petition, it is hereby ordered that the defendant shall on or before Friday, June 2, 1976, at a time convenient to counsel for plaintiff and at the defendant's place of business, produce for inspection the following:

A. Log 1-3- (2 P.M. - 7-4 3 A.M.) ER.

B. OR Log - 5.

C. Minutes or reports of any meeting of the Emergency Room Subcommittee relating to the admission of Mary Jones.

D. Minutes or reports of the meeting of the Emergency Room Subcommittee on the first Friday of January, 1975.

E. Minutes or reports of any meeting of the Utilization Committee relating to Mary Jones.

F. Minutes and reports of the meeting of the Utilization Committee occurring next after January 1, 1975.

G. Minutes or reports of any Medical or Surgical Committee or Subcommittee relating to Mary Jones.

H. Minutes and reports of each and every Medical and/or Surgical Committee or Subcommittee which held a meeting next after January 1, 1975.

I. Copy of Medical Staff By-Laws, Rules and Regulations adopted pursuant to Standard VI of the Standards for Accreditation of Hospitals.

J. House Staff Manual.

K. Any evaluation of the case involving Mary Jones by the Medical Staff organization pursuant to Standard III of the Standards for Accreditation of Hospitals.

L. Minutes and records of those Medical Staff and Departmental meetings held pursuant to Standard V of the Standards for Accreditation of Hospitals held next after

M. Records and minutes of any meeting of a Nursing Committee or Subcommittee relative to the matter involving Mary Jones and, in addition, the records and minutes of any Nurses' Committee meeting or Subcommittee meeting held next after January 1, 1975.

IT IS FURTHER ORDERED that counsel for plaintiff may use defendant's facilities, if any, for copying any portion of the aforesaid documents that he so desires and that counsel for plaintiff shall pay a reasonable charge to the defendant for the use of such copying machines and that, if defendant has no such facilities, counsel for plaintiff may take from defendant's place of business any or all of the aforesaid documents to his office for copying upon his signing a receipt for the documents, and that the documents shall be returned to the defendant hospital within one day thereafter.

BY THE COURT

J.

Take a look at the last paragraph of the Order. Be sure to include something like this in your Order. Otherwise, a miserable and officious supervisor or manager will fuss with you that (1) you can't use their equipment to make copies; and, (2) you can't take the papers from the building. Then you're back in Court again.

### Ask for More Than You Need

You know that after you receive your Order you will go to the defendant's place of business to inspect the records. Once there you will be held to the very letter of the Order—nothing more, at all. Accordingly, when you prepare your Motion ask for the right to inspect everything relevant that you can think of and even then try to be general. For example, don't ask for letters from A to B during the week of July (unless you're sure that is all you want) but ask for all letters, correspondence, memoranda, reports, and notes relating to so-and-so a subject during the month of July. If you ask for too much, the defense attorney and the judge will hold you back; if you ask for too little no one will say a word.

### Let's Go on a Fishing Expedition

That's exactly what you're doing when you file a motion like this. Usually you don't know for sure what you're going to find and you barely know where to start looking. Let defense counsel complain all he wants—in point of fact you really are fishing through somebody's files for data that can help you. With perseverance and a little bit of luck you may catch a big one.

### What Can They Have That You Want?

The data that is available to you is too numerous to mention. As I have said many times, you must once again use your imagination and ask for everything you think they may have that can help you. We can compile a small list of items that might be in the files of the average organization or corporation:

Standard Operating Procedures
Records of Repairs
Records of Prior Similar Incidents
"In-House" Investigations
Records of Performance
History of Machines
Payroll Records
Health Records
Blueprints, Surveys and Photographs
Work Progress Reports
Personnel Records
Correspondence and Memoranda
Records of Complaints from Others
Inspection Reports of Government Agencies

The list could go on and on. Suffice it to say that if you need something and you think someone has it, file your motion.

## REQUESTS FOR ADMISSIONS

This is a discovery tool which really isn't used very often. It is somewhat similar to an interrogatory in that it is used to establish beyond question certain "static" facts. A Request for Admission is nothing more than a statement which the opposing party must admit or deny under oath. Look at the following:

### EXHIBIT 5-4

IN THE COURT OF COMMON PLEAS OF ALLEGHENY
COUNTY, PENNSYLVANIA.
CIVIL DIVISION.

JOHN SMITH,
      Plaintiff,
                  :
                  :
                  :
    v.              :       No. 27 April Term, 1976.
                  :
SAMUEL BROWN,
      Defendant.   :

REQUEST FOR ADMISSION OF FACTS,

TO: JOSEPH B. JONES, ESQUIRE
Attorney at Law
123 Jones Building
Pittsburgh, Pennsylvania   15219

You are required to answer, under oath, the following request for admission of facts pursuant to the Pennsylvania Rules of Civil Procedure and Local Rules of Court:

1. The Defendant is required, for the purpose of the above captioned Civil Action only, to admit the genuineness of each sheet of paper attached hereto. (Each sheet of paper has been given a specific number at the lower left corner.)

ANSWER:

2. These documents describe the business relationship existing between Plaintiff and ABC Corporation during the period January 30, 1975, and April 10, 1975.

ANSWER:

3. On or before January 30, 1975, said documents were not on the physical premises of the ABC Corporation at Pittsburgh, Pennsylvania.

ANSWER:

4. From January 30, 1975, through April 10, 1975, said documents were physically at the premises at the ABC Corporation at Pittsburgh, Pennsylvania.

ANSWER:

5. The Defendant had access to said documents during the period of time January 30, 1975, to April 10, 1975.

ANSWER:

6. The defendant utilized portions of these documents at meetings with plaintiff prior to January 30, 1975.

ANSWER:


7. The defendant failed to record these documents during the aforesaid period of time.

ANSWER:


Respectfully submitted,

John A. DeMay,
Attorney for Plaintiff.


The major problem with this device is that it has rather limited applicability. The statement of fact must be so precise and narrow in scope that the defendant cannot evade or avoid a positive or negative answer. If you try to make a broad or general statement, defendant is sure to respond with "The statement as set forth cannot be answered affirmatively or negatively." Or simply "The statement is too vague and general to be answered positively." You must be careful to use Requests for Admissions only in those instances in which you can be precise and defendant can do nothing more than answer "Yes" or "No." It is not to be ignored, however, since from time to time it is a handy discovery technique.


## DEPOSITIONS BY WRITTEN INTERROGATORIES

The Rules of every jurisdiction make some provision for this procedure. It is simply a means of taking a deposition of some distant witness by serving him with a set of questions which he must answer under oath. It is usually unsatisfactory and should only be done when you and the defense attorney cannot go to the witness for a deposition and it is not feasible to bring the witness to you. Fortunately in this day of high speed and relatively inexpensive transportation it need rarely be done.

### Keep The Jury in Mind When You
### Frame the Questions

In preparing the questions you have to keep in mind how they are going to sound to a jury since they, with the answers, are to be read at the trial. You might give thought as to what period of the trial you intend reading them. For example, if you read them at the start of the case when the jury is not well acquainted with the facts surrounding the time, place, and people involved your questions might contain a lot of detail that would be unnecessary if the questions and answers were to be read at a later time. If the witness has knowledge of only a few essential facts so that your questions can be concise, then you can only use the questions and answers after someone else has filled in all of the background details so that the jury can appreciate where this particular testimony fits into the overall picture.

### Ask The Questions in Alternative
### Forms to Avoid Evasive Answers

Don't forget that this witness, like all witnesses may be a little frightened and troubled at being called in to give answers to your questions. If he is a citizen of a foreign country he will be appearing in a lawyer's office, perhaps in a nearby metropolitan area, or before a United States Consulate officer or some other official and he may understandably be reluctant to give full and complete answers. About the only thing you can do is to ask the important questions two or three times, changing the phrasing each time so that you get all of the facts that you want. Of course, you run the risk of confusing the witness but, on balance, that is a chance you have to take. With several similar questions to work with, both the witness and the interrogator will warm to the subject and the answers will get longer and more complete.

### Have The Questions Translated Here if You
### Are Sending Them to a Foreign Country

Don't forget that words can lose their meaning in translation! The only way you can be sure that they will not is to submit them to a local interpreter and discuss each question with him so that he understands the exact meaning of every word. Interpreters are available in every major city or at your local bank or high school. You will have to work with him so that when the questions and answers come back they are not so much useless gibberish.

In that connection you cannot use local idioms or popular American phrases in your questions. The "old ball game" may mean baseball in the United States, but it probably refers to soccer in most of the rest of the world. Therefore, restrict your choice of words to easily understood and proper ones—no slang, please.

# PART II
## Trial

# CHAPTER 6

# Preliminary Trial Observations

As we begin to talk about the trial of a lawsuit it is worthwhile to give some thought to the various persons who are involved in a trial, and the place where it is to be conducted. The individuals each have a distinct personality that you are going to have to deal with and the room has structural and acoustic problems that you will have to adjust to. It will take some time and thought on your part to analyze these things. As you think about your trial you have to take into consideration the six elements involved—the room, the judge, the jury, the witnesses, the defense attorney and yourself. It will do you a lot of good to anticipate some problems that may arise in each instance and decide upon a solution well before you walk into the courtroom.

## TAKE A LONG LOOK AT THE COURTROOM

If you try cases day in and day out you know every courtroom in which you might be working and its little peculiarities. These are second nature to you. But if you are not a daily trial lawyer or are trying a case outside of your home town, you must take the time to go to the room where the case is to be tried and look it over. What you find may surprise you. There are several things to look for:

A. Size and acoustics.

B. Placement of jury box and counsel table.

C. Disconcerting sights and sounds.

D. Availability of visual aids.

Let us consider these separately.

### A. Size

Most courthouses are old. They were generally built in the era of 1900-1940 and the architecture of the time stressed a very long, wide, high-ceilinged room. They are usually very beautiful and give you plenty of room to move around, but the acoustics are terrible. That spaciousness almost makes the spoken word evaporate. If you put a soft-spoken witness on the stand and let him speak normally, no one will hear him. Most of these courtrooms will have microphones, but even then you will have to remind the witness to speak directly into the microphone and to speak loudly. Be sure to position yourself, when on direct examination, at the far end of the jury box. If you can hear you know the jurors can hear.

Adequate space is no problem in these rooms so plan to spread out. There is plenty of room to place your easel, photographs, model, diagrams, shadow box and other paraphernalia. Try to visualize where you intend to put them. They should be out of your way but immediately available, and if appropriate, in a place where the jurors can peruse them at their leisure. Don't forget that you are bringing them into the courtroom to be looked at.

The more modern rooms are, naturally, just the opposite. They are small in dimension—too small, usually—with low ceilings. You can hear so well that even a whispered conversation with your client will frequently be picked up by one and all. In this situation you had better warn your client and witnesses to be careful about what they say. A derogatory remark about a witness, the judge, or defense counsel might be heard by the jurors and may well be prejudicial. Tell them to go into the hall outside of the courtroom if they want to make small talk.

A small room will also inhibit your movement and the amount of papers, photographs and demonstrative exhibits you bring into the room at any one time. If you know in advance that you can keep a large exhibit in the room only during direct and cross-examination of one or two witnesses, and will then have to remove it to make room for another one, I suggest you lengthen your direct examination relating to the exhibit. Let the witness spend more time than usual with it and after he is through ask permission for the jurors to take a few minutes to examine the exhibit carefully. You don't want to lose the value of the exhibit merely because space requirements will not permit it to remain in the room.

Another problem is that the intimacy of the room can dampen your normal techniques in interrogating a witness, responding to defense counsel, or relating to a jury. For example, you can't very well raise your voice during cross-examination—it will sound as if you are bellowing, and the jurors will wince at the noise you make. If you are sitting almost shoulder-to-shoulder with defense counsel you might be inclined to get personally argumentative with him, which won't do. That turns the trial into a cat-and-dog fight between the two of you and in these personal duels I have found that the plaintiff—who has the burden of convincing a skeptical jury—usually suffers.

Finally, you may have to sit at counsel table, or stand adjacent to it, while interrogating which isn't the best situation. It is so much better to be able to move away from counsel table, away from the defense attorney, and make your interrogation an isolated matter in which only you, the witness and the jurors are involved.

The intimacy of a small room does pose its own problems and you had better figure out in advance just how you are going to cope with them.

## B. Placement of Jury Box and Counsel Table

Traditionally the jurors sit to the right of the Bench as one faces the judge. However, space limitations and architectural problems sometimes require the jury box to be on the left side. Novelty and innovation have placed them in a semi-circle facing the judge, but behind the counsel table, and I am sure that there are numerous other configurations. In any event, you had better be aware of where they are and how that location is going to affect your procedures. It may be that in showing a movie, for example, the judge is going to have to move from the Bench or that, depending on where they are, the jurors will have to move about.

Likewise, the location of counsel table will have to be noted. Sometimes there is one big table with each attorney at either end, sometimes there are two separate tables side by side and other times two separate tables front to back. Where you sit, where you are going to spread out your papers, and the ease and manner with which you are going to converse with defense counsel are small but important matters and you have to keep them in mind as you look over the courtroom.

## C. Disconcerting Sights and Sounds

There are all kinds of little things that you have to look for and give some consideration to. All courthouses are located in busy downtown areas. Will there be traffic noise to contend with? Is the room air-conditioned? If not, and the windows have to be opened in the heat of the day, will the noise interfere with the interrogation? You might have to use your best witnesses in the morning and early afternoon, well knowing that between the heat and the noise the jurors will miss some of the late afternoon testimony. Or, alternatively, save the late afternoon for showing pictures or demonstrative exhibits that capture the attention of the jurors rather than have them listening to the drone of testimony.

Are there windows on the wall opposite the jury box? Will the afternoon sun be shining in their faces? Are there blinds or shutters that will block out the light so the room can be made dark enough to show movies or project slides on a screen? Where will your witnesses sit? Are they conveniently accessible to you? Is the area between the jury box and counsel table so narrow that you cannot easily set up an easel or a screen without blocking the way? If so, where will you place them? If there are several defense attorneys, just where are they going to be seated? Is the room so small that they will get in your way? What are the local rules about recesses? Where will the jury be at such times? Can bulky exhibits be conveniently brought to the courtroom or must special provisions be made? How embarrassing it is to bring in a large model, which fits through the courtroom doors, only to find it cannot be wheeled through the railing separating the spectators from the participants. These are things you should think about ahead of time.

### D.  Visual Aids

Every courtroom should have a blackboard, but when you want more than this you had better check to see if it is available or whether you have to bring your own. You may find that the room contains one easel, but for your purposes of showing several large photographs at the same time you may want two or three. A shadow-box for showing X-rays is usually necessary, but not always among the standard equipment, and TV sets (for video-taped depositions) are usually not available. Don't forget to inquire about extension cords, chalk, pointers and the like. These are always supposed to be in the room but are frequently misplaced or lost. A few minutes of your time to be certain that they are present are absolutely essential. You will be lost without them.

## A FRANK TALK ABOUT JUDGES

If, in your jurisdiction, there is more than one judge, and you are notified that you will begin your case on a particular day, your first question has to be: "What judge do I have?" That judge will be a major participant in the trial and he will have a profound influence on your attitude and actions. Accordingly, it behooves you to know everything possible about his personality, attitudes, beliefs and mannerisms.

We lawyers may dislike many things about our judges—the manner of their selection, the type of person who is appointed, their actions on and off the bench and their personalities, but one thing is sure—we are stuck with them. You know that on a certain day, at a particular time and place, you are going to be trying a case before Judge Jones and it matters not one whit that he is a political hack, that you and he have fought in the past, that his entire legal upbringing is hostile to yours, that he drinks too much and works too little. He is your judge and there is nothing you can do about it. Your sole job is to use every talent you possess to win his favor or dampen his antagonism and to see to it that he handles your case fairly and judiciously. Whatever else that takes—hard work, humility, whatever—it is going to require you to know him well, or to know of him, and to make an adjustment to his demands and his quirks of behavior.

Certainly the best way to appraise a judge is to know him personally. You should make every effort to meet him, chat with him in chambers, or join him at some Bar Association function. Inquire about his school, his legal experience, his family and his attitude on various social, political or sports issues of the day. By watching him, listening to him speak, and hearing him express his attitudes you can get a fair impression of the kind of person he is.

Other sources of information about a judge are the courthouse personnel. His immediate secretary, tipstaff and law clerk will be very protective, of course, but they can, and will readily, tell you his likes and dislikes as far as trial practice is concerned, his background and how he came to be a judge. Critical evaluations can be gained by talking to other court personnel and, in a large court, at least, they are not loathe to give it. You can ignore the obvious slander you are sure to hear from some people but most of them do have solid, honest impressions and evaluations that will stand you in good stead. It is interesting how people get labeled, and while the labels are only a rough and general analysis of a personality, they are reasonable enough to give you some idea of the type of person you are dealing with.

Finally, you can talk to other attorneys and get their impressions of the judge. You will note a very sharp difference in the tone or nature of the evaluation by a lawyer from that of a member of the courthouse staff. The staff member will always analyze a judge from the "me-him" point of view; the lawyer will speak in terms of "him and the Law." Thus a secretary will tell you that Judge Jones is "great" to be around, a tipstaff will say he is "lazy" and a clerk will identify him as "generous." The lawyers will look at this man and tell you "great for settlement," "gives a fine charge" or "knows the law well."

After you have inquired around you should come up with some good impressions of the kind of person you are going to be dealing with for the next several days. Then you have the job of adjusting your attitude to his. If he is punctilious, you be on time; if he likes to keep things moving, you see to it that you have more than enough witnesses for each day so that you won't run short, and perhaps review your notes to see if you can make your direct examination a little shorter and more concise; if he is dumb (and some are) have a trial brief to present to him at the beginning of the trial and prepare Trial Memoranda on the two or three evidentiary or procedural problems you anticipate arising during the trial. It isn't necessary to flatter an egomaniac or toady to a fool, but it is necessary to let him run his courtroom his way—not only necessary, but fair. A judge has a few rights just as you have. The judge may want to settle your case and you may want a verdict; nonetheless you can cheerfully put up with numerous bargaining sessions, make some minor adjustments in your demand so as not to be obstinate, and courteously reject the offers. The judge may be disappointed that the case does not settle, but he won't be angry about your conduct.

My point is that it is important that you know, in as much detail as possible, what manner of person your judge is and knowing that, to make adjustments in your method of operation to coincide with the judge's attitudes. This will insure the fact that your client gets a fair trial. There will be no personality conflict between you and the judge that will influence his rulings on evidence, his demeanor toward you and your witnesses, or his charge to the jury. Conversely, if you can make the relationship a pleasant one, the judge will give you a break when you ask for a recess out of time, or a witness is late, and on a very fine point of law you might find that the decision will be favorable to you solely on the basis of your cheerfully professional conduct. If you want to fight the Establishment or the System or even this particular judge, you have plenty of time and opportunity to do it without starting during this trial.

## YOUR WORTHY OPPONENT—THE DEFENSE ATTORNEY

Just as a judge has individual foibles that you should learn so does your defense attorney. If he has tried many cases, he too has developed a style, technique and mannerisms that people know about and will talk about. It is best to learn these facts from talking with other plaintiffs' attorneys, but other sources would be court reporters and tipstaffs—those who see the man in court frequently. They can tell you how your defense attorney operates. They usually cannot tell you what to do about it. Everywhere you will find the type who might be labeled "The All-American

Boy," the "Comedian," the "Humble and Innocent Litigator," the "Suspicious Inquisitor." You might approach each one of them somewhat differently and it's helpful to know, in advance, just which type of man your defense attorney is. If he is pompous, should you be a humorist? If he habitually makes blatant asides to the jury, how do you plan to control it? If he is suspicious, irascible and demanding, should you deliberately provoke him to the point that he explodes in the courtroom—and can you control things when he does so—or should you put on the air of "innocence abused." If the defense attorney is a young man, you might easily take advantage of his inexperience—but—will it cast you in a better light and result in a better verdict if you adopt the role of a benign and helpful adversary? Think about these things and make some plans before your trial begins.

Some people complain about trial lawyers analyzing people and making plans in this manner. They feel it is too theatrical. They ignore the fact that this is life. "All the world's a stage" and so it is to a certain extent and a trial is a condensed portion of that world. The fact that you act in one way with a particular defense attorney and judge, and another way in the next trial does not make you an actor, or theatrical, or hypocritical or an impostor. Your neighbor will act one way at 6:00 P.M. at home with his wife and children and be an entirely different person at 8:00 P.M. at a party. Have you heard the expression "house devil, street angel" applied to people? Each of us acts differently at home, the office, on a tennis court and at a party. The trial lawyer merely recognizes these differences in personality, demeanor and manner and deliberately puts them to use under varying circumstances. It is a talent you will want to develop to the utmost.

## THE FINDERS OF FACT—THE JURY

How is it that you can take twelve (nine or six) ordinary men and women and somehow completely change them by the simple expedient of calling them a jury? Citizens are proclaimed, jurors defamed. Newspaper editors and writers proudly stand by the "people" and viciously attack high "jury" verdicts. Somehow it's lost on them that jurors are people, citizens, human beings.

Lawyers sometimes share this wrong attitude. How often have you heard your fellow attorneys express reluctance to try a case before a jury or speak in a derogatory manner about them? Yet that man may at that very moment be on his way to address a meeting of the Kiwanis Club or the League of Women Voters and hopes to deliver a persuasive speech. I can only call such an attitude "unreal." Jurors have neither fangs nor claws, but a lot of common sense. As you look about the courtroom you can readily fill the jury box with your relatives, neighbors, friends and the strangers who live in the next block. They are plain ordinary people who, in general, do an excellent job of providing justice for us all. They are certainly not to be feared as many people do fear them. They do have a variety of backgrounds, life styles and experiences and part of your job is to try to match up the personality and background of your plaintiff with as many jurors as possible who will face you on *voir dire*. You can begin now to ponder whether you want women or men, young or old, rich, poor, bankers or steel workers, Irish, Blacks or Jews, the gregarious type or the introvert. This is not the kind of thing you can decide upon easily and quickly. Take your time and let the subject come to mind time and again as you prepare for trial, so that when the day comes that you must select the jury you will have a clear idea of whom you do not want even though you haven't finally decided whom you do want to sit in judgment on your case.

### THE WITNESS—TELLER OF TALES

Every witness is called to the stand to tell a story—a true story as he knows it. Whether you will win or lose a case depends upon the quality of your witnesses—and the plaintiff is the foremost of them. They will be judged by the jury and sometimes that judgment will be based not only on what is said but the manner of its saying and the appearance of the person who speaks. Clothing, hair style, manner of speech, gestures, wit, articulateness, self-confidence—all of these come into play as elements to be considered when the jurors decide whether a witness is to be believed. You must analyze every witness as objectively as you can and decide whether he is to be used, how much of his story is to be told, when the testimony is to be presented and in what manner you will show this witness to a jury. An articulate engineer will testify while standing before the jury and will use a blackboard; a shy child will testify from the witness stand and his testimony will be brief and to the point. A person who claims to have pertinent knowledge, but whose word is suspect, may be discarded. The mannerisms of another person may have to be corrected, and that near-juvenile delinquent who is so necessary has to get a haircut—which you will probably have to pay for. There is no such thing as trusting to luck that your witnesses will be models of propriety and decorum with the silver tongue of an orator. They will not. They have many faults and in a short period of time you have to correct the most obvious of them before they go on the witness stand.

The Judge, Defense Attorney, Witnesses, Jurors, the Courtroom itself—all of these are worthy of your serious attention and reflection many days before your case begins. The time and effort devoted to this part of your preparation work is well worthwhile.

CHAPTER **7**

# The Pretrial Preparation Agenda

The seven days before your trial begins are going to be hectic since you will be involved in a dozen and one last minute details, each of which is important.

## WHAT TO DO?

I suggest that you cancel or severely restrict all other work and turn your attention completely to pretrial preparation. Unless you have help there is no other way. To be sure, you can give many of the chores to your secretary or your investigator but only you can make the decisions. A secretary cannot decide the order in which you are going to call witnesses, nor can an investigator decide whether a deposition for use at trial should be taken of a witness who is currently ill and who may or may not be available for trial.

If you have another attorney who will work with you during the trial, he can provide invaluable service in helping to share this preparatory work. This could reduce the time that you spend by as much as 75 percent but even then you will have to spend a portion of each day with him and surely all of the last two or three days. But even he cannot go over the direct and cross-examination with the witnesses and be sure that they are prepared the way you want them to be.

There is no substitute for your judgment and experience when it comes to making decisions regarding the testimony, soothing a nervous witness, preparing schedules or deciding on exhibits and their order of introduction. Therefore, you must resign yourself to the fact that you must curtail your office routine and devote your attention single-mindedly to this case for several days before trial. Let us go through some of the things that ought to be done.

### Notify Witnesses Promptly

As soon as you learn of a trial date notify your witnesses. This can be done by phone or letter and is in the nature of what I call a preliminary notice. You need not give them a precise date and time—especially since you probably don't know it. The fact that a case is listed for January 7th does not mean that you will use the witness that day. Routine delays, selecting a jury, a little argument and other normal but obscure problems could well delay the start of the trial to January 9th and you may not plan on using a particular witness until a day or two thereafter. Nonetheless, the witness has to make some plans and is entitled to as much preliminary notice as possible. This is the time when you will learn of impending vacations, hospitalizations, out-of-town business trips and the like and can either work with the witness to change his schedule or, if he is un-cooperative and adamant, prepare to subpoena him. Everyone will appreciate your courtesy in giving this notice and will understand your problem in being unable to be precise as to date and time.

### Work Up a Schedule

When you are within a few days of the trial date it is appropriate to check with the court and the defense attorney to try to determine accurately when the case will begin, excluding the time that will be spent in jury selection, preliminary arguments and settlement negotiations. If you can be reasonably sure, now, that the actual trial will begin on a date certain, then you must begin to work up a schedule for witnesses based on the order in which you intend to call them and the amount of time you expect each to be on the witness stand. This will require some guess work regarding the length of cross-examination, the length of recesses and other time-consuming parts of the trial, but it can be done. Then you can plan on bringing in each day only those witnesses you expect to use that day.

There is no point in summoning all of them to your office or to the court for the first day of trial when you know very well that there is no chance of using them that day. Waiting is wearying and aggravating and under the best of circumstances we have enough of that. There is no reason to antagonize your people just because you have not planned a sensible schedule for their appearance. My only caution is that you do not un-derestimate the number of persons you need each day and, as a result, are

THE PRETRIAL PREPARATION AGENDA

embarrassed before the judge and jury when you have no one else to call to the stand and there is time left in the day. Accordingly, always have two more witnesses available than you think you will need. If you think you will use five witnesses, have seven in court.

The witnesses should be fully prepared, in court, and ready to go. Don't fall for the solemn promises of some witnesses that they will stay available at their home or on the job and will come into court on a phone call. None of that. When it suddenly appears that you are running short of witnesses and you need Miss Jones who is working downtown you will find: (a) she is out shopping for a "few minutes"; (b) she is taking dictation at an important Board of Directors meeting and cannot be disturbed; (c) her boyfriend just called from San Francisco and she had to leave work to go to the airport to pick him up.

Don't rely on these assurances from any witness. Too many unforeseen problems can arise that will interfere with your plans. Medical doctors are famous for being "called to the emergency room" just when you need them to come in. In fact, they are busy, disinterested in your case, and just don't want to be bothered that afternoon. Protect yourself. Have those witnesses—all of them that you have scheduled for that day in the courtroom so that they are available when you need them.

### Issue Subpoenas

Most people don't like to be subpoenaed for two reasons: it is a coercive act that gives them little chance to avoid compliance; and second, it is a formal matter with a sheriff or investigator knocking on their door and handing them a piece of paper, and it frightens them. Those are precisely two excellent reasons for serving subpoenas on unreliable persons. This is no time to be playing games. Good will and promises are casual things—tritely given and blithely ignored, and all with a good deal of self-justification.

Disappointments and misunderstandings are easily avoided by the simple expedient of issuing a subpoena. Many attorneys feel that this creates antagonisms and ill feelings between witness and lawyer. I think that is greatly exaggerated. If animosity exists because of the subpoena, it really doesn't last long, especially if you take a few minutes to explain the purpose and necessity for the subpoena. If the witness won't listen and wants to stay angry then ignore him. I have never seen a witness who would commit perjury on the witness stand just because he was served with a subpoena.

These remarks apply especially to professional people. If you have a good rapport with them, you probably need not subpoena them; but if there is the slightest indication that they will give you trouble, subpoena them. Do you believe that a treating doctor who is subpoenaed into court will deny that the plaintiff had a broken leg? Will an architect deny his findings regarding the collapse of a building because of a subpoena? The answer is clearly no. They may not give you as much as you want—the icing on the cake so to speak—but they will not lie. And, presumptively, if you had not subpoenaed them and let them come into court at a time of their own choosing, you would have had a cooperative witness but an angry judge and jury who have their own way of dealing with witnesses who keep them waiting. If someone has to be unhappy, let it be the witness.

Of course we know that it is futile to subpoena an expert—he can refuse to express an opinion at any time and, almost, for any reason. If you are having scheduling problems with this man, there is nothing to do but to discuss it with the judge, secure his cooperation and make the necessary adjustment in the court schedule. Finally, with video-tape depositions becoming more prevalent, and given their excellence as an alternative to "live" testimony, the problem with the expert will tend to be minimal in future years.

Friends, close acquaintances, and witnesses who can be definitely trusted need not be subpoenaed so long as you recognize that you are the one taking the risk of non-appearance. It is a matter of using your good judgment. Some of my friends habitually forget birthdays, miss airplane flights and show up at 10:00 for a 9:00 o'clock meeting. These persons need a stern reminder that you are not going to subpoena them as a courtesy based on your trust in them and that neither you nor the judge is going to abide any dalliance on their part.

### Talk to Every Witness

It is really sad to watch an attorney put a witness on the stand whom he has not met or has not talked with at length. As soon as you look at the witness you know he is not prepared—slovenly clothes, unkempt in appearance, hesitant in movement and speech. Even if he is well dressed, you can tell when the questioning begins—the attorney either has to lead him because he dare not let the witness testify properly, or if the attorney tries to ask proper questions, there are pauses, stammerings and misunderstandings between the witness and the lawyer. This leads to a bad impression and a poor result. It is unnecessary and wrong despite the boasts you sometimes hear of people who pick up a file in the morning and go off to court without even knowing who their witnesses are. Check the record—these braggarts are losers.

You must meet every witness personally, appraise his appearance carefully, and go over his testimony in detail. With rare exceptions I can honestly state that I have, in my office, examined and cross-examined every witness I have put on the witness stand. You must know the witness' story and you must give him a "feel" for the courtroom atmosphere. As you and he discuss the facts it is a simple matter to launch into a direct examination of the witness. He won't even realize, until you tell him, that this is exactly the way you are going to examine him in the courtroom and precisely the questions you are going to ask. The important thing is that now you can correct his peculiar idiom, mode of expression, loose usage of words, annoying habits and the scope of his testimony. So many people want to tell the "whole story" when in point of fact they personally know only a part of it and have learned the rest from hearsay. That's not the way they tell it to their friends and neighbors but that's the way it is.

Now is the time to explain to them that they can testify solely to what they saw, did, or, if it is admissible, heard, at the scene of the events and not what others told them. This is the time to show them that irrelevancies, even if true, must be excluded because of practical time limitations. Have you encountered the witness who wants to describe an event minute by minute and, almost, second by second. Given the opportunity he (though it is usually a she) would take an hour to tell you whether the sun was shining on the day of the accident. Such persons have to be taught to limit their comments to the question asked. You will never have the opportunity to correct this problem if you have not met the witnesses and listened to their answers to your questions.

The voluble witness, the soft-spoken one, the person who puts his hand to his mouth when he speaks, the one who hesitates before giving every answer—all of them need help. You can learn about their problems and correct them in your office if you will take the time.

Cross-examination is a peril to which most persons have not been exposed in their lifetime, except the errant husband who faces an irate wife and tries to explain his whereabouts of the night before. Witnesses are not used to it, don't quite know what to expect, and worry about it. Since you know that some of them, at least, will be vigorously cross-examined by defense counsel it is only fair that you acquaint them with the subject, identify specific portions of their testimony which are likely to come under attack, and help them to prepare for it.

The best way to accomplish all of these objectives is to cross-examine them yourself. You can vary the amount of time involved and the extensiveness of your cross-examination with the importance of the witness and the scope of his direct testimony. Often your work with a witness will be brief—perhaps just to point out to him the sensitive parts of his testimony—but with key witnesses you have to go through the whole routine. Time-consuming though it may be, it is good for both you and the witness since the witness will be well prepared for whatever the defense attorney throws at him and you will be much more deeply immersed in what your witness knows and can say. This can be a satisfying experience and time well spent, but, like it or not, it must be done.

### Instruct Witnesses Regarding Dress and Demeanor

It is surprising how many witnesses think nothing of appearing in court dressed in the most casual attire or barely dressed at all. They won't dress properly unless you tell them to do so. It should be like a litany for you to recite over and over again with each male witness "suit, white shirt and a tie" and with each female witness "dark dress, little jewelry and a new hair-do." Appearances are important. As one of my judicial friends likes to point out, the President of the United States could be sworn in while wearing nothing but a swimming suit and roller skates and he would still be President—but it's not the same. Your witnesses dress up to go to a party—they can dress up to come to court.

Demeanor in the courtroom, the adjoining hallways and in the vicinity of the jurors or parties should also be discussed. There is nothing worse than people at the back of the room practically applauding when the witness on the stand gets the best of the defense attorney. The big smiles, the nodding of the head, the rush of words back and forth—always too loud—may very well ruin whatever effect your witness has created from the stand. Caution your people, therefore, that your trial is not a ball game where one cheers for the home team and applauds a good play. Their job is to sit in that courtroom, keep still, listen attentively and, in due course, take their turn on the witness stand.

Talking about the case in the hallways or near the jurors is another subject you should discuss. Tell your witnesses not to discuss the case at all in such places, but if they must, to speak in low tones and in a place where they are sure no jurors are present. It's always possible that someone might talk too much and too loud in the vicinity of a juror, that the juror or defense counsel would report it to the judge and you could be faced with a motion for a mistrial with a consequent loss of time, energy and money. A few words of caution to your witnesses will help to dispel this onerous possibility.

### Make Sure Your Bills Are Up-to-Date

Whether your case is a personal injury claim, a property damage case, or a suit for breach of contract there are going to be bills and estimates that have to be presented to a jury. Are yours current and complete? This is the time to check and make sure that they are. It is possible that your client just recently secured additional medical treatment and you will have to get that bill. An estimate for repairs to a building, made two years ago, is woefully out of date. Construction costs have soared and you will have to get a revision of that item.

In many instances you are going to have to make changes to take into consideration inflation, rises in the cost of living, higher wages and the like. If you are claiming lost wages and have a statement from the employer which you want to introduce into evidence, check the date. If it is more than a few months old you had better call to inquire if the information is still valid. There could well have been a new wage pact negotiated that would increase base pay, incentive pay, overtime and some fringe benefits that will substantially alter your claim. All of these items will have to be gone over so that you can be sure that they are complete and current.

### Double-Check Exhibits and Number Them

Photographs, wage records, tax returns, weather reports, hospital records, car repair estimates, doctor bills, drug bills, hospital bills, nurses bills, car rental bills, diagrams, models, life expectancy tables, present worth tables, medical books, books of accounting—the number and variety of your exhibits, or potential exhibits, can be surprising. Because of this you will have to spend several hours going over them to make certain that you have everything you need. In addition, you may have to have some of the documents authenticated. It will be very helpful if you can get the defense attorney to agree to waive formal proof as to some documents—a hospital record or weather report for example—so that you need not call a witness to prove it. But he may legitimately ask you to have a cover letter or authentication on the document, signed by a competent person to the effect that it is all that it purports to be. This may take some hurried running around.

This is also a good time to number your exhibits. You should have a pretty clear idea of the sequence in which you want to offer them and it will facilitate everything to number them now. At the very least it is a handy way to keep track of them since you, your secretary, investigator and witnesses are going to be handling them before and during the trial. In addition, once you get into court you will not have to constantly be handing them to the court reporter or clerk for the purpose of putting a number on them. It's very convenient and I recommend it even if your local practice requires that court personnel number exhibits.

### Decide on Photographs and Prepare Diagrams

You are going to be talking with your investigator or expert at length and it is appropriate now to decide how best to depict some object or scene so that the jurors can understand what is going on. It is the opportune moment to go over photographs and decide which you shall use, which will be enlarged and what size they should be. I hold to the belief that an 8-1/2" x 10" photograph is next to worthless. The ideal size for both physical handling and use on an easel is the 16" by 20" size. Witnesses and jurors can handle them with ease and pass them about; at the same time when you place them on an easel everyone can see them. A selected few photographs should be enlarged to the 28" x 40" size. The impact of these large pictures is tremendous and their size and detail are a delight to everyone in the courtroom.

Diagrams have to be large for reasons of clarity and information. Don't let your expert make tiny little notes or labels on them—tell him to write with big letters and with short words. Thus, all can see clearly and the point he desires to make will be easily understood. Be sure to enlarge to the 28" x 40" size certain other exhibits—nurses' notes or doctors' orders from a hospital record; a page from an accountant's work sheets; a blueprint—anything that is complicated, needs explaining and is important. The jury will thoroughly enjoy these exhibits and your experts can present a fine explanation while standing before them with the exhibit.

## Take Nervous Clients or Witnesses to a Courtroom

Can you guess how many people have never been inside a courtroom? Well, it has to be a guess but I hazard 90 percent of our adult population. These people include your plaintiff and witnesses, and some of them will describe their current condition as "petrified," "I'm a nervous wreck," "scared to death." They mean it, it's not put on. Do them a real favor—make a joke out of their fears and then take them to the nearest empty courtroom. Let them see where the judge will sit and let them have the fun of sitting in the witness chair and the judge's chair. Show them where you and the defense attorney will be. Take the time to ask them a few questions while they are on the witness stand.

It is interesting to observe what a great sedative this experience is. The person will settle down quickly and begin to make his own jokes about his fears. It is helpful if a trial is going on in a nearby room to drop in there for a few minutes but that isn't always possible and can be unnecessarily time consuming. Your witness may not want to leave. The time that you spend with your client and witnesses is well worthwhile and is always appreciated by the people involved.

## Do Last-Minute Investigation

Under the best of circumstances there is always some last-minute investigation to be done. Usually it is something simple like locating a witness who has moved, or securing a photograph with a different view from the ones you presently have, or sending out to get a complete hospital record because the one you have is a summary chart. Sometimes, however, when you have talked things over with all of the witnesses you learn that there was another person at the scene that you hadn't known of before, or that there is a very important object that is available that you thought had disappeared long ago. Very suddenly you can find yourself running a full-scale investigation that has to be completed within a few days. Then you will bless the fact that you started this pretrial preparation a week before the trial and not the day before. You will also appreciate the fact that you have a good investigator who already knows the case well. There is nothing to do but to pitch in, help wherever you can, and get the job done.

Success in these last-minute investigations can improve your case substantially. I clearly recall a case in which an important witness moved overseas shortly after the accident. I never had a chance to interview her or to take her deposition. While interviewing the other witnesses in preparation for trial, it came out that this person was now back in the United States, but no one knew exactly where she lived. My investigator worked furiously to locate her, did so, and she agreed to come and testify in the case. This sort of thing happens often enough so that you should always have the thought lingering in the back of your mind and allow yourself an extra day or two in the event it does occur.

## An Ill or Absent Witness—Rush Depositions

It is not at all uncommon that when your secretary calls witnesses to arrange appointments for them to see you that she will find one who is either in the hospital, incapacitated at home, or is just about to move. Upon learning this you are going to be faced with the decision whether to postpone the trial in the hope that the witness can appear at a later date or take the deposition of that person for use at trial. It seems to me that if everyone else is ready to go and the witness involved is not of overpowering importance, the best decision is to take the deposition.

A video-tape deposition really makes an excellent substitute for a "live" appearance and even if you don't use video-tape, a transcript of a deposition can be effectively handled in the courtroom without too much loss of effect. In fact, with some witnesses I would rather use a deposition transcript because of their poor appearance, speech defects or poor memory. It's less painful. If the alternative is to be a delay of several months and the ever-present possibility that someone else may then be unavailable, I vote in favor of proceeding now and deposing the witness.

You may run into a problem with defense counsel if he is busy, since this may require that the deposition be taken at night or at some considerable distance from the courthouse. If that happens, you will have to go to the judge to get the matter attended to. I might add that if it happens, you might re-examine your relations with that defense attorney. They are usually cooperative and understanding of this type of problem. If your defense attorney is not, it could be that he is merely difficult and hard to get along with—or it could be that he is recalling a time when your cooperation was needed and not given. Perhaps your poor manners are being repaid in kind.

### The Witness Fee

Often this annoying subject is avoided by many attorneys until after a witness is discharged. At that time the attorney either hands the witness a fee arbitrarily set by him (always too low) or the witness submits a bill (always too high). This is no way to handle the payment of a witness fee. The witness has done a genuine public service by appearing in the trial, he has assisted you and your plaintiff, and in so doing he has lost time from his work, incurred parking fees and luncheon charges and has been generally inconvenienced. We know that the law has established a witness fee which provides both a daily and a mileage rate, but this is usually so low that your witnesses will end up losing money for their cooperation. They cannot afford it and it is not right. Each of them is entitled to payment of his lost wages and expenses, and reasonable compensation for the inconvenience.

These figures are easy to establish if you will spend a few minutes discussing the subject with your witness. If he is on an hourly rate or a monthly salary, it is a simple mathematical calculation to determine his lost wages. You should know the parking rates in your area and can approximate a reasonable luncheon expense. If you will add another ten or fifteen dollars to this total sum, most witnesses will be perfectly happy. As a rule of thumb, I estimate $35.00 to $50.00 per day for each witness and this figure seems to cover the majority of cases. A little adjustment is necessary if a person has a very high-paying job or if I have to bring him into my office for a meeting at night or on a weekend. The important thing is that you discuss the subject with the witness and have a clear understanding with him.

Experts are in a class by themselves. When dealing with them it is mandatory that you discuss fees because there is no consistency in their charges and they are not at all reluctant to send you a fantastic bill if you have not agreed upon a set amount. Medical doctors are most frequently used by us as experts and their fees, in my area, bound all over the place. I have routinely seen bills come in varying from $75.00 to $500.00 for a court appearance. Happily most of them seem to be in the range of $150.00 to

$200.00, but past experience, or general experience, can never be relied on in a specific case. You have to discuss fees at an early stage and get a firm commitment from the doctors as to what they are going to charge.

This principle applies with equal force to any other kind of expert whether he be a pilot, engineer or architect. Many times these persons are uncertain what to charge since there are no established guidelines. The egotist will want to charge too high a sum for his services; the opportunist will keep one eye on the potential recovery in the case, the other eye on your possible fee and will suggest an extravagant sum. If these men are sincere, you can reason with them and arrive at a sensible arrangement; if they are simply greedy, try another expert. Sometimes you will run into a humble person who suggests a figure that is obviously too low. This is your opportunity to be fair about the matter and to advise him what you have found the going rate to be and what you think his services justify.

When you deal with out-of-town experts you know the price is inevitably going up and since you will now deal in large sums it is mandatory that you arrive at a specific charge well in advance of trial. (It is understood that travel and lodging expenses will be paid by you.) Unfortunately, here again we have few established rates. My experience has been that these people will charge between $500.00 to $1,000.00 a day as a fee. Anything lower than that is a bargain and anything above that is gouging. This is a broad range but I have not noticed that my bills have established a sufficiently consistent pattern to narrow it, and my conversations with other attorneys reveal that they have much the same experience. This points up the necessity for discussing fees ahead of time and making a clear and definite arrangement with your expert.

When using out-of-town lay witnesses I suggest that you stick pretty much to the same rules that you use with your local people plus the addition of travel and lodging expenses. If the person comes a long way at considerable inconvenience, you could well justify paying him $75.00 per day.

You cannot forget that questions regarding your payment to any witness constitute legitimate cross-examination bearing on credibility. Be prepared then to have your witnesses ready to answer these questions. Remember, they are not being paid for their testimony! They are being paid for their lost wages, expenses, cooperation and inconvenience. You must be certain that your witness understands this so that he, and you, are not embarrassed should the subject come up in court.

### Trial Briefs and Memoranda

Certainly not every case requires a trial brief. The question is whether this particular case does. It is only when you have gone through it carefully that you will be able to decide whether there are any legal problems of a sufficiently novel or difficult nature that a brief should be written. Generally that is going to be true if you are trying to change the law of negligence in your jurisdiction or if your case is so "borderline" that a judge will have to be convinced to let your case go to a jury. Since you know there will be serious argument on the question of liability you might as well prepare your brief before trial and give it to the judge at once. In that way he will understand your theory of liability and the law that you are relying on, and will be able to do some research on the problem before argument on defendant's motion for a non-suit. I find that this is far superior to waiting until the time of argument to submit a brief.

Legal memoranda of two or three pages should be prepared to cover anticipated evidentiary or procedural problems that a judge does not routinely encounter. A good illustration would be the instance in which you plan to prove a hearsay statement and are going to offer it as an exception to the Hearsay Rule. A judge doesn't come across that kind of problem very often and would welcome a short brief giving some good authority for your offer. Another example would be your attempt to offer an official document from a foreign jurisdiction and a question arises whether you have complied with your own statute in having the document properly authenticated. The judge can use some help in this type of situation and since you know in advance that it is likely to arise take the time to prepare a memorandum.

# CHAPTER 8

# Selecting the Jury in Personal Injury Cases

The selection of the jury is a skill which must be mastered and put to good use by each of us. It requires us to devote a considerable amount of time thinking about our client, the nature of the case, and the defendant, and relating the characteristics and peculiarities of each to whatever we may learn about the individual jurors. It requires us to watch the jurors carefully, to pick up every detail possible in their appearance and behavior, and to listen attentively to their answers and the manner of their response to the questions posed to them during the interrogation. Finally, the selection process demands that we make a careful judgment as to which jurors should be stricken and which ones will remain to hear the trial. In developing and improving our skill in this area we have to use our own reason and experience, but we can also rely upon certain well-established principles that have considerable validity. We will look at these in a few moments. First I would like to discuss a constant problem—time.

## TAKE YOUR TIME—IF YOU CAN!

If we grant that jury selection is one of the most important parts of the trial—the method provided by law to determine which persons will actually hear the case—then it stands to reason that the process should take a reasonable amount of time. Yet, for some reason unknown to me, there is more pressure brought to bear on the attorneys by the judges and court personnel to rush through this procedure than in any other part of the trial. With the exception of a few prominent cases—usually criminal cases—wherein jury selection can take many, many days, in the average civil case there is an uproar if you take so long as a few hours. There is a constant pressure to rush—hustle, bustle—get it over with and get the trial started. It is almost as though the average judge, or clerk who may conduct the proceeding, is personally affronted if you just don't take the first twelve jurors and get on with the case. They proceed on the absurd assumption that any twelve jurors will do; and that you are somehow trespassing on their valuable time if you insist on being careful and deliberate. I wonder if you have shared with me the ordeal of selecting the jury in a courtroom with the presiding judge sitting on the bench? Every time you take a minute to scrutinize your notes the good judge either bellows: "Now let's get on with this; we don't want to waste any time"; or he fidgets, shuffles papers, or otherwise gives every indication that his patience is being tired. Remonstrate if you will: he merely takes that as further evidence of your dilatory tactics. It is sad to be faced with this problem and it shows a lack of understanding on the part of the Court of the importance of the jury selection process.

What can you do in this situation? You must enter on the record a formal objection to the coercion on the part of the judge. That will protect you to some extent and might make the judge reconsider his attitude. If it is a clerk who is pressuring you, a visit to the judge to register an objection may well solve the problem.

The only other way to handle this situation is to deliberately take your time—using any subterfuge available—up to the point of a contempt citation. In point of fact you should be able to select a jury within a two- to three-hour period and if you have a legitimate one or two hours given you, it should not take too much imagination to squeeze out an extra thirty or sixty minutes. It's very unfortunate that you have to resort to this tactic but we must deal with practicalities. Count yourself lucky if you are given all of the time that you need!

## THE INTERROGATION OF THE JURY

The only way you are going to find out any information about the jurors is by asking them questions. The manner of interrogation varies in different jurisdictions—in most areas a court clerk will ask the questions of the jurors but in some cities the attorneys conduct the examination. In either event the nature of the questions will be essentially the same. If you are going to question the jurors, be certain that you have prepared a written set of questions so that you do not overlook anything important. The following list constitutes an essential set of questions that should be asked in every case:

1. What is your name?
2. What is your street address?
3. In what part of this city do you live?
   (I believe this to be important. A street address is frequently meaningless, but the identification of a locale will help you to place the juror in a particular social, economic and political setting.)
4. What is your occupation?
5. For whom do you work?
6. What is your religious persuasion?
7. What is the name of your doctor?
8. What is the name of your lawyer?
9. How many children do you have?
10. What are their occupations?
11. For whom do they work?
12. Do you drive a car?
13. Do you own your home?
14. Are there any adult persons living in your home besides your spouse and children?
15. If so, identify them and their relationship to you.
16. What is their occupation?
17. For whom do they work?
18. Have you ever been involved in a lawsuit?
19. If so, state the type of case it was, whether you were the plaintiff or defendant, and the result of the case.

The answers to these questions will give you a good general knowledge of the background of the jurors. It will be enough that you can begin now to "rough out" your ideas as to the jurors whom you will want to reject.

**Special Questions on Voir Dire**

Every case is individualized to the extent that it involves specific persons and a particular accident or incident. Accordingly, there are additional questions which must be asked in each case that are peculiar to its facts and the persons involved. These are usually a part of the routine interrogation:

1. Do you know the plaintiff?

2. Do you know the defendant?

3. Are you, or any member of your family, a stockholder, officer, or member of the board of directors of the defendant corporation?

4. This accident occured on (here follows a brief statement of the accident). Do you know anything about this accident?

5. Do you know the plaintiff's attorney?

6. Do you know the defense attorney?

7. Have you or any member of your family ever been represented by them or their law firm?

Then should come the questions that are most specifically pertinent to your case—and here come the problems. Usually you have to get the permission of the court to ask these questions and, probably, simply because you want them asked, the defense attorney is going to object. This will require an appearance before the court and some argument. I suggest three things:

1. Have the controversial questions typed as a pleading so that they can be filed as a part of the record.

2. Try to have the court reporter present at the time the questions are presented to the court so that all of the argument can be recorded.

3. Force the court to make a formal ruling on each question.

If your questions are not important enough to justify this procedure, then they are probably not important enough to bother with at all.

When should special questions be asked of the jurors? This depends upon your plaintiff and your case. Here are a few illustrations of problems which will call for specific questions to the jurors:

1. If the accident occurred in a bar, or if drinking was in any way involved, even inferentially, you have a right to know the attitude

of the jurors concerning the use of alcohol. There are some persons in this world who are so completely prejudiced against the use of alcohol that if your plaintiff was drinking they will find against him even if the alcohol had nothing to do with the accident.

2. Your plaintiff may be well known in the community, and in a somewhat controversial manner, that could engender prejudice or hostility. A good example is the politician. Let the plaintiff be a councilman, legislator or mayor and you may be sure that those of a different political persuasion are going to be hostile. Similarly, if the plaintiff is the child of a prominent, wealthy family there is going to be a natural feeling that the child "doesn't need any money" and therefore should not be fairly compensated for injuries received. This type of prejudice will also be present when the plaintiff has a criminal record or when the accident occurs when the plaintiff was with a person not his, or her, spouse.

3. There are incidents which, when they occur, receive widespread publicity. Television broadcasts spread them throughout the community and they are the subject of much discussion in the newspapers. Frequently the news coverage is biased or becomes partisan as to cause, effect, responsibility and persons involved. A simple illustration would be a tragic airplane accident in a small town in which many persons, including some local people, were killed or injured. Aside from the immediate news coverage the matter will probably be discussed for months as the appropriate authorities make their lengthy investigation and issue reports from time to time. The event will be widely discussed among the citizens and opinions formed well before your case comes to trial.

When you have a case in which any of these unusual, novel or peculiar problems exist, there is simply no other way to determine prejudice, hostility or bias on the part of the prospective jurors except to prepare a special set of questions and ask them. It's my observation that the average judge will allow some questions in this area, but will try to limit the number—once again illustrating the attitude of "rush rush" to get the jury selected. Since you can reasonably anticipate that this will be his attitude, make your list of special questions a very extensive one so that when the judge eliminates some questions you have enough remaining to give you a good idea as to the attitude of the jurors.

## Challenge for Cause and Peremptory Challenges

There are, of course, two types of challenges—the challenge for cause and the peremptory challenge. The first requires little discussion since it is so obvious. Either during the interrogation, or at its conclusion, it may become clear that some of the jurors simply cannot serve in this case. This is nearly always due to a personal relationship with one of the parties or the attorneys, a personal knowledge of the case or a preconceived, prejudicial opinion that has already been formed. Under these circumstances the clerk or judge, as the case may be, will quietly excuse this juror and draw another to take his place. This poses no real problem. It is in utilizing the peremptory challenges that you have to be very careful. The number of such challenges will vary from area to area, but I have found that on the average each attorney is allowed four such challenges. Your concern is how best to use those challenges.

### Watch the Jurors Carefully—Things You Can Learn by Looking

Since your goal is to learn as much as possible about the jurors, and since the number of your questions to them is limited, great emphasis must be placed on your ability to learn about them by observing them. There are a host of things you can learn about the jurors simply by studying them carefully. Use this observation to the fullest while you have the opportunity. Much will depend on where the jurors sit during the interrogation. If they are in the jury box and you are at the attorneys' table the sheer distance will inhibit you. Happily in my area the attorneys sit together at a table with a court clerk and the jurors are brought to the table, one at a time, to be interrogated. This is an excellent system and gives the attorneys a good chance to observe the jurors. What shall we look for?

### 1. MANNER OF DRESS

While no man should be judged by the "cut of his clothes" there can be no question that a person's manner of dress betrays important facts about his wealth, life style, and attitude. A woman who reports for jury duty in a well-fitting, neat, obviously expensive dress is certainly a different person from another juror who is wearing blue jeans and a sweater. Consider two male jurors who each appear neatly dressed in a pin-striped suit, white shirt and tie. Note that one suit is frayed at the sleeve ends, the crease in the trousers and around the collar, while the other suit is in good shape. You may conclude that one man is an active, working businessman while the other is either living on Social Security benefits and a small pension, or, if he is too young for that, he has come on hard times financially. The difference may be important to your case. Look at the male juror who wears a pair of slacks and a brightly-colored sports shirt open at the neck. He leans back in his seat with arms outstretched and laughs and jokes with the people around him. This man is a casual, out-going, gregarious type who, if you keep him, may well end up being the foreman of the jury.

Clothes are important. It is your job to note whether they are casual or formal, dirty, frayed, clean, neat, expensive-appearing, or bargain-basement. Each of these characteristics reveals a little more information about the juror.

## 2. ORNAMENTATION

People use ornaments to send a message. It's your job to be receptive to what that message may be. Two or three jeweled rings on a woman's hand represents a proud proclamation to the world: "Look, I'm wealthy and I want everyone to know it." A tiny Purple Heart emblem in a lapel signifies that the juror is a veteran of some war, was in combat, was wounded, and is proud of those years of service. He is hardly the type of juror you want to hear the case of a young "hippie" who has never come closer to violence than participating in an anti-establishment demonstration. The Masonic button, Knights of Columbus pin, the school ring, the diamond tie-tac are all worn for a purpose. The wearer is proud of something and he wants everyone who looks at him to know of it. Your job is to receive the message and, utilizing this information with the other data you learn about the juror, decide whether he should be retained as a juror in the case.

## 3. ACTIVITY AND BEHAVIOR

As you sit in front of the panel watch the way the jurors act, talk and conduct themselves. Granted that the strangeness of the situation and the solemnity of being in a courthouse (for the first time, as to most of the jurors) will have a restraining effect on their conduct, nonetheless they will, after a short period of time, begin to "be themselves." The quiet, withdrawn person will stay quiet and alone; the garrulous, gregarious types will gather together telling jokes or complaining loudly about delays which they don't understand. Make note of these things. If you can observe the jurors during a recess, try to see which one or two are the persons around whom the others naturally tend to gravitate. That person, or those people, will probably be the leaders in the jury room and you had better analyze them carefully. Always pay close attention to the person who makes the others laugh. He will be popular and even though he may not be a leader on the jury his good natured joking will sway several jurors for or against your cause.

Several jurors may be reading before or during the interrogation. The fact that they are glancing at the local newspaper has no significance but if one is reading *The Wall Street Journal,* you might ask yourself "why?" Some jurors will have paperback books with them to while away the time and there is some meaning to the fact that one is reading "The Brothers Karamazov" while another is reading "Monsters From Outer Space." It takes only a moment to discover these facts and they represent one more bit of knowledge that you can use in making your judgment.

### The Purpose of This Fact Gathering—Finding a Common Bond

The reason—the only reason—that we go to all of this trouble to find out as much as possible about each individual juror is so that we can match up, in as many ways as possible, our client with the jurors who share the same background, attitude and beliefs. We know that sympathy and understanding come much more easily when one shares common experiences with another person. Some of these common experiences are very powerful forces such as one's ethnic background or occupation; others are less significant—belonging to the same club (Elks, American Legion) or living in the same section of town. The important task of the lawyer is to find as many areas of similarity as possible between client and juror. In order to do this there must be some considerable time spent in reviewing your client's background.

### KNOW YOUR CLIENT—WELL

Up to the time of jury selection each of your conferences with your client is going to be directed to the facts surrounding the accident, the nature of his injuries, and the type and extent of his losses. As we approach the time when we are to select the jury the emphasis must shift entirely away from these areas. At this point we want to know in the greatest detail about the client as a person. What is his ethnic heritage? What schools did he attend? What skills has he developed, what occupations has he had and, specifically, for what companies has he worked? His hobbies, clubs, and social activities should be part of the dossier that you are preparing. Certainly you want to know about his wife, children, parents and family activities. Essentially what you are doing is working up a psychological profile of your client which you hope to match with as many jurors as possible. You are going to have to spend quite a bit of time with him going over these matters—several hours, at least—and despite your pointed questioning you are still going to have to let him ramble and reminisce. When you finish you will have a pretty clear idea of the type of juror you would like to have and some definite ideas about the types of persons you do not want on the jury.

In thinking about your client's background, occupation, and personality, and how you might match him with the various members of the panel, there are a few characteristics that are worthy of special mention and discussion:

### Ethnic Heritage and Religion

The two frequently go hand-in-hand. We speak of an "Irish Catholic" or a "German Luthern." I recall a history professor who was very proud of the fact that during the 1700's the pioneer movement in the United States from the eastern seaboard into the western wilderness was led by a hardy breed of "Scotch-Irish Presbyterians with a rifle in one hand and a Bible in the other." Naturally he was a descendant of one of them.

This bond of heritage and religion is so strong that it alone can make a difference in the outcome of a case. The fact that one is of English or Italian ancestry conjures up a veritable host of lifelong associations. Family training, education, aptitudes, attitudes,—one's whole way of life is, to a great extent, built upon these twin pillars of ethnic origin and religion. When one meets a person with the same background there immediately arises an empathy and understanding, identification and comprehension, that requires neither word nor contact. Of all of the areas of mutuality between your client and the jurors this is the strongest.

There is one curiosity about this bond that I want to call to your attention—don't get a majority of these people on the jury. When they are in the minority—let us say four or five of the same heritage as the plaintiff—they will fight tooth and nail on his behalf. I suggest that this comes from a feeling that they must support and defend their compatriot and in so doing they are supporting and defending themselves and their group against the other, majority, jurors. Take the same group and put them in control of the jury—let us say they number ten members—and the situation becomes very different. Now they are in a dominant position, sure of themselves, and it is unnecessary to defend their group against the other jurors. Under these circumstances they will adopt quite a different attitude toward your plaintiff. They become much more critical and more willing to return an adverse verdict. It is almost as if they say to one another, "We're in charge of this jury. We don't have to defend or protect ourselves, or the plaintiff, because of our background. Now we'll take a very critical look at our plaintiff's case." And they do—sometimes even a hyper-critical look at the plaintiff's case, much to your chagrin.

### Occupation

The second most important bond is vocation or occupation. It takes years of training and education to become expert in many kinds of work, and after having spent that time in preparation the individual spends the rest of his life performing in that occupation. Naturally he learns or assimilates many definite, unique ideas, attitudes and prejudices. Bankers simply "understand" each other; so do railroad men, steelworkers and coal miners. Each lives in a world that the rest of us know little about and this uniqueness leads them to an affection for, and an understanding of, one another. There are enough associations attached to one's job that when your plaintiff and a juror share them you begin the case with that juror in your corner. Whether he stays there depends on other things. Lest anyone scoff at the power of occupational bonds, consider the well known and widely recognized "community of silence" among the members of the medical profession when the subject of malpractice is brought up. It is highly effective and common enough to have been specifically mentioned by a Pennsylvania Appellate Court. See *Cooper v. Roberts*, 220 Pa. Super. 260, 267; 286 A.2d 647, 650 (1971).

### Schools and Clubs

Of lesser importance but still highly significant are the ties existing because of membership in various social organizations, clubs, and attendance at a particular college. A person wears a class ring because he is proud of the fact that he graduated from a certain school at a particular time. We are all aware of the good-natured "elitist" attitude shared by graduates of Harvard, Yale and Princeton. The esprit-de-corps among Notre Dame graduates is proverbial. Therefore, it is important that you notice a class ring on a juror's finger. If your client graduated from the same school, he had better wear his ring too.

The same principle applies to membership in the various social clubs such as the Elks, Lions, American Legion, the Masonic Order and the rest. If a juror is wearing a pin identifying his membership in such an organization and your client is also a member, let him also wear such a pin. It represents an external expression of the fact "Look, we're the same kind of people."

### Neighborhood and Social Standing

These represent "weak links" in the chain of community of interest but they are "links." Frequently they are the only connection between client and juror and as such they have some value. There is a certain "snob appeal" in living in certain neighborhoods and a juror will tend to identify with the plaintiff if that relationship exists. The fact that they come from the same neighborhood causes the juror to think that he and the plaintiff probably have about the same life-style—houses, cars, children, clubs, activities and the like. This can bring about an aura of understanding—quite unspoken—between plaintiff and juror.

Remember that no one of these things by itself means that a juror will favor your client. All that it means is that when the common bond exists you and your client walk into the courtroom with a "friend in court." You begin the case among acquaintances, so to speak, rather than absolute strangers, and remember that there is an air of hostility and suspicion when strangers meet. The more numerous the ties between your client and the jurors, the stronger the bond between them. If the juror and the plaintiff are both Scots, that's fine. Let them also be salesmen for major steel companies and that is better still. Finally, let them both be members of the Masonic Order, the American Legion and graduates of the University of Pittsburgh and you have a real friend on that jury. It is the number and type of mutual relationships that create the common bond that will make a big difference in the way a jury views your plaintiff's case.

## THINK ABOUT THE NATURE OF YOUR CASE
## WHILE CONSIDERING JURORS

While a common bond between your client and a juror is very important it is not enough that you can stop your analysis simply because that bond exists. Don't forget—brothers do quarrel! You must go further and give serious consideration to the kind of case you are trying.

The kind of case you are going to present has a great effect upon your decisions in jury selection. The average person will tend to consider a breach of contract action a little differently from a personal injury lawsuit; a juror who is a member of a minority group may be quite interested in a claim for violation of civil rights and be completely bored in an antitrust suit. Therefore, you must analyze the juror in the light of the nature of your lawsuit. In addition keep in mind the locale, the manner in which the events occurred, the type of person involved, the time of day at which significant events happened, and other salient facts. These can all have an effect on the attitude of the juror. Let me illustrate what I mean by a few definite examples:

1. Suppose your client is Irish and so is a juror. So much to the good. The case arises out of an intersection collision with a taxi—a difficult liability situation—and the juror is a taxi-driver. Watch out! You keep that juror at some considerable risk.

2. Your client was injured when a new bar stool collapsed while he was having a few drinks at the neighborhood tavern. That should be a pretty fair case—but, the juror before you belongs to a religious sect which abhors drinking. He has to go.

3. If your case involves the crash of an airplane due to the negligence of the crew, don't permit a pilot's wife to remain on the jury; but if the accident was due to the negligence of an air-traffic controller, she will probably be a good juror.

4. In an action for breach of a fiduciary's duty between an estate and a bank where you know you are going to be delving into books and records, using charts, and trying to make clear complicated financial transactions you should try to keep on the jury an accountant, bookkeeper, or a retired businessman who is well acquainted with these things. The ordinary jury consists of eight women and four men—none of whom routinely handles anything more complicated than the family budget (and they probably do that job poorly). You had better have someone on that jury who understands what you are driving at.

5. The juror in number 12 seat is a nice old man who seems to have much in common by way of heritage and background, with your young client. Your case involves an accident which occurred at 4:00 A.M., while your client was driving home from a night club. Is the juror the kind who goes to bed after the eleven o'clock news and takes a dim view of young people who stay out late? You must think about this fact—the juror may well be psychologically primed to find your client contributorily negligent for being on the road at that hour of the morning.

6. Your client sustained the loss of a leg in an industrial accident and you are bringing a products liability case against a third party. It appears that your client and a juror have much in common—heritage, age, education. But the juror is walking with a marked limp and it appears as though he has an artificial limb. Be very careful of this person. He may be quite bitter about his loss and cynical of all others who share the affliction. If he is living on workmen's compensation or disability benefits, is he going to give your plaintiff a substantial award for his loss? I'm sorry to say the answer is, usually, no.

7. If your case is a substantial breach of contract action against a small corporation, what will be the attitude of juror No. 7 who has stated on *voir dire* that he once owned a small business but was forced into bankruptcy? Is he going to remember, with anger, that it was cases like yours that brought about that difficult event?

These are the types of matters that you have to be thinking about. They are serious considerations that can and should influence you profoundly in making your decision whether to accept or reject a juror. The fine point in judgment, the point at which skill and experience come into play, is determining which influence is the most important—the kind of case you are trying or the common bonds which exist between client and juror. Here it is fundamentally a matter of quantity or weight. If there are numerous common bonds but the case is going to be offensive to a juror, he must be stricken. If the case is of a neutral character or only slightly negative as to a particular juror and the common bonds exist, keep the juror. I would be willing to keep a claim adjuster for an insurance company on a personal injury case if liability and damages were clear and he had much in common with my plaintiff. It is strictly a matter of gathering together all of the facts that you have observed and heard, putting them in the balance, and watching the way the scales tip. When those imaginary scales refuse to tilt either way, cast your lot in favor of the jurors who have the most in common with the plaintiff.

## THINK ABOUT THE DEFENDANT

The identity of the defendant and his or its background are also important and must be taken into consideration. Your analysis in this regard is almost the same as the matters you considered when you thought about your plaintiff, vis-a-vis, the jury. We know that the best defendant is a corporate entity because it has absolutely nothing in common with the average juror. There is no emotional attachment to a corporation. If the defendant is an individual, that is a different matter and you had better know as much about him as you can possibly learn. Your deposition of him will be of some help and a little investigation of his background will add to your knowledge. Thereafter, it is simply a matter of striking those jurors who have much in common with the defendant.

## STUDY YOUR NOTES

After the interrogation has been completed, after you have spent a few more minutes carefully observing the jurors, it is time to withdraw from the scene, find a quiet corner and study your notes. This is a good time to ask for a recess or simply tell the court that you need the time for reflection. Somehow try to get away so that you have some solitude to analyze what you have learned. You must review your notes as to each juror and jot down short comments about your feelings concerning the person. Very quickly you will find that most of the jurors are relatively neutral persons in your view—there is really nothing to be said of them, very strongly, either pro or con. A few others are going to be definitely favorable and they can be disregarded. The defense attorney will strike some of them and if the rest remain, so much to the good. A very few will be obviously unfavorable and you can note them as persons who must be stricken.

Finally, you are left with a group of five or six persons who are the problem cases. They have some definitely good characteristics and some positively bad ones. These are the ones you have to think about. You must remember what you heard and saw and how you instinctively felt about the jurors. Now it becomes important to recall that a juror was reading "The Brothers Karamazov" and not "The Monsters From Outer Space." If your case requires a serious, sober, highly educated mind that fact may solve your problem. If your injury is a serious one, calling for substantial damages, and most of the jurors are of modest means, it is well to remember that juror No. 15 is the nice-looking woman who wore three jeweled rings on her fingers and comes from an affluent neighborhood. She would not be afraid of awarding a high verdict, whereas to the other jurors $10,000.00 would be a monumental sum. You might keep her. As to another questionable juror you might be swayed by the fact that he mentioned that he was a retired truckdriver and was once an official in the Teamsters Union—especially if the defendant is a corporation which is very much in the news because of a running battle with that very union.

So it goes, a constant juggling act of personality, background, cause of action, observed behavior, ornamentation—trying to piece together that combination of jurors who will go best with your client and your type of case. It is a delicate work and you must have the time for sober, quiet reflection.

## STRIKING THE JURORS

When you return to the room in which the panel is seated all eyes will be upon you. The jurors know that they all cannot serve on the trial jury, that some must go, and they are curious as to who will go and who will stay. It may well be that this is the only significant event in a long tiring day. You should by now have noted or memorized the numbers of the jurors who must be stricken and the three or four who are questionable.

Most jurisdictions provide for the attorneys to alternate striking the jurors, one at a time. Assuming that you have a panel of twenty persons (which seems to be the most common number) each attorney will be allowed four strikes. Let your first two be the necessary ones, noting meanwhile who it is the defense attorney is striking. You will be surprised at how often he will strike one of your questionable jurors. That narrows the field, and your problem. At this point study the remaining worrisome jurors again. You may see or remember something specific that will help you to make up your mind and lead to your third strike. If there is nothing new, look to the sex balance on the jury. The usual problem is that there are too many women. Therefore, all other things being equal, if one of your questionable jurors is a woman and the other a man, strike the woman. The last strike should be fairly easy because at this point you should have only two or three "question marks." One of them should, rather clearly, be more objectionable than the rest and he should be stricken.

Your strikes, whether they are made by calling out the name of the juror, or his number, or by drawing a line through a name on a piece of paper, should be made quietly, unobtrusively and soberly. You don't want to embarrass anyone. If the panel has been together for a while, some of the jurors have become friendly and the one you strike may be a friend of one who remains. If you make a scene out of your actions, or treat it like a joke, you may well antagonize the juror who is staying behind to hear your case. Such unnecessary antagonism is to be avoided at all costs.

## MAKE A CHART OF THE JURORS

It is handy at this point, when the trial jury has been selected, to take a few minutes to prepare a chart listing the jurors by name and number as they will be facing you in the courtroom. From time to time there may be something that comes up where it would be nice if you could refer to the juror by name instead of number. It is much better to say to a witness: "Please speak loudly enough for Mrs. Jones in seat number 12 to hear" rather than refer to her as "Juror Number Twelve." It is a little thing but like many small attentions it is appreciated. You will not be with that jury for a long time—perhaps three or four days—and the more intimate you can get with them in that time the better off you will be.

## SOME GENERAL STATEMENTS

There are a few general rules about jurors that attorneys are always talking about and which ought to be mentioned. We place little credence in them since they are so general and vague as to be substantially valueless in application. Nonetheless they properly belong in any discussion of jury selection.

### 1. Stay Away from Young People

In the last few years persons eighteen through twenty-one years of age have been permitted to serve as jurors in many states. As a group they are disinterested, inexperienced and usually have only a high school education. They tend to be quite cynical about injuries and are completely incompetent to award damages. The reason for the latter is obvious enough—they've been cared for by their parents for all of their young lives. Usually, they have never worked, never had to budget money, don't know the cost of goods and services, and have had little acquaintance with the worry of illness, injury, loss of income and accumulated bills.

### 2.   Beware of Engineers and Accountants

These persons are very literal-minded, inflexible and unimaginative. They demand that a case be presented with the same precision with which they conduct a laboratory experiment and they expect the outcome to be as crystal clear as the "read out" of a computer. Since the plaintiff has the burden of proof, they will quite readily find for the defendant if there is even the slightest element of doubt in the plaintiff's case.

### 3.   Strike Spinsters and School Teachers

Traditionally spinsters are considered to be unloving, unloved, sterile and mean. They are thought to be so unhappy and bitter about their station in life that they will not exercise a sense of charity or understanding toward a plaintiff. (Somehow, nuns are excluded from this analysis.)

School teachers should be stricken because they are weak, usually under-paid and contentious. The fact that they are not well-paid for their work generally means that they will not award a substantial sum to the plaintiff. Their pedagogic attitude is a source of constant argument and friction in the jury room during deliberations and could lead to a "hung jury." Their weakness stems from the fact that they pride themselves on "looking at all sides of the issue." This frequently means they cannot make up their minds.

### 4.   Farmers Do Not Make Good Plaintiffs' Jurors

It is well known that farmers lead a very hard life. They tend to be self-sufficient, independent and resigned to the problems of illness, injury, suffering and pain. They are contemptuous of those who complain of anything less than a major injury and physical disability is to be borne in dignified silence. As a group they are hostile to lawyers and lawsuits.

### 5.   Avoid Bankers and Businessmen

These men are the very elite of the Establishment. By virtue of their nature, training, occupation and associations, they are unmitigatedly hostile to anyone who seeks anything, especially money—from a corporation, business, or a person who is closely associated with these entities. Hospitals, churches, schools and governmental agencies are also sacrosanct and must not have verdicts returned against them.

**6. Do pick for a plaintiff's jury** a salesman, stock broker, union leader, the banker's wife, a mother of a large family, an explorer, any kind of skilled mechanic or tradesman, politician, most priests or ministers, and, if necessary, a professor of psychology or economics.

These are some of the generalized, over-simplified "do's and don'ts" that one constantly hears bantered about. There is a certain element of truth in these "old lawyers' " tales, but they cannot easily be applied to your plaintiff and your case. *My suggestion is to ignore them.* Rely instead on your detailed study of your plaintiff, the nature of your case and your knowledge of the defendant. Then listen attentively to the interrogations of the jurors and observe them as carefully as you can. Then, and only then, are you going to be able to select those jurors who will approach the case with an attitude most favorable to you and your client. That is the proper way to select a jury.

# CHAPTER 9

# Making a Good Opening Address

An opening address serves two functions, i.e., to explain to the jury what the case is all about, and, second, to acquaint the jurors with yourself. Do you remember when you were selecting the jury how deeply interested you were in each and every one of them? It may come as a surprise, but they are just as interested in you. They want to know what kind of a person you, the plaintiff's attorney, are. Your opening address gives you an opportunity to show them and tell them. It is important to realize that what you say, and the manner in which you say it, is going to have a lot of influence on the twelve people before you. To a great extent it will set the tone for the trial itself since it will put the jurors into a mood, feeling or "psychologic set" that will stay with them throughout the trial.

If you make a good impression, the jurors begin the case with an attitude that is kindly disposed toward you and the plaintiff. A poor opening will leave the jurors either completely neutral or, even worse, just a little bit suspicious of the validity of your case. You will be somewhat like a runner in a race who trips and falls right at the start—he might still win but by the time he picks himself up and gets started again the other runners are a good distance ahead. Accordingly, it is important that your opening speech be well prepared and delivered.

## THE JURORS ARE AN INTERESTED, CAPTIVE AUDIENCE— TAKE ADVANTAGE OF IT

It isn't often that you gather twelve people into a room and compel them to listen to you give a speech. Yet that is exactly what your jury is—a captive audience, but an interested captive audience. Everyone is curious about the lives of other people—which is why gossiping is so popular—and if the story involves something dramatic such as an accident, a large sum of money, or allegations of libel or slander, so much the better. The jurors have to be there—and they realize this—so they are prepared to listen with interest and curiosity to what the case is all about. They want to hear you! Take advantage of this by making a good, informative, enjoyable speech.

## GET CLOSE TO THE JURY

Since it is so important that you establish a good rapport with the jurors as promptly as possible and since this is the first time they really find out what kind of a person you are, try to get as close to the jury as you can and speak to them in a friendly manner, on a person-to-person basis. It is simply no good to stand at a lectern some six or eight feet away and deliver a lecture to them. This smacks too much of a teacher-pupil relationship which they will resent, and they will accept your speech in much the same, bored attitude they had when they listened to a lecture in high school or college. It's even worse if you read a prepared speech. It's far better to stand right at the jury rail and talk to them as a friend or acquaintance would. Move about a few steps to your left and right so that you can make contact with the jurors at the ends of the jury box. Look the jurors in the eye and talk to them on a personal basis. If you can use a blackboard or photograph in your opening speech be sure to do so. Your purpose is to sell yourself to the jury and also to make them as aware as possible of the facts you intend to prove, and it's much more effective to have something for them to look at while they are listening.

## BE FRIENDLY, COURTEOUS AND CONFIDENT

This is the one time in your day when you have to go out of your way to be friendly and courteous. Everyone approves of the person who "has manners" and if he is obviously friendly and cheerful, we like him even more. If you are a witty person, then by all means make them laugh— a trial is a serious matter but it need not be a somber one. Whatever little thing you can do to impress the jury with your thoughtfulness or consideration of others should be done. Take a moment to introduce the judge (they probably forgot his name moments after they were told because of the excitement and novelty of being in a courtroom for the first time). Reintroduce the defense attorney and say a few pleasant words about him. If there is a clerk, bailiff or tipstaff who will be working with the jury introduce him with some good-natured comments. Let the jury have the feeling that you know these people well, that you are comfortable around them, and that the jurors can be too.

Above all, be confident. For the first time they are going to be learning the facts of the case and you should leave no doubt as to what you expect the facts to be and the conclusion to which you expect those facts to lead the jury. You may be worried about the outcome but there is no reason to share your doubts or fears with the jurors. Speak firmly, positively, loudly enough that all can hear, and with a sense of conviction that what you are telling the jury is exactly what you are going to prove through your witnesses and exhibits.

## IDENTIFY THE PLAINTIFF, THE SPOUSE, AND THE CHILDREN

The jury knows that "Joe Somebody or other" is the Plaintiff but they don't know who he is. They are anxious to relate the name with the person. Your opening address is the time to do this. Identify the plaintiff again by name and then introduce him by having him rise in the courtroom for all to see. Now he becomes a person and not a name—the case itself begins to become real rather than an abstraction. Almost at once the jury is going to begin to judge the plaintiff—whether they like him or not, whether he looks clean-cut or not, whether he is the kind of a person who gives the appearance of being truthful, whether he is the kind of person they could have as a friend. For this reason your client should be dressed in his best clothes—a suit, white shirt and tie if he is a man, or a subdued, well-fitting dress, with a minimum of jewelry if she is a woman.

Don't overlook this matter of dress; impress your client with its importance. Unless you tell him clearly and in unmistakable terms how you want him dressed he may come to your office the morning of the trial dressed in a sports shirt and slacks—and possibly dirty ones at that. More than once I have sent a secretary scurrying to a nearby department store to buy a white shirt and tie while I and my associates have frantically searched for a jacket that would fit the client and match his trousers.

Since the jury is starting to make some judgments about the plaintiff right away, be sure to have the spouse present and all of the children who can conveniently be in the courtroom (babies excluded). These persons should be pointed out to the jury though they need not stand for a formal introduction. Give the jurors a chance to look over the whole family and let them know that their verdict will not only affect the husband and wife—it will also affect that pretty little girl who is with them. If the children are small and apt to get boisterous, just keep them long enough for the jurors to get their image fixed in their memory and then quietly, without fuss, let them be taken from the courtroom to the hallway or a waiting room. A relative, neighbor or friend should be along to give assistance with the small children so that the plaintiff and spouse can stay in the courtroom.

If this sounds like a play on the sympathy of the jury, so be it. In point of fact the spouse and children have been affected by the injury to a husband or wife. Sometimes their loss is compensable—as a loss of consortium on behalf of a spouse or a loss of nurture in the case of the death of a parent—and sometimes it is not, but irrespective of the legal right to recover there is always a practical loss when a parent or spouse has been injured, and the jury might as well see those who have shared the suffering. If the jury considers these people in making their award they are doing justice—call it a kind of "social justice" if you will—despite the fact that the technical points of the law are stretched a bit. Don't let this aspect of the matter inhibit you when bringing the family group before the jury.

## EXPLAIN THE PROCEDURE TO BE FOLLOWED

Most—nearly all—jurors know absolutely nothing about courtroom procedure. For example, many jurors will expect the defense attorney to make an address to them when you have finished. They think objections are meant to hide evidence which they should hear. They don't understand the role the judge is to play (beyond the vague idea that he is "The Boss") or specifically what their function is. This is the time to explain the entire matter to them in a very simple, straight-forward manner. Tell them that this is your opening address, that thereafter you will put witnesses on the stand and introduce evidence to prove your case. Explain that objections are made to exclude what the attorney believes to be improper evidence and that the judge will then rule whether the objection is proper or not. Tell them that delays may occur from time to time when complicated legal problems develop and that the judge and attorneys may withdraw to the judge's chambers to thrash them out.

If your case is to be tried in separate segments—liability first and damages later—tell the jury about this so that they are not puzzled when the plaintiff fails to mention his injuries and losses during his initial testimony. Mention the fact that at the conclusion of your case the defense attorney will go through the same procedure as you have outlined for your case. Finally, conclude with an explanation of the court's charge on the law and the jury's duty to find the facts and apply the law to those facts in reaching its verdict.

While this sounds like a great deal to say to a jury before you even get to a discussion of the facts, it really need not be lengthy. You could probably do an adequate job of explanation in 7 to 10 minutes and the time spent is well worthwhile.

In my area—both in the State Common Pleas Court and the Federal District Court—some judges have begun to make this explanation themselves. This is a fine idea since it shortens the time you must devote to miscellaneous matters and enables you to begin at once to talk about the case itself. Another innovation which has begun to take hold among local judges is to continue their discussion with the jurors to include part of the regular charge—on matters involving burden of proof, credibility of witnesses, definitions of negligence, contributory negligence, the functions of both the judge and the jury, and a little about the applicable law. I think this is an excellent approach and I commend it to you if your Court is adaptable to change.

## GIVE THE JURY A GENERAL OUTLINE OF THE FACTS— THEN GO BACK AND GIVE A DETAILED STATEMENT

Within the bounds of reason you can't spend too much time in an opening address. Most of those which I have heard—and made—were woefully brief. The sad part of it is that there is no good reason for brevity at this point in the trial. The jury wants to know what the case is about in as much detail as is reasonably possible. It is understood that you don't want to bore them with minutiae—but you can avoid that hazard and still give a good summary of what happened on that "fateful night of January 25th." I have a friend who likes to comment about his opening that: "I tell them what I'm going to say, I say it, then I tell them what they heard." While your opening need not be quite like that, you can rest assured that my friend's opening address leaves a jury completely informed and secure in the knowledge that they know what is going to happen during the trial.

My recommendation is that you should begin by giving the jury a good, thorough summary of the case and then follow up with a more detailed, step-by-step statement of the facts you intend to prove. In this way you will have twice impressed on them your side of the case. The first statement—the summary—will orient them in terms of what happened, when and where, who was involved, the various acts of negligence on the part of the defendant, the nature of plaintiff's injuries and a general statement of his losses. Such a summary might go as follows:

Identity of
Parties

Date of
Accident

Scene of
Accident

Time and
Weather

Facts of
Accident

Injuries
Sustained

Damages

Pain and
Suffering

Permanency

"Ladies and Gentlemen, the case you are about to hear is a claim for damages on the part of Sam Jones, the Plaintiff, against Robert Smith, the Defendant. This claim arises out of an automobile accident that occurred on October 25th—almost exactly two years ago. The accident occurred at the intersection of Forbes Street and Grant Street in downtown Pittsburgh—and I'm sure all of you are familiar with that corner. If you're not, you're going to get familiar with it quickly while you're on this jury, since it is the corner right outside the front of this building and you will be passing it several times each day. The accident occurred at about 8:00 A.M. that Tuesday morning. The weather that day was warm, dry and bright—much like today. Sam Jones was on his way to work and was proceeding in a northerly direction on Grant Street—he was going right past this building and heading toward the U.S. Steel Building several blocks down the street. As he approached Forbes Street he saw that he had the green light and entered the intersection.

"He passed through the first lane of traffic and as he entered the second lane of traffic the defendant, Robert Smith, coming down Forbes Street went through a red light and crashed into the right side of Sam Jones's car. As a result Sam Jones not only suffered severe damages to his car, he also sustained a broken right arm, a concussion, an injury to the muscles of his neck—and was a nervous wreck for several weeks. He was unable to work for four months so that he lost nearly $2,800.00 in wages and his medical expenses amounted to about $1,400.00, including charges for a week in the hospital. He still has pain in his right arm and difficulty in some movements of that arm, which the doctors will tell you is permanent in nature. It is to recover damages for these injuries and losses that we are before you.

"Now let's go back a minute and take a closer look at this accident . . . . . ."

This is a reasonable way to begin your discussion of the case. The jury is well-oriented with this explantion. They know what happened, the scene of the accident, the parties involved, and the nature of the plaintiff's injury and losses. Now you can go back and acquaint them in detail with the widths of streets, location of traffic signals, amount of traffic, the details of the hospitalization and medical treatment, the kind of work Jones did and the specifics of his current physical problems. Most important, because of your summary the jury is ready to accept and understand these details.

## TELL THEM THE WITNESSES YOU WILL CALL

Since you are going to be calling several witnesses to the stand to give testimony, this is a good opportunity to acquaint the jurors with their names, the role they play in the case—eyewitnesses to the accident, medical witnesses on the subject of causation or treatment, or condition witnesses to the plaintiff's incapacity—and what they are going to say. It helps to tell the jury:

> "Alex White will be called by me as a witness in this case. He was standing at the northeasterly corner of the intersection—over here (if you have a picture or have made a drawing on the blackboard) and he was waiting to cross Grant Street. He is an important witness because he actually started to cross Grant Street when the light was red for Grant Street traffic. Then it turned green and he had to return to the sidewalk. He can testify to that fact, but in addition as he was standing idly by, he actually saw the accident occur and will tell you about that.
>
> "Another witness we will bring before you is Sally Young. She was a passenger in the right front seat of the defendant's car. She will explain to you why this accident happened—that Smith was clipping along at a pretty good speed for this hour of the day, that he tried to light a cigarette but the lighter struck in its compartment and that Smith was actually leaning down to twist the lighter free when he proceeded right through the red light into the intersection and struck the car of Mr. Jones."

Go on in this manner with each of the witnesses. If several persons—such as condition witnesses—will testify to about the same facts, group them together and instead of using names (which might be forgotten quickly) refer to them as the next-door neighbor, the plaintiff's boss at work, one of the members of his bowling team, and his sister. In this manner you not only introduce the witnesses to the jury and place them in the framework of the case, you also begin to impress the jury with the fact that you know what you are doing and that you have a good case.

## EXPLAIN ANTICIPATED PROBLEMS

There are going to be practical problems arising in every case and some of these you are going to be aware of before you even get to the courtroom. I refer to delays caused, perhaps, by a doctor whom you have scheduled to testify at 1:30 P.M. but who calls just as you leave for court to state that he can't be in until 3:00 P.M.; a witness who doesn't speak English well and with whom you may have to use an interpreter; a large, bulky exhibit that you could not bring to the courtroom earlier because the room was occupied and which will require a recess so that it can be brought into the room at some appropriate time during the trial. You must explain these problems to the jurors.

Time-consuming delays—usually unexplained—and seemingly unnecessary, are the biggest gripes that all jurors have about our trial system. If you doubt my word, just bring up the subject with some friends who have completed a tour of jury service. The wrathful blast which follows will blow you right out of the room. Wasted time, boredom and ennui are the foundation for most complaints about jury service. Then, when the jurors get into a foul mood, every little inconvenience becomes exaggerated. Avoid the problem and save yourself some grief by the simple expedient of telling the jurors that there are going to be some delays, what the cause may be and about how long you believe the delay will last. If you will remember your days of military service and "hurry up and wait," you may recall that it was never the waiting that really bothered us, it was the fact that we never knew why we were waiting or how long the wait was going to be. Be sure your jury knows these facts.

I have commented earlier about your explaining the occasional disappearance of the attorneys and the judge into chambers for a discussion. Since you know that this is going to happen, be sure to mention it. Another matter you might honestly discuss is the problem of a hostile witness. If you have had to subpoena a doctor to get him into court, you know he is going to come in an angry mood. It's proper to mention this—at least the fact that you did have to subpoena him and that most subpoenaed doctors are unhappy witnesses. If you have a young child as a witness, tell the jury that you may have trouble developing his testimony, that he may speak too softly and that he may become easily confused; and if one of your witnesses is an elderly person who is hard of hearing then say so, and explain that you are either going to be bellowing if you stand back from the witness or you will have to stand beside him with your back to the jurors and talk directly into his good ear.

Whatever the problem may be, if you know that it is likely to occur and will be disruptive or troublesome, explain the matter in your opening. The jurors will really appreciate it.

## TOUCH ON THE APPLICABLE LAW

You will have to tread lightly on this matter. To begin with, an opening address is generally restricted to a statement of facts, and facts only, which you intend to prove. In addition we all know that it is the duty of the judge to charge the jurors on the applicable law and many judges consider this to be a unique privilege of theirs, and theirs alone. Last, but definitely not least, defense counsel is going to be a little nervous about how far you intend to go in this area and what you intend to say. On the other hand, it is patently absurd that the jurors know absolutely nothing about the applicable law until the end of the case when they get it explained to them in one generous dose that simply must leave them confused and uncertain. It is in recognition of this possibility that the judges in my area have begun to charge the jury, in part, at the beginning of the case.

From your point of view the one thing you don't want are confused, uncertain jurors. Accordingly, take it upon yourself to explain to them as much as possible the law that applies to the case. I feel so strongly about this that I will discuss the law—within reasonable limits—until either the judge or the defense attorney stops me. The important thing is to get some knowledge of the law into the minds of the jurors so that they can apply it to the facts as you unfold them. Actually if you will use a little common sense, tell the jury the applicable legal principles without distortion, and don't get too deeply involved in this matter, the average defense attorney and judge will let you speak. So speak out—firmly and accurately—and give your jury a good legal basis, as well as a factual one, for finding a verdict in your favor.

## DON'T EXAGGERATE—DON'T TELL THEM ANYTHING
## YOU CAN'T PROVE—THEY WILL REMEMBER

It is surprising, but true, that some lawyers will try to "con" a jury in their opening address. What naive duplicity! It boomerangs every single time and the poor attorney wanders around asking everyone: "What happened." What happened is that he lied or told half-truths to twelve people who simply didn't forget—especially when opposing counsel in his closing address reminds them what they were told in Plaintiff's Opening and what was actually proved. It is simply poor practice, so don't do it.

Don't tell the jury you are going to call a witness and then fail to do so without a good explanation. Don't exaggerate the testimony of a witness or tell the jury he is going to testify to certain facts when you know very well that he can't testify to those facts. If your case is sound enough to justify a trial, you don't have to resort to these tactics. The saddest point about all of this is that it is a self-defeating, pointless, useless approach. The average civil trial is so short—requiring four to six days—that the jurors will remember on Friday what you told them on Monday and if you told them half-truths or exaggerations, they are going to be very unhappy. Need I remind you that jurors who are angry or disturbed at Plaintiff's counsel frequently return defense verdicts? Since this whole subject requires an unnecessary and unjustifiable risk—don't do it.

## USE AN OUTLINE—BUT NO READING

Despite the fact that by this time you know your case very well, it is still appropriate to have a brief outline before you when you make your opening address. It should not be anything detailed—just some short phrases that you can glance at from time to time. This will lend coherence, organization and thoroughness to your speech. It will insure the fact that you cover everything that you think is going to be important and will enable you to move logically from one point to the next. Your speech must have a certain spontaneity about it and should be colloquial, but if you don't have some kind of an outline, you're going to be naming witnesses in the wrong 'er, or you will be switching too soon from liability to damages, or forgetting some of the medical aspects of the case. An outline simply enables you to keep everything in order. However, don't use a detailed outline and don't read. A detailed outline will confuse you and reading a prepared speech will bore the jurors. They don't want to hear it so why do it? Your problem is to be organized without being a lecturer. A simple outline will do the job. Try something like this:

OPENING

I.  Introduce Judge and All

II. Facts—Accident—Tuesday, October 25, 8:00 A.M., Grant and Forbes

III. Witnesses—Who, Where
     Alex White    Corner
     Sally Young   In Car
     3 Condition Witnesses—Boss,
        Friend, Sister
     Dr. Block    Orthopedist
     Dr. Brown    Neurologist

IV.  Problems—
    Conferences
    M.D.s on time?
    Sally Young—may have to be
      hospitalized tomorrow

V.  Injuries and Losses—
    Concussion
    Broken right arm—permanent
      disability
    Whiplash
    Nervousness

| Wages | $2,798.54 |
| Medical | $1,466.00 |
| Life Expectancy | 26.2 years. |

VI.  Law—
    Intersection
    Speeding
    Failure to Look Ahead
    Red Light

VII.  Summary

You can work up something like this in a few minutes and it will be of great value when you begin to speak. At least if you get carried away with one aspect of the case, it will help to remind you that you have other things to talk about.

## HOW MUCH TIME SHOULD YOU TAKE?

It is trite to say that in a simple case you take a little time and in a complicated case you take a long time. Trite and untrue. In every case you will want to introduce various persons; you will discuss anticipated problems and the applicable law, the injuries, damages, and the facts on liability. The only area in which there is a major difference will be in discussing the liability facts and possibly in identifying the witnesses.

Accordingly, I recommend that you select a typical case of yours, work up an outline and proceeding slowly, time yourself to see just how long you do take to make an adequate opening. I have found that, on the average, 30 minutes is just about right. In that period of time you can touch upon all pertinent subjects without rushing. If the case is extremely simple (such as my hypothetical intersection collision) with few witnesses, you could reduce the time to 20 minutes. But why hurry? If you have a good reason to try a simple (on its facts) case take the extra ten minutes and do a more thorough job. If you have several defense attorneys, numerous witnesses and a complicated factual situation, you might speak for as long as 45 minutes. I doubt that any ordinary case will require more time than this. The important thing is that you don't rush. No one is going to give you a medal for making a ten-minute opening and you can't possibly have done your job in that time.

## TRY TO USE PHOTOGRAPHS, DIAGRAMS, OR BLACKBOARD TO ACQUAINT JURORS WITH THE SCENE

This is valuable in any opening but especially so if you must speak for 30 to 45 minutes. The jurors do tend to get tired listening to you droning on and if you can switch their attention to something visual, it is a big help. In addition to showing a photograph or drawing try to use one upon which you can write. Note on it the placement of witnesses with a symbol or write their names, draw a little box to represent a car or truck. If you're using an enlargement of a written document (such as a page of nurses' notes from a hospital record) underline the pertinent material. By doing this, then, at one and the same time, you are talking, showing a visual aid, and demonstrating the essential facts on the visual aid. Naturally, you can do the same thing with a model or a blackboard.

The big problem with this technique is doing it without objection from defense counsel. I can only say that it is important for you to know defense counsel well and know just how far he is going to be willing to let you go. Only experience and camaraderie will provide an answer to that question. However, don't let either your ignorance of opposing counsel nor his suspected hostility deter you.

To begin with, Pretrial Conferences are utilized nearly everywhere. This is an excellent time to try to get the picture or drawing admitted into evidence and then to try to get the agreement of defense counsel to use it in your opening. This can be done if you are honest and open with him as to what you're going to do, and when he agrees, be sure to get that agreement into the pretrial record. If you forgot about this at pretrial, or the drawing was prepared later, or you made up your mind to use it at the last minute, then, when you are sent out to a courtroom ask for a conference with the judge and bring up the subject at that time. Most of the time the judge will understand your problem and agree to let you use something—if not the photograph or drawing, at least the blackboard.

The vital, crucial aspect of this consent is that you stick to the facts and never go beyond the bounds of your agreement with defense counsel or the Court. If you do they may forgive but they won't forget—and it will be a long time before they trust you again. If you plan to try lawsuits on any kind of a regular basis, there will be many occasions when you are going to need the consent and cooperation of opposing counsel and the court, so you had better establish a firm reputation for reliability—especially in matters like this where you are given a certain degree of latitude and discretion.

## TELL THE JURORS YOU HAVE TALKED WITH YOUR WITNESSES

Many attorneys who are not actively engaged in trial work have a reluctance to admit that they have talked to their witnesses before trial. This is a strange attitude but it apparently springs from a feeling that they will be accused of "telling the witness what to say." Of course it's wrong to suborn perjury, but it's equally wrong not to have gone over, in detail, the testimony of every witness. Wrong? The word is not strong enough. I would assert that an attorney who fails without good cause to talk to a witness before putting him on the witness stand is guilty of malpractice! How could it be otherwise?

To put a witness on the stand when you are ignorant of what that person is going to say is to invite destruction of your case. Your client hardly needs a lawyer to ruin his case—he can do that poorly himself. The client retains the lawyer to insure that the best possible case will be introduced on his behalf and this means that the lawyer must know, in detail, all of the evidence he intends to produce. The only way he is going to know that detail is to talk with the witnesses.

The jurors, in their honest ignorance, may also wonder about your having talked with the witnesses and the propriety of doing so. Meet this issue early and head-on. Tell the jurors that you have talked to the witnesses at length, that it is your duty to have done so, and that the facts you are telling them now were learned as a result of those conversations with the witnesses.

This will satisfy the jurors and also take away a ploy that some defense attorneys use. If you haven't mentioned this subject in your opening, then at some point in the cross-examination of your witness defense counsel will interrupt his routine questioning to ask, in varying degrees of length:

Q. By the way, did you talk with Mr. DeMay about this case?

A. Yes.

Q. How long did you talk with him.

A. About an hour.

Q. Did you discuss the facts of this case?

A. Yes.

Q. Did he tell you what to say?

A. (Here, it had better be): "He told me to tell the truth."

That puts an end to that line of questioning. I always tell my witnesses to tell the truth on the stand, to be prepared for this type of interrogation, and if they are asked about our conversation in a manner suggesting impropriety to roar out the fact that I told them to tell the truth in all things.

There is one other matter that needs explaining to the jurors about your conversations with the witnesses—the possibility that you misstate what the testimony will be. This happens from time to time. You will sometimes get confused about who, exactly, is going to say what; or you get carried away with an explanation of the facts and forget that you began by mentioning that "Jones will testify" and now you're talking about Smith's testimony—having long ago concluded with your summary of what Jones will say. On other occasions you will innocently but plainly misstate portions of the testimony of the witness. These mistakes are easily handled. Tell the jury that you have tried to summarize what each person will say, but that if they do not so testify, the problem and the fault are yours alone in misunderstanding or misinterpreting what they have to say. I suggest a comment somewhat along these lines:

"Now, Ladies and Gentlemen, I have tried to summarize for you the testimony of the several witnesses I will bring before you. There is one matter, however, I do want to mention. If by some chance the witnesses, or some one witness, does not testify as I have stated here before you, please understand that it is undoubtedly my own fault. It is possible that I may have misunderstood the witness or perhaps in talking with all of them I've confused John's testimony with Joe's testimony. I don't think I have—I hope I haven't—but if it does occur please excuse me and don't take it out on the witness. He will be on the witness stand to tell his own story in his own way and you rely on what he says at that time."

Such a brief statement will help to take away the sting of any conflicts between your statements and the witness' testimony.

## LEAVE SOME THINGS UNSAID—BUILD A LITTLE SUSPENSE

This may be a little contradictory to my insistence throughout this chapter that you thoroughly advise the jurors of the facts you intend to prove. Perhaps it is, but it is an acceptable exception. There is always a little psychology that has to be used in a trial and part of your problem is to keep the jurors interested, listening, and subject to being pleasantly surprised by the testimony of someone they didn't expect to hear or testimony that is stronger than you lead them to believe. This can be accomplished if you have an especially good witness who need not testify in the early stages of the case. Save him to provide that surprise for the jury.

For example, you might discuss in detail the testimony of the attending physician of your minor plaintiff, then mention casually that you will probably call another medical expert on the problem of the permanency of the disability. What a pleasant surprise it is for the jury to learn that the expert happens to be the well-known and respected Dr. Spock. Likewise you might mention in an automobile accident case that you have one or two "other" witnesses, and then produce the mother, sister or girlfriend of the defendant who testify honestly, though unhappily, that he was driving 50 miles per hour in a 35-mile zone. If you can, try to hold back on your comments about one or two witnesses for the surprise or shock value it will have.

In conclusion I urge you to consider your opening address as truly a vital part of the trial. It is too often treated in a casual manner as though it were an unnecessary appendage to the whole procedure. It is not. Treat it instead as a fine opportunity to let the jury get to know you and your clients, and to learn clearly and thoroughly what your case is all about. Let your first important contact with the jury be a good one.

# CHAPTER 10

# The Plaintiff's Case-in-Chief

The Plaintiff's Case-in-Chief represents the heart of his lawsuit. All of the months of preparation are brought to culmination in this phase of the case. You could forego everything else—Opening Address, Closing Speech, Cross-Examination of Defendant's witnesses—and still win a case on the evidence you produce in your case-in-chief; conversely you could do well in every other portion of the trial, but if you perform poorly at this point you are most likely going to lose. This is the time when you must prove all of the facts that the law requires and do it in a manner sufficient to convince the jury that yours is the cause of justice.

To repeat, there is no part of a trial which equals in importance the presentation of your case-in-chief.

## BEGIN WITH ADMISSIONS IN THE PLEADINGS

Having concluded your Opening the next order of business is to offer, and read into the record, all of the admissions that defendant has made in the pleadings. This is the moment when all of the time, thought, imagination, and labor that you put into discovery really earns its reward. The more facts you have forced the defendant to admit the happier you can be.

Reading these admissions at this time is important for three reasons:

1. It has great psychological effect on the jury.

2. It puts into the record the necessary, but uncontested, facts that you need to prove your case.

3. It permits you to concentrate your attention on the remaining contested issues in the case.

Let us take a closer look at these factors:

### 1. The Psychological Effect

Try to put yourself in the position of a juror. You are a little nervous, but very interested, anxious to do a good job, and wondering how this trial is really going to proceed. You have heard the plaintiff's attorney tell you about the case and all of the things he is going to prove. When he finishes you are skeptical—at least to the point of trying to retain an "open mind"—but curious. Can he really prove all of the things he said he would? At this point the attorney stands before the judge and asks permission to read portions of various papers he holds in his hands. The judge agrees and turns to tell you that plaintiff's counsel is going to read admissions that defendant has made and that you must accept these facts as proved and true. Then counsel reads to you:

"Paragraph three of the Complaint—At all pertinent times plaintiff, Sam Jones, was the owner and operator of a certain Ford Sedan proceeding in a northerly direction on Grant Street. Answer—Admitted.

"Paragraph four of the Complaint—At all pertinent times defendant, Robert Smith, was the owner and operator of a certain Plymouth Sedan that was proceeding in a Westerly direction on Forbes Street. Answer—Admitted.

"Paragraph five of the Complaint—This Accident happened on October 25th at 8:00 A.M. Answer—Admitted.

"Paragraph six of the Complaint—The accident happened at the intersection of Grant Street and Forbes Street. Answer—Admitted."

On and on it goes. He continues:

"Interrogatory No. 15—Was Sally Young riding in the right front seat of Smith's car? Answer—Yes.

"Interrogatory No. 19—What were the weather conditions at the time of this accident? Answer—It was warm, dry and clear.

"Stipulation No. 3 from the Pretrial Record: The Plaintiff, Sam Jones, was employed at the Wesson Company as a welder. He earned $4.11 per hour. He did not work for seventeen weeks following this accident. The amount of money he could have earned during this period was $2,798.54."

You as a juror, cannot help but be quite impressed by this recital. The very things plaintiff's attorney told you he was going to prove are being proved right before you. There is no argument—these are the facts of the case.

The result of this presentation is an inevitable feeling on the part of all of the jurors that (1) the plaintiff's attorney really knew what he was talking about during his opening address, and (2) it appears as though the plaintiff ought to win this case.

This procedure gives you a fine, early advantage over the defendant. Everything the jury hears is favorable to your position and is beyond dispute.

## 2. Necessary Facts Are Placed into the Record at an Early Stage

You must always protect the record. Try every case with an awareness that an appellate court may have to review it some day and the only data those judges will have before them is the transcript of the record. Accordingly treat the court reporter and his little stenotype machine with the greatest respect. No matter how small or seemingly insignificant a fact may be, if it is agreed to by defense counsel or constitutes an admission read it to the jury and the reporter. You must remember that if the fact is admitted, it can never be the cause of a reversal. If you have not offered it and made it a part of the record, it always represents potential trouble and you will have wasted your time in having established it as a fact during discovery.

## 3. You Can Concentrate on Contested Issues

As a human being there are just so many matters to which you can give particular attention. The fewer there are the better you will be able to concentrate on them. Therefore, reading admissions into the record promptly relieves you of concern about proving some of the necessary facts. You are now free to devote your time and talent to those matters which are going to be seriously—perhaps, bitterly—contested by your opponent. The extent to which you will be relieved of the burden of proving all of the facts in the case is dependent upon how well you have done your job during discovery and at pretrial. If you were lazy or slovenly, you will pay the price now. If you were diligent and imaginative, you will now be able to concern yourself with proving only a relatively small portion of the numerous facts involved in the case. The others can be read to the jury as admissions and then you can forget about them.

## SCHEDULE YOUR WITNESSES

I would hope that you would have at counsel table a detailed schedule of the witnesses you intend to call, the order in which you will call them and an estimate of the time they will testify. Granted that you can never accurately estimate the length of cross-examination, nonetheless you can make a sensible guess and if you are off a little on one witness you will make it up on the next. Also, on the list, make a notation of the exhibits you will offer with each witness or admissions you may read into the record before or after the witness testifies. Incidentally, reading some admissions before or just after the testimony of a witness is an excellent way to give credence and support to what the person has to say.

Be certain that you have more witnesses on hand than you will need for both the morning and the afternoon sessions. It is very embarrassing to run out of witnesses—for whatever reason—and have to stand up and make apologies to the court and jury. This is especially so if it occurs midway through the session and there is possibly another hour of trial time available. I used the word "embarrassing"—it is sometimes worse than that. I know some judges who would consider it a personal affront and either hold you in contempt or dismiss the case. So avoid this at all costs. If any persons are going to suffer a little with time on their hands, let it be the witnesses. A few hours one way or another really don't mean that much to them and your failure to have them around can mean a great deal to you.

To get back to that schedule, why don't you try to work up something like this:

MORNING SESSION

9:30                    John Jones—Plaintiff
                       Introduce Exhibits:
                           1-5 Photographs of scene
                           6-8 Photographs of car
                           13  Hospital bill

Identification and Payment Only—14 and 15
—Doctors bills
Read Stipulation 4—Life Expectancy

11:00      Alexander White—Eyewitness

11:45      Sally Young—Eyewitness

12:15      Clem Smith—Boss
Introduce Exhibit 9—Wage Record

### AFTERNOON SESSION

1:30       Barbara Anderson—Nurse
Introduce Exhibit 10—Hospital Record;
Exhibits 11 and 12—Blow-up of
Nurses' Notes

2:00       Dr. George Strait—Orthopedist
Use Exhibit 10—Hospital Record
Introduce Exhibit 14—his bill—fair and
reasonable.
Get shadow-box—use X-Rays.

3:00       Dr. John Carroll—Neurologist
Use Exhibit 10—Hospital Record
Use Model of Elbow
Introduce Exhibit 15—his bill—fair and
reasonable.

4:00       Mrs. Mary Jones—Wife
Had to hire help during John's illness
Introduce Exhibits 16 and 17—bills she
paid for help

Available —

Dorothy Schurtz—neighbor—condition
Samuel Cardiff—friend—condition

A schedule like this keeps everything in order. As you finish with one witness you need only glance at the sheet to know whom you are going to call next, the exhibits you will prove through the witness, items you intend to use for demonstrative purposes, and little points that you are liable to forget.

### Your First Witness—Make Him a Good One

There is no rule of law that says the plaintiff must be your first witness. There is an axiom of trial tactics that your first witness must be a good one. Once again we are back to that basic proposition of making a good first impression. If you believe the aphorism that "first impressions are lasting impressions" the reason is obvious.

This witness should be a person who can testify positively with force and believability, and be of strong character. He must be in command of himself and the English language. You must be sure that he can stand up well under cross-examination. Therefore, go over your list of witnesses, find the one that will really stand out, and begin with him. The only restriction that I can think of is that in the order of things it will have to be a liability witness and it should be a person who can stay on the stand about thirty minutes,. at least. You hardly want to start with a fine witness whose testimony will take only a few minutes. Whatever effect you gained by putting him on the stand is quickly dissipated by the brevity of his testimony. But you could use a photographer for example who can testify about his taking of photographs, identify the exhibits, discuss the scene generally, and then describe measurements he made at the scene.

In a medical malpractice case you might use a Resident who can describe plaintiff's arrival at the hospital, his physical condition, the personnel and equipment available, and what was done in the Emergency Room before the defendant doctor arrived. The point that I want to make is that the witness must be a very fine person, but his testimony need not be specifically directed to the negligence in the case. He can be called to provide necessary general or background information—in effect prepare the scene for the witness who will follow.

Inevitably some of your witnesses are going to be of poor quality. Sometimes it is because they are not blessed with handsome or beautiful countenances; at other times it will be because they speak crudely and use slang expressions, and on occasions because they are just stupid. We don't choose witnesses to events—we are stuck with the persons who were there.

If you must use such persons, try to work them into the middle of each session. Secure the testimony quickly and get them off the witness stand. In this way they will be preceded and followed by better witnesses and any poor impression they make will be masked by the other witnesses. Try to be careful that a poor witness is not on the stand when the luncheon recess occurs or at the end of the day.

Remember the basic rule: Begin with a good witness and finish with a good witness.

### Be a "Clock Watcher"

The daily routine of every court follows a pattern similar to this:

| | | |
|---|---|---|
| 9:00 A.M. | — | Trial convenes |
| 11:00 A.M. | — | Recess |
| 11:15 A.M. | — | Reconvene |
| 12:30 P.M. | — | Luncheon Recess |
| 1:30 P.M. | — | Afternoon Session begins |
| 3:00 P.M. | — | Recess |
| 3:15 P.M. | — | Reconvene |
| 4:30 | — | Adjourn |

I believe that at the conclusion of each of these time periods you should either be continuing with direct examination or should have just concluded direct examination. The reason for this is that during the recesses and at lunch the jurors are going to be gathering together and talking—usually about the case, at least about the witness. No matter the court's admonition that the case should not be discussed and opinions formed until its conclusion. Human nature being what it is there is no way on earth to stop jurors from discussing the testimony they have just heard and the person who gave it. In addition, I believe, they begin to form an opinion early in the trial, beginning with your introduction of the plaintiff, and that throughout the trial the original opinion is modified slowly and reluctantly if at all. This is why a good opening address, the reading of admissions and a strong first witness are so important.

Since we know this process is going on we should try to take advantage of it as much as possible. If the jury has a recess at 11:00 A.M., isn't it wise that they should talk about your direct examination of a witness—rather than how well defense counsel is doing on cross-examination? During the lunch break which would you have them discuss? Above all, when the day ends at 4:30 P.M. should the jurors leave with the strong testimony of your direct examination to sleep on or the damaging results of cross-examination? The answer is clear—let every time period end while you are still on direct-examination or just as you are concluding it. This is not hard to do if you will only watch the clock.

If your first witness is on direct from 9:30 A.M. to 10:15 A.M. and under cross-examination from 10:15 A.M. to 11:00 A.M., there is no problem. Your next witness will easily be on direct when the 11:15 A.M. recess occurs. Later, as you approach 12:30 P.M. and are nearing the end of direct-examination with a witness, check the time closely. If it is 12:10 P.M., ask a few miscellaneous questions or ask the witness to come down to the blackboard again for a few minutes. If you have exhausted the questioning by 12:17 P.M., don't turn over the witness to defense counsel—

keep the witness on the stand, but now offer some exhibits that this or a prior witness may have identified. It should now be about 12:22 P.M. At this point you might tell the judge that you have finished, but suggest that this would be a good time to recess for lunch. He will probably agree that cross-examination should begin after lunch.

I never object to cross-examination at the beginning of any session. If the witness does poorly, you have plenty of time to rehabilitate him or to dissipate the effectiveness of the defense attorney by calling other witnesses. Cross-examination does its greatest damage when it has been effective and the jurors have a long time to reflect on it. It is bad practice for you to conclude direct-examination at such time as to permit the cross-examination to be continuing at recess time and terrible if defense counsel finishes effective cross-examination at the end of day. Just watch the clock and do a bit of juggling and you'll be all right.

I grant that if you're successful the advantage is a minor one, but the cumulative effect of these minor advantages can be overwhelming. Just remember—if it is the defense attorney who is getting all of these minor advantages, will you worry?

## Use This Approach for Lengthy Testimony

The desirability of achieving both a verbal and visual effect from a speaker was commented on in Chapter 9 relating to your Opening Address. The same reasoning applies to a witness—he is a speaker too. Since there is a dialogue between you and the witness, the droning, dulling effect of lengthy testimony is not quite so deadly as in a long monologue but it is possible. This can be avoided by getting the witness down from the witness stand, putting him directly in front of the jurors, and eliciting his testimony while he demonstrates with a photograph or diagram or draws on a blackboard. This is very effective when you have an expert, many of whom are present or former teachers, who can use a blackboard to illustrate the technical problems he is, at that very moment, talking about.

Completely aside from the value of imparting greater knowledge to the jury in this manner you must consider the "getting to know you" and the "friendliness" aspect of the witness and his testimony. I have discussed this at greater length, previously, with regard to you and your plaintiff. The same principles apply to the witness. How can you possibly arrange for the jurors to get to know the witness and to like him? There isn't very much you can do. You are limited in time, space, and movement. One thing is sure— if you keep him on the witness stand he is (1) some considerable distance from the jury (especially those at the far end of the jury box); (2) he is speaking only; and (3) he is relatively stiff, formal and physically confined. There isn't much room on the witness stand for him to express any personality or individuality.

Now, take the same person and put him before the jury with a blackboard. He comes alive. He moves about, he gestures, he dramatizes and he emphasizes important points by writing them on the blackboard or underlining them on a chart. This is an ideal way to make that witness a likable human being—and a knowledgeable one. Now the jurors will say "I really like that man" or "He really knows his business." That is exactly the impression you are trying to develop. The only way you can really create this aura of empathy and friendliness is to get the witness out of the witness box and down on the floor standing before the jury.

### Should You Use an Outline?

I am tempted to say that you should throw away all papers when you interrogate a witness. The art of direct-examination is in the nature of a stylized conversation between you and another person. You should know this witness so well, and what he is going to say, that there is simply no need for you to have an outline. You simply know what you want to develop and the questions should flow naturally and spontaneously. But—as a cautionary matter only—let there be at counsel table one piece of paper with the witness's name and three or four words written on it which identify the substance of his testimony. If it is a doctor just write:

Dr. Paul Canyon          —          History
                                    Diagnosis
                                    Treatment
                                    Prognosis
                                    Causation

I suggest this only so that you might avoid the human frailty of forgetfulness. It is always possible to forget. Those few words on a scrap of paper will help you to remember.

Unless—you want to forget. Let me explain. Suppose you have a good witness who you know will be extensively cross-examined and you're not too sure how well he will do. It is helpful, sometimes, to remove the sting of the cross-examination and to divert the jury to have held back on one aspect of your direct-examination. Then when defense counsel has finished you can interrogate the witness about this phase of the matter. For example, if the witness is a doctor, you might say—

> "Doctor, on my direct examination, I forgot to ask you about the history you received from the plaintiff. Now what did he tell you when he first appeared at your office?"

Then proceed to develop this for a few minutes. That does some good in that it requires the jury to turn their attention to a new matter and forget about the cross-examination for the moment, at least.

You must be a little careful of this technique, however. You know that redirect-examination is limited solely to new matter developed on cross-examination. A good defense attorney will be on his feet quickly to voice an objection to this line of questioning and the judge should sustain the objection. You take your chances. Accordingly, never leave anything really important to this moment in the interrogation. In my illustration a simple history can be developed any number of other ways than through a single doctor.

### One Interrogating Approach to Avoid—Always

Don't repeat the answers: To do so is the clear mark of a neophyte, a slow thinker, an uncertain lawyer or worse. It is also maddening to everyone in the courtroom. If you are not a novice, dim-witted or unsure of yourself then it is simply a bad habit which must be broken. If you want to know how irritating it is let one of your children try it out at the dinner table:

| | | |
|---|---|---|
| Husband | — | Where did you go, dear? |
| Wife | — | I went to the store. |
| Child | — | She went to the store. |
| Husband | — | What did you buy? |
| Wife | — | A few groceries. |
| Child | — | She bought a few groceries. |
| Husband | — | Who was with you? |
| Wife | — | Betty Bairlee. |
| Child | — | Betty Bairlee was with her. |
| Husband | — | How long were you gone? |
| Wife | — | About an hour. |
| Child | — | She was gone an hour. |
| Husband | — | See anyone I know? |
| Wife | — | No. |
| Child | — | She said "No". |

Five minutes of this and your child is in big trouble. So are you when you keep it up in the courtroom.

If you think about it for a moment you will realize that lawyers do this for the purpose of gaining a few moments to think of their next question. A good lawyer doesn't need those few moments. He knows the case and the witness so well that the questions are practically tripping over themselves in his mind. The key to the solution of this annoying problem is, simply, preparedness. If you are well prepared you are so busy asking questions you don't have time to repeat answers.

### Where Are You Standing? Get Close to the Jury

Thus far you have done everything possible to create a close relationship between yourself and the jury. Continue this effort by standing next to the jury box while interrogating the witness. By so doing you develop or reinforce the attitude that you and the jurors are on the same team, that you and they are trying this case together. That feeling is lost if you stay apart from them—whether it be by asking the questions from your chair at counsel table or if you stand in front of the table to ask your questions. Why be a stranger standing eight feet away from the jurors when you can be a friend standing in their immediate proximity? An adroit defense attorney will never cross-examine from his side of counsel table. Instead he will move over by the jurors and sometimes, if he must sit, will place a chair between you and the jury and ask his questions from this position.

I recommend that your position should generally be at the end of the jury box—by jurors 6 and 12—and that you feel free to move forward from time to time, even going directly to the witness stand when appropriate. But all movements should be done immediately adjacent to the jurors.

Another reason for my recommendation is that most of your jurors will be in the 40-60 age bracket—and some of those people are hard of hearing. They may not require a hearing aid, but they certainly lack the audition of a young person. To complicate this problem further, the jury box is about fifteen feet long and its near end is still about six feet from the witness stand. Thus, if you interrogate from your chair or in front of counsel table, the jurors at the far end of the jury box may be straining to hear a conversation occurring ten to twenty feet away from them. No wonder they can't hear! Now if you will stand adjacent to the jurors at the end of the jury box, then every juror has to hear your questions and if you can hear the answers of the witness, so can they. In this manner the conversation between you and the witness takes place right in front of and around the jurors. You and the witness will have to raise your voices a little but that is no problem.

By placing yourself in this position you accomplish two purposes: empathy with the jurors and the certainty that they can hear what is being said.

## USING THE EXPERT

The purpose of calling an expert witness is to establish that, in his opinion, a given set of circumstances caused an accident or, in the case of a medical doctor, caused an injury. The expert is permitted to express this opinion because the subject matter is beyond the knowledge of the ordinary juror and is within the field of expertise of the witness. Since the expert is a person who has specialized in a very limited and technical vocation the introduction of his testimony is going to pose some unique problems.

### 1.   The Language Barrier

The first of these is the language barrier. Every specialist has a language of his own. If you put an atomic physicist and an orthopedic surgeon in a room together, they will not be able to engage in an intelligent conversation until they begin to talk about women, sports, or politics. Unfortunately these highly educated, skilled men are so steeped in the technical words of their work that literally they are each speaking a foreign language. Without a dictionary they have no common basis for understanding each other.

It is the job of the trial lawyer to take this person who speaks so incomprehensibly and force him to use the English language. To do this you have first to understand his language so that you know what he has to say to the jury and how he is going to say it. This calls for long meetings with the expert. At these sessions you will have to ask constantly for definitions and use all of the mental capacity you have to understand the technical principles that are involved in your case. You will have to go to his office where he will have books, papers, diagrams and models to show you. You may have to spend time in a laboratory while he demonstrates experiments or techniques that he has told you about. Above all you have to read the journals and books that he gives you or to which he refers you. Only after you thoroughly understand his language and the scientific principles that he is using can you help him to reduce all of this to a form that will be understood by the jurors. During these long hours of preparation you must be careful not to fall into his jargon. You're supposed to be educating him on how to speak even though he is teaching you what there is to say.

A long time ago I had a bitter lesson in this matter. I had a case involving the causation of a cerebral thrombosis—a type of stroke. The defendant doctor was one of the leading neurosurgeons in this area. In preparation for my cross-examination of him I read every book, pamphlet and medical extract on the subject and talked with several other neurosurgeons. My cross-examination lasted two hours and afterwards the doctor congratulated me on the fine job I had done and how well I knew the subject. The jury retired shortly thereafter and returned a defense verdict. I discussed this matter with a colleague to inquire what had gone wrong. After listening to my story he commented, among other things, on the cross-examination:

> "You understood the doctor; he understood you; but the jury didn't understand either of you."

After you have absorbed the expert's knowledge you must work with him to make it understandable to the jury. Go over his testimony time after time. Correct him constantly, and don't hesitate to be a little dictatorial and insistent. Get tough—you don't dare let him confuse the jury with his technical language.

## 2. The Expert's Opinion

If you practice in a jurisdiction which permits the expert to express a qualified opinion, count your blessings. If he is allowed to say that "A probably caused B" or that "A was the most likely cause" or the "single most significant cause" you are fortunate. Your burden is light. In Pennsylvania and some other states, the expert must testify positively that in his opinion "A caused B." There can be no qualification to this opinion. This judicial ruling has been the cause of constant battles between lawyers and the experts. As one electrical engineer said to me, "I just don't think in terms of positive statements—even 99 out of 100 is a qualified statement." To them the rule is absurd. No matter. We must abide by the rule. What shall you do?

First of all try to reason with the expert. Tell him that it is only his opinion which must be positive—he is not stating that the fact is positive. The fact may be the subject of widespread controversy—does smoking cause cancer?—but it is only the opinion that has to be definitive. I like to point out to the expert that it is something like taking a firm stand on who is going to win the World Series. Usually the man will understand and conform with your desires. If he does not or cannot, you will simply have to get another expert. You must not take a chance at trial with an expert who cannot be trusted to express a positive opinion and stand by it if that is what the law requires.

### 3.  Presentation

The expert is the one witness who should not be permitted to get his point across by words alone. He should testify at length and if all he is going to do is talk you run the danger of putting some of the jurors to sleep. He must testify before the jury. He must have props—models, photographs, drawings, charts, blackboard and preferably a combination of some of these. Just remember that his function is to explain a technical subject so that the jurors will understand the nature of the subject and the basis for his opinion. He can do this beautifully with visual aids. Help him—suggest different ideas, work with him. Find out which type of exhibit he is most comfortable with and which ones will help him to do the best job. When you get this witness well prepared with several exhibits, he can do a grand job of testifying before that jury.

### 4.  The Hypothetical Question

It baffles me that there should be so much concern about a hypothetical question since it should be a reasonably simple matter. The expert must express an opinion. That opinion is based on facts. You have to prove those facts in the courtroom to lay the foundation for the opinion. You and the expert should decide, in advance, just exactly what you have to prove. You can make a list of these facts if necessary, and check off each one as you prove it. Then simply read the facts as the initial part of your question and ask the witness if he can form an opinion from those facts. When he says "Yes" ask him what the opinion is.

The defense attorney can only argue: (1) that you didn't prove the facts (which is a simple matter to establish one way or the other); or (2) that the facts are insufficient to enable the expert to express an opinion—and that is usually a matter for the expert himself to decide. If he feels that the facts are sufficient to enable him to express an opinion, the Court will generally not intervene. In the usual case it is the first objection which leads to the courtroom argument. If the defense attorney is correct it is entirely the fault of Plaintiff's counsel. If this happens, the only course available is to withdraw the expert for a time and introduce testimony to establish the missing facts. Then return the expert to the witness stand, rephrase the question and secure the opinion.

I can only say that while you are working with the expert you have to sort out the facts you must prove in order for him to express the opinion. Prove them systematically and one at a time—using a checklist if you must. Prepare a question that includes each fact and ask for the opinion. Don't worry if the question is a long one and incomprehensible to the jury—the question is for the record—the opinion is for the jury.

## READING A DEPOSITION—USE YOUR BEAUTIFUL SECRETARY OR DISTINGUISHED-LOOKING PARTNER

If you have taken a deposition for use at trial, the time will come when you must read it to the jury. Do not do this by yourself. Such depositions are often lengthy and if you stand before the jury reading questions and answers for half an hour they are going to get tired and miss part of it. A much better approach is to bring your secretary or partner into the courtroom, put him or her on the witness stand, and then interrogate in the usual way from the deposition. If the girl is pretty or your partner is a very distinguished-looking person so much the better. This is a good time to relax a little and make a few humorous remarks. You needn't worry about the testimony: since the judge and the defense counsel have copies of the transcript, everyone but the jury knows what it is. All you are doing is reading it to them. So take the time to joke a little about your secretary being the equal of the female witness of stage and screen with the pretty face and the beautiful legs, or needle your partner about the fact that he hasn't read so well since he left Miss Farragut's sixth-grade reading class. Say something that will attract attention to what is going on and that will give everyone a chance to relax from the concentration they usually give to a witness. You certainly want the jurors to pay attention, but you don't want to have them sitting on the edge of their seats.

Be certain that whoever is answering your questions has read the transcript several times and knows it thoroughly. You should have gone over the reading with him and made sure that he knows which portions are to be emphasized and which are routine and can be read unemotionally. I once had an associate who was superb at this task. He had a mane of snowy white hair, a ruddy complexion and a face that could look, now mischievious, now as somber as the judge who sat beside him. He didn't read a deposition—he acted a part. He looked upon the transcript as a script for a play. His voice would rise and fall; sometimes thunderous and at other times so soft that the jury would have to lean forward to hear him. When he had to read the answers to the cross-examination you would be surprised at how quickly he would rattle them off—and drop his voice; and the pained expression he would get on his face if defense counsel objected! It was always fun with him on the stand. The jurors loved him and even the judge and defense attorneys enjoyed him. That is the kind of person you want for this job.

### The Video-Tape Deposition

This is the coming thing and I believe it will be almost universally utilized in the next several years. It is certainly far superior to the reading of a transcribed deposition. The witness is in court for all practical purposes—the jurors can judge the way he looks and testifies, and can pick up those little pauses and nuances which lend credibility to the testimony or suggest doubt and evasion. The direct and cross-examination are the same as they have seen in court. It is an excellent way to present the testimony of a person who is unavailable for some good reason.

In my area, the Bar Association has purchased the necessary equipment, provides the operator—both when the deposition is taken and in court—and assumes responsibility for the storage and safekeeping of the film. The camera and other necessary items are easily transportable so that the deposition can be taken almost anywhere—at a bedside, in a doctor's office, or the study of a home. During the taking of the deposition the attorneys make all of their objections but the witness answers every question. Before the trial, or at some other appropriate time, the judge and attorneys view the deposition. The judge rules on the objections. When he sustains an objection the operator notes the section of film with a marking device on the equipment. These short segments are blocked out in some appropriate manner and not shown to the jury. However, they remain part of the entire film for the purpose of appellate review.

The cost of producing such a deposition is insignificant. Our Bar Association charges as follows:

| | |
|---|---|
| Flat Fee for the first two hours of tape | $ 75.00 |
| Each additional Tape | 25.00 |
| Fee of Operator—per Hour for Taking Deposition and Showing in Court | 7.50 |
| Plus Mileage—per mile | .15 |

The average cost of a deposition is about     $100.00.

When the deposition is to be shown the operator brings one or two television sets into the courtroom, sets up his equipment, and in a matter of minutes the jury is watching and hearing the witness give his testimony.

This device completely eliminates the problem of the dying witness, the doctor who suddenly finds that he cannot go to court the next day and the person who breaks his leg shortly before trial. Now you don't have to continue the case. Gather together the operator, his camera, and the defense attorney and go to where the witness is. In two hours the job is done, you are on your way home and the film is ready for use the next day. Try this the next time a key witness slips on a banana peel while on his way to the courtroom.

## HOW TO DEAL WITH FOUR UNEXPECTED WITNESS PROBLEMS

When you are dealing with people you are bound to have problems. These will come in so many sizes, shapes and varieties that it is impossible to mention any but a few of the unusual and nasty ones. The others you will have to solve on the basis of your experience and common sense. The ones that I would like to discuss are:

1.  The emotional witness who breaks down;

2.  The witness who tells a lie;

3.  The confused witness; and

4.  The hostile witness.

Granted, these are not common troubles but they occur often enough and are sufficiently difficult to handle that they deserve special treatment. Let us look at them for a few moments:

### 1.  The Emotional Witness Who Breaks Down

This person is nearly always a close relative of the decedent in a death case or of a very badly injured plaintiff. On some occasions it is a witness to a horrible accident. It is usually a woman. In either event the testimony is vital and you have to figure out how to get it into the record either before the tears start flowing, after they have stopped, or in-between the teardrops. Since you know the witness is going to cry, faint or become speechless, you might as well discuss the matter frankly with her in your office. Explain the importance of the words that are necessary—the essential nature of the testimony—and the fact that she must exercise iron control over her emotions so that the jury will hear what she has to say. Go over the testimony several times so that she can say the words even while she is crying. Make it a matter of pure memorization and conditioned reflex if you must, so that she blurts out the answer upon hearing your question even if she cannot think at all.

When you get to the courtroom do not let this person listen at great length to the testimony of others. Certainly she has to stay in the room long enough to get adjusted—but not so long as to begin to get upset. When she is on the witness stand keep your questioning brief—skip some of the usual background type questions. Get to the point. Try to get the essential answers into the record and then let the witness cry. Sometimes I find that if you are stern, direct and to the point the witness will give you what you need. Then you can relax and ask a few more questions to fill in the details before things get out of hand.

If the witness breaks down at an early stage, you will have to ask the court for a recess. Do what you can for a few minutes and try again. Usually, after the first gush of emotion the witness will settle down long enough to enable you to interrogate her. If it becomes obvious that the witness cannot testify in court—and this is very rare—the only recourse is the use of a deposition.

I am not in any way suggesting that tears are prohibited in a courtroom. When the emotions run high and feelings are overwhelming the jurors should see it. This is a part of life that is just as real as the dry sterile words used by a pathologist in describing his findings during an autopsy. My point is that you cannot let the passions of the witness interfere with your eliciting crucial testimony.

### 2. The Witness Who Tells a Lie

I am not talking about the confused or mistaken witness. I refer to the person who tells a deliberate lie in the erroneous belief that he is helping the plaintiff. This is usually a friend or co-employee who is always relatively unintelligent. His motives are good but his ways are base. When this happens continue with your questioning. Hopefully there will be a recess at the end of his direct-examination; if there is not, ask for one.

At this point you have one of two choices—go to the defense attorney or go to the judge. If you know the defense attorney well, and are sure he will not take undue advantage of the situation, go to him. Now, using every euphemism you know for the word "lying" explain what has happened. Tell him that you want to talk it over with the witness, put him back on the stand on direct-examination, that you will suggest to the witness that he was mistaken or confused as to a particular fact and get the truth from him. If your defense attorney is a decent person, he will let you do it. No one wants to make a criminal out of a witness because of one stupid act.

If he promptly recants and defense counsel is allowed to vigorously cross-examine from the approach that it was a mistake, and that if he was mistaken on this matter he might be mistaken on others, there is no serious harm done. As far as the defense attorney is concerned he probably knew of the lie before you told him. He undoubtedly has a statement, or deposition, of the witness so that while he is surprised that it occurred he knows when the mis-statement was made. If he can force the witness to "eat humble pie" and cast some doubt on the balance of his testimony he has done his job.

If you feel you cannot approach defense counsel, then you must see the judge. Usually a conference in chambers will resolve the matter as previously described with the addition that the court may well chastise the witness outside of the hearing of the jury. If the judge insists on criminal action, the matter is out of your hands.

So far as you, the plaintiff's attorney, are concerned, never let a falsehood stay on the record. No case—no verdict—no witness—is worth it. If you have a conscience, it will plague you. If you haven't, you might think about the fact that these things often get out of hand. The witness will brag of his wrongdoing in a bar, or on the job; he will tell his friends and neighbors. On occasion word gets back to the defendant, the court, or the defense attorney and suddenly you're confronted with a charge of having deliberately used perjured testimony. The lying witness, like poison, is to be avoided by all means.

### 3.   The Confused Witness

This person is very hard to handle. How can you get him straightened out without actually telling him what to say? In point of fact you probably can't and will have to lead him as much as you dare. If the confusion stems from nervousness you might try asking as many miscellaneous questions as you can to try to get him settled down; then turn to the material facts. If he is slow of thought keep your questions as simple as possible so that his answers are obvious and brief. You can't go wrong with:

Q. "What color was the traffic light?"
A. "Red."

If he suffers from a poor memory you will have to limit your questions to a basic few. I presume, however, that you will have gone over the testimony prior to trial so that the witness knows what he will be asked and therefore can be prepared to answer those few questions, at least. Your interrogation will, of necessity, be brief and with a little bit of work you can hope that the witness will remember why he is being called to the witness stand.

The most difficult time with this witness will be on cross-examination by defense counsel. The witness, if he is easily confused, is bound to contradict some of the things he said on direct. Unfortunately, he won't even realize what he has done. From your point of view it is a comfort to know that the witness' confusion will be readily apparent to the jury and that it will evoke some sympathy from them. However, you will have to straighten out the contradictory testimony. When it occurs take up the matter on redirect and meet it squarely. Try something like this:

> Q. "Now, Mr. Smith, you have just told Attorney Brown and the jury that you were talking to Betty Burke when the accident occurred. Now earlier you had told me, on direct examination, that you actually saw the accident. Now will you please tell us, straight out, which of these is correct. What were you doing and what did you see?"

Naturally the defense attorney will object. Your argument to the court will be that the witness is obviously confused, that both answers cannot be correct, and that you have the right to develop an explanation of the basis for the confusion. The judge will nearly always let you do this—especially if it is obvious that the witness is honest but simply mixed-up. Now let the witness answer that he was talking to Betty Burke but was facing the scene of the accident and saw it occur while he was speaking with her. This will mollify the jury. They will understand that the witness was telling the truth on both direct and cross-examination. You may be sure that the defense attorney will go into this matter again on recross-examination but it probably won't do him much good. Your witness, now alerted to the problem he has created, will be able to fend off the questioning.

In conclusion I must point out that you should have become aware of this type of difficulty with this witness when you cross-examined him in your office. Accordingly, you should have deliberately arranged to keep his testimony brief and limited only to the salient facts of which he has knowledge.

## 4.  The Hostile Witness

This is the easiest of the "witness problems" you will have to handle. Your biggest worry is whether the witness is clever enough to hide his hostility.

Nearly always, this person is a close friend or relation of the defendant or is appearing in court reluctantly and because you have subpoenaed him. A treating doctor is illustrative of the latter situation.

I have found that most subpoenaed witnesses may come into the courtroom in a rage, but become quite docile when they are on the witness stand. The unfamiliar environment has something to do with this. In addition, when they get on the witness stand and all eyes are turned upon them they have the normal desire to make a good impression and not to make fools of themselves. They also recognize the coercive authority of yourself and the Court. Finally, they have enough honor and moral integrity so that they will not lie. So, treat them with respect, be firm, develop the facts you need and let them go. Don't bother asking them questions which call for discretionary or judgment answers. Why ask an angry doctor if your client was in great pain throughout the course of his lengthy treatment? You know the answer will be negative. You can develop that type of testimony from other, more friendly, persons. Instead, stick to the basics and let the witness go.

Sometimes, though, you have to call a witness who is positively hostile. By all means encourage him. If he wants to be nasty, mean and crude do everything in your power to have him demonstrate these qualities before the judge and jury. Then when it is clear, especially to the judge, you have a right to ask the Court for permission to interrogate the witness by means of leading questions as on cross-examination. That privilege should be granted. Then you are free to ask him in a direct and leading manner the questions that will bring out the facts you need. If he is evasive, insist on a direct answer to your questions and solicit the court to order the answers. The judge will do so. If he wants to joust with you on matters of semantics, ask him to define the word and to answer your question on the basis of his own definition. If necessary, ask for a dictionary, read the definition, and ask for an answer in accordance with the dictionary definition. If you are getting stubborn "I don't know" answers relating to plain facts, ask him questions that are so obvious that he dare not answer in this manner for if he does he merely makes himself look foolish. Before very long the witness will realize that he can't win, that there is no point in venting his anger at this time and place and he will begin to answer directly and honestly.

The key to the handling of a hostile witness is to make sure he adequately deomonstrates his hostility in court and then to interrogate him, by leading questions, persistently and diligently until he realizes that he will either make more of a fool of himself or else answer the question. Unless you have a neurotic on your hands he will choose to answer the questions.

## REHABILITATION OF THE WITNESS— BEWARE OF THE "RED HERRING"

If your witness has done poorly on cross-examination there is not a great deal that you can do to rehabilitate him. I have already mentioned how you can help the confused witness and the possibility of reserving a small part of your direct examination to this period of time.

The principal question, though, is whether the witness really did perform poorly and whether he did so in matters that are really material. Your tendency will be to exaggerate the effectiveness of the defense attorney's cross-examination. It is helpful, therefore, to find someone to talk with who is not so intimately and immediately involved in the case as you are. Your partner would be a great help, but you can also turn to a friend among the court personnel or even one of the witnesses who has been sitting in the courtroom. After hearing their comments you may decide that no further interrogation is necessary.

If the witness really does need help, try to keep your redirect examination on a narrow basis. Each question you ask may open the door to further cross-examination and if the defense counsel has been successful the first time around, he is likely to be equally so the second time. In addition, having already damaged the witness, he will be quick to object to any questions that try to take away the effect of what he has done.

If you know that the witness has previously given a statement to an insurance adjuster or claims agent, this is a good time to bring it out. It is very effective to force the defense attorney to produce a prior, written, consistent statement, prove it through the witness, introduce it into evidence and read it to the jury as proof that the witness has been consistent and truthful as to most of his testimony on direct examination.

Another similar approach is to use the history in a hospital record to establish that the testimony of the witness has been consistent. Finally you might try to find a photograph or drawing or map that would help the witness to clarify discrepancies between his testimony on direct and cross-examination.

You will note that I am referring you to items of a documentary nature as assistance for your witness. The reason is that the cross-examination has raised doubts about the validity of the witness' oral testimony. The doubts are best resolved if you can support the witness with a written document. For reasons best left for explanation by a psychiatrist we are always more prone to believe something that is written rather then something that is verbal. Your jury will be much happier if you can support the witness with a written document rather than to try to rehabilitate him through his own words.

I mentioned in the caption to this section that you should beware of following a "red herring." This is the major and serious problem in deciding whether the witness even needs rehabilitation. If your witness really knows what he is talking about, and has been well prepared, and nonetheless the cross examination disturbs you, the odds are 100 to 1 that the effective cross-examination was on irrelevant, immaterial, miscellaneous matters. Think of that for a moment. What else can the defense attorney do if the witness is unshakable on the basic facts? He must attack on matters that are not directly involved in the case. These are "red herrings." Thus it is that he will ask the doctor: "How much are you being paid to come here in court to testify?" or "Have you talked to the plaintiff's attorney about this case?" This is when you can expect questions about prior injuries to plaintiff, an old criminal offense, a former marriage, the fact that he was 4-F during one of our nation's wars, or if the lawsuit involved damage to a building, the fact that it was once used as a house of ill-repute.

Since you may not have known these things you could not prepare your witness concerning them. He is surprised, shaken and answers poorly. But these things have nothing to do with your lawsuit. Don't rise to the bait—don't follow the red herring! Let it go. Give the defense attorney what little gain or pleasure he may have achieved through this line of questioning. It really has not hurt you. If it is embarrassing to you, the witness or the plaintiff, you only exacerbate the embarrassment by continuing to keep it before the jury. Don't do it.

This is why it is so important to analyze the cross-examination before you think of rehabilitating the witness. In most instances the matter is either beyond your control or the cross-examination was effective on irrelevant matters and should not be answered. If there is sincere doubt in your mind, take the conservative course and let the witness alone.

## EXHIBITS AND DEMONSTRATIVE EVIDENCE

A great deal has been written and said about collecting these items for use at trial but not enough about using them. Motion pictures are a fine tool, but if you have to disrupt the trial to get the equipment set up or if the courtroom lacks window blinds to keep out the afternoon sun, your effort may have been a waste of time. One of the "miscellaneous" duties of the plaintiff's attorney is to anticipate these problems and to have resolved them in advance.

Consider plain ordinary photographs for example. Anything less than an 8 x 10 picture is useless. Even that size photograph has to be passed from juror to juror. Why not get it enlarged to a 30 x 40 size and put it on an easel where all of the jurors can see it at one time? If you want the jurors to handle pictures, the 16 x 20 size is perfect—it can be passed from hand to hand and yet it is big enough to be seen from the easel.

If you decide to use movies, slides or any other exhibit that will be shown on a screen, get someone to help you. You have too many responsibilities to be worried about setting up and operating the equipment. The cost is minimal and the effort leaves you free to work with the witness—

interrogating or demonstrating—while the exhibit is being shown. It is wise to go with the operator to the courtroom before the trial and make decisions as to what he will need, where the equipment is to be placed, when it is to be shown, and to discuss any other problems that arise when you tell him what your purpose is in showing the exhibit.

Flimsy objects such as maps, charts, blueprints and drawings should be glued on or tacked to heavy cardboard so that they can be easily handled in the courtroom. There is nothing worse then trying to hold up a blueprint before the jury only to have the ends start rolling in—when you grasp one place another end flops about and you suddenly look like a comedy routine on a television program.

Large models are excellent for demonstrative purposes, but if they are specially made they are extremely expensive. In addition their size makes them difficult to handle in terms of where you intend to put them and keep them. You can't very well let a model the size of a Ping-Pong table remain placed between counsel table and the jury box or blocking the entry and exit to the courtroom. These things always tend to end up being shoved into some far corner of the courtroom and have no utility at all after their immediate use. A drawing or picture can be kept in constant view of the jurors for them to look at and think about. Accordingly, unless you have a special reason I suggest you avoid the large model.

If you do use a model be certain that it accurately illustrates some important principle you are trying to make, and that nothing about it is going to "boomerang" on you. I well recall a case in which a trainman, while on a locomotive, had to restart the engine by reaching under a cover and pulling on a lever. When he did so his elbow struck a fixed projection severely injuring his ulnar nerve. The railroad made an exact replica of those portions of the engine. The only problem was that nearly every person who demonstrated the use of the equipment banged his elbow! The only ones who didn't were obviously not tugging on the lever with any spirit. That kind of demonstrative evidence you can do without.

## ARE YOU GOING TO HAVE A VIEW?

I realize that a view is generally utilized only in condemnation cases or those involving property damage. The question is whether it should be used more frequently and whether you feel one is desirable in your case. I can think of several situations in which a view would be helpful:

1. Where an accident occurs on one of our intricate highway junctions where neither an aerial photograph nor a verbal description can adequately explain the problems confronting the motorist.

2. In a case against a hospital in which the precise layout of an operating room, and the positioning of personnel, are in question.

3. Where a huge machine, performing a multiplicity of functions, in a mill or a foundry, is the cause of an accident and should be seen in operation.

These are the kind of cases in which you may want a view and the Court may well agree with you.

Therefore, if you're going to have a view, the time to do it is after the opening address and after reading admissions into the record.

If you decide a view is appropriate, you will have to discuss the matter with the Court and defense counsel to work out an agreement concerning problems relating to it. Some of these problems are:

1. Is the judge going to participate?

2. Will the court reporter come along?

3. What specific areas or objects are the jurors to see?

4. Who is going to point out these things to the jurors?

5. What statements or comments are to be made to the jurors and who is going to make them?

6. Can the jurors ask questions? How shall they be answered?

7. If the attorneys travel with the jurors, are non-trial conversations to be permitted or shall counsel maintain silence?

8. Shall the court reporter take down everything that is said at the scene or merely agreed-upon excerpts?

9. Shall expert witnesses come along?

It is difficult to give positive answers to these questions since so much depends upon what the jurors will be looking at; what, specifically, you want them to see; and just how you want to relate to the jurors when you are with them. Consider the matter of talking with the jurors—I definitely like this. I consider a view as a break from the usual routine for all concerned and would prefer that the judge, attorneys, reporter and jurors travel together in a bus and engage in normal good-humored conversation while on the trip. This attitude springs from the fact that I am a gregarious person and believe that the plaintiff's attorney should get as close to the jury—physically, verbally, and emotionally—as he possibly can.

It works to my advantage—vis-a-vis most defense attorneys—to laugh and joke with the jurors.

If you are concerned that you may be out-talked and out-witted or otherwise taken advantage of in this type of arrangment, then press for a plan in which the jurors will travel to the scene in a bus and the judge and attorneys go together in a car. If you are worried about the questions a jury may ask at the scene, then try to prohibit them. There is nothing wrong with this since jurors rarely ask questions in the courtroom. On the other hand, the purpose of the view is to show the jurors something that cannot be adequately explained in the courtroom and it's normal that they will have some questions which should be answered by someone. If the matter is so simple that it does not provoke questions you probably did not need the view at all. Therefore if you will accept some generalizations, I would like to recommend the following answers to the questions previously posed:

1. The judge should accompany the jurors. The trip will aid his understanding of the case and he will be present to rule on the disputed matters that will arise.

2. The court reporter is essential. He can take down all formal statements of counsel and the court's ruling on objections or arguments.

3. The attorneys should agree in advance on where the jurors are to go when they arrive in the area and the specific objects they are to look at.

4. and 5. When the group arrives, each attorney should make a statement, on the record, of what he wants the jurors to look at and how these objects fit into his case or why he deems them important. Perhaps the "why" approaches argument and may be objected to; the "how" is acceptable as part of a legitimate explanation of the manner in which the several facts relate to one another. Following this, the jurors can either stroll around the area by themselves or be led, as a group, by the tipstaff or other court-appointed officer.

6. The jurors should be encouraged to ask questions while they are at the scene. The questions should be taken down by the reporter, the judge should rule on the validity and propriety of the questions and each attorney should have an opportunity to answer.

7. The entire party should travel together. Conversation among the members of the party should be permitted so long as the case is not discussed and so long as neither attorney tries to take advantage of the situation. If the latter occurs, a whispered objection to the judge followed by a curt word or two by him to the miscreant will correct the situation.

8. The court reporter cannot take down everything that is said. Usually there is no convenient place that he can set up his equipment as the group wanders along. It is a practical impossibility. Instead, select two or three appropriate sites where the reporter can get set up and then record comments of counsel, questions of the jurors, and rulings of the court.

9. Expert witnesses should come along since if you have to use an expert the case obviously requires technical knowledge and skill. The expert should be permitted to make a statement to the jurors, on the record, concerning important things to be seen and perhaps demonstrate the use of equipment. If a machine is the object which is the cause of the trial, the jurors might as well have its parts and functions explained to them and see it in operation.

A view is always informative and is a welcome respite from the ordinary routine for everyone involved in a case. I encourage you to utilize it since I believe that, on balance, it generally inures to the benefit of plaintiff.

# CHAPTER 11

# Skillful Cross-Examination—
# Method over Myth

How much has been written and spoken on this subject! It sometimes seems that success in this area is the sole criterion for winning a lawsuit. Certainly there is no part of a trial which commands attention so much as cross-examination. Much of this over-emphasis and exaggeration is due to the setting—witness on the stand, attorney pacing the floor firing questions, witness sweats and squirms, attorney ruthlessly and relentlessly presses on, witness collapses and screams out the truth or cries and whispers the truth or runs from the courtroom. It's pure drama—colorful, exciting, climactic. It's drama, all right, but it's not life.

Your case is simply not going to succeed or fail on the basis of the cross-examination by either you or the defense attorney. That part of the trial is rarely dramatic or climactic. In fact most cross-examination that I have heard is dull and pointless and should never have been carried on—except for a few questions asked because "everyone does it." That is a poor reason to cross-examine, but it takes nerve to say "I have no questions of this witness."

A good plaintiff's case is less analogous to a duel of the Three Musketeers than it is to the construction of Notre Dame Cathedral. The former is short, violent, depends on one single ability; the latter is a long-range project requiring careful planning, adherence to blueprints and drawings, careful execution and the combining of the talents of several specialists. The end result is beautiful, but the process itself is laborious, detailed, time-consuming and generally unappealing to the layman.

The advice on "how to cross examine" is seemingly endless and always conflicting. It calls to mind two old aphorisms I've always enjoyed contemplating: Should you "Look Before You Leap" despite the fact that "He Who Hesitates Is Lost"? What does one do?

I've been told "Never ask a question unless you know the answer" but I always ask questions to learn the answers. Trial lawyers often warn in whispered voice "Don't ask that one question too many," but they have never given me a list which says that eight questions are O.K., but the ninth is disaster. I can understand the advice, but I have problems in applying it—and honestly I don't think the great lawyers can answer the question either, at least not on any logical basis. With them it's instinct, not learning, and therefore their advice is so much hot air because it can't be followed. I watched a fine trial lawyer start to cross-examine a doctor one time and almost immediately the doctor began to give him all that he wanted. To me it was simply a matter of asking some logical questions and getting honest replies. The lawyer turned to me for a moment, however, and whispered, "I offered him combat and he refused." Maybe that's what it was. I don't know. I do know that I have offered combat to a witness—the offer has been accepted and the witness has won! I don't do that very often.

It is my opinion that every lawyer has a particular aptitude which is expressed in the way he tries his case. If you have the ability to win your case on cross-examination, go ahead. Of course your success is contingent on the defense attorney being decent enough to offer you the witness—and the right kind of witness—to examine. You may find that as your reputation grows, competent defense counsel begin to restrict the number of witnesses they will call and then choose among that number persons of wit, charm and intelligence who will accept your offer of combat. That can lead to trouble.

To those who lack a natural instinct for cross-examination I can only suggest that the "art" be taken out of the subject and that it be approached with care, attention and planning. That, too, is a road to success. The requirements are those stressed throughout this book—detailed knowledge of your case, careful planning, an outline of the subject matter you want to discuss with the witness and an approach that is pleasant and methodical. If you make headway with the witness, keep going; if you are obviously failing, stop—you can rest confident in the fact that your case is not going to collapse because of your failure to triumph over a witness, and that with careful preparation you will elicit most of the facts that you need to be successful. Your cross-examination may not be the kind to make headlines but it can be the kind that helps you to win lawsuits.

## A CUTTING TOOL

The purpose of cross-examination is to elicit favorable testimony which was not brought to the attention of judge and jury in the direct examination of the witness. Since the witness must answer your questions and since he can be pretty much restricted to a "Yes" or "No" answer, you are in a position really to force him to make damaging admissions. Cross-examination is frequently referred to as "slashing," "cutting," "pointed," and the like—and it is. You control the questioning—the witness has no place to hide—and a judge is there to prod him should he become shy, hostile or evasive. In addition to his being forced to answer your questions, a jury of twelve men and women is watching the scene and noting how he reacts to your questions. The more reluctant he becomes to give answers freely, the more obvious it becomes to the jury that he is hiding something and is not telling "the truth, the whole truth and nothing but the truth." The result can be devasting to his cause.

## FREQUENTLY AND HARSHLY CRITICIZED

The constant analogy of cross-examination as being akin to the use of a knife or sword has caused it to be popularly criticized even while it is popularly enjoyed. It is true that cross-examination can play havoc with the nerves and emotions of a witness, can be confusing, and, if carried to extremes becomes unfair. Unfortunately no one has yet come up with any other system to my knowledge (much less any better system) for eliciting from a witness all of the facts of which that witness has knowledge. People will not voluntarily tell everything they know that pertains to an event. This can be due to fear, to a natural reluctance to speak out, to ignorance of the importance of certain facts, to lying, to mistake, to exaggeration, to bombast. It makes no difference so far as the search for the truth and justice are concerned. Someone has to ask searching questions—sometimes embarrassing or humiliating ones—so that all of the witness' knowledge is brought into the open. That someone is the trial attorney and the process is cross-examination.

## FIRST, LET'S LOOK AT THE CROSS EXAMINATION BY DEFENSE COUNSEL

Since the Plaintiff's attorney is the first to proceed with the presentation of witnesses, the defense attorney is going to be the first to cross-examine. Knowing this you should be well prepared for what is to come, both personally and insofar as your witnesses are concerned. If you have been thorough, everyone of your witnesses has already been subject to cross-examination—by you.

Thirty minutes to an hour of good, stiff interrogation in your office—the length of time dependent on their importance and the extent of their testimony—will do wonders for your witnesses. It gives them a "feel" for what to expect, alerts them to matters that are important, instills confidence, and gives you an opportunity to correct poor speech patterns (the "ah" and "uh-huh" habits or the "long pause syndrome"), inflections of voice (the whine, the inaudible answer), and annoying personal habits (hand over the mouth, chewing gum, looking at the ceiling as if to pray for Divine Assistance).

Take all the time necessary to be sure your witness knows how to appear and how to speak forth his testimony. Some critics will call this "coaching" and so it is. But if it is necessary for the President of the United States to hire a coach so that he will make a good presentation on television, it is equally important for you to coach your witnesses so they can handle cross-examination in the courtroom.

### The Worst Time for You

Watching one of your witnesses undergoing cross-examination has to be pure agony. It's terrible. The tension becomes almost unbearable. The witness never follows your instructions completely. He says the wrong things at the wrong time. Undoubtedly this is the worst part of a trial for you. You watch in anguish as the jurors at the end of the jury box strain to hear the soft-spoken, but crucial testimony; you become disgusted when the witness gives a mistaken answer; you get weary when an angry judge upbraids the witness for rambling far afield from the subject matter of the question.

Relax. You can't do the testifying—even though you wish you could—and, without realizing it, you are exaggerating the effect of the witness' mistakes. This is the low point of every case. Nearly always you will think that your witness has testified poorly. At times like this go to a friend in the courtroom—the reporter or law clerk, your assistant or one of the other witnesses—and get the benefit of another viewpoint. You'll be surprised at how often they remark at how well the witness has done! Someone said, "Never take counsel of your fears." That surely applies at a time like this.

### Listen Carefully—Put Your Pencil Down

This is no time to be making notes. It is imperative that you listen to every question and every answer. During cross-examination of your witness your job is to ascertain what facts defense counsel is trying to develop, what approach he is trying to use, what objectionable questions he is asking, what harm is being done to your cause, how the witness is being received by the jury, and what, if anything, you are going to do in the next few seconds or minutes. You have no time to write. If you do want to make notes during cross-examination, bring an assistant or your secretary in the courtroom to do so for you. This is one time when your eyes and ears have to be receptive to what is going on and, with your mind racing to evaluate and analyze the information, you must decide what you are going to do.

### Be Alert—What Is the Defense Attorney Driving At?

We know that all defense counsel are excellent trial lawyers. If your adversary in this case is not, pretend that he is—you'll make fewer mistakes. Accordingly, there must be a purpose—a good reason—for the questions he is asking. Be alert—try to figure out where he is going. It may be that he just wants to ask a few questions to test your witnesses' memory—in which case you can relax. Again, he may make it a habit to cross-examine every witness for a few minutes because he thinks it looks bad in front of a jury not to do so—in which event you can again relax.

Some defense counsel make it a practice to cross-examine over the entire length of the direct examination and if you have one of these, pay attention. He is probing for contradictions and he is relying greatly on his own notes of the answers elicited on direct examination. His notes are brief jottings, fragmentary, incomplete and he has the human failing of writing down what he wants to hear.

Be ready to move quickly when he begins a question: "Now, I believe you previously testified......" or "You told us earlier......" or "Your testimony indicates......" He may quote the witness correctly or his misquote may make no difference, but be ready to quickly challenge his statement of the witness' testimony if it is incorrect and the matter is important. If he wants to make an issue of it, the matter must be important to him, so take the time to have the court reporter read the testimony back exactly as it was given. In this way the witness knows for certain what he said previously and he has had a few moments to reflect on his answer.

The defense attorney can cross-examine your witnesses from several areas—he can test memory, attack credibility on the grounds of friendship, power of observation or self-interest, he can raise the issue of antagonism to the defendant or simply suggest that the witness is lying. Your job is to listen, watch and evaluate the effect of these questions and how well your witness is responding. Your mind has to be considering several items:

1.  Shall I object to this question, or this line of questioning?

2.  Is the witness handling himself well?

3.  Shall I ask any questions on redirect examination or simply get this witness off the stand?

4.  Shall I try to rehabilitate the witness?

5.  Can I, shall I, try to use a prior consistent statement? (How devastating it is, where the witness has become confused, to ask him whether, before trial, he had given a statement to an investigator for defense counsel. When he admits that he did, demand the statement and try to read it or admit it into evidence. The more defense counsel objects, the more you remove the sting of his cross-examination).

6.  Do I have a witness who can corroborate and support this witness?

7.  Can I use a photograph or document to support the witness.

8.  Shall I, on redirect examination, just go back over a few "safe" questions to try to remove a little of the onerous effects of the cross-examination?

In short, you have to be thinking. If things are going poorly you must do something.

### Can Your Witness Handle the Questions?

One of the things you have to watch and listen for is the ability of your witness to respond well to the questioning. If he is doing well, you might ignore even legitimate objections. You can use such a person as this—one who is confident, knowledgeable and articulate—as bait for an ambush of defense counsel. Tell him to answer freely and, given the opportunity (which he must judge for himself) to respond with an answer that will do the utmost damage to defendant's cause. This can be highly effective.

As defense counsel asks him questions and continuously receives hurtful answers from a self-assured witness, he is placed in the uncomfortable position of facing an embarrassing cessation of the questioning with a jury knowing that he has been bested or, going further and trying to break down the witness. Inexperience and frustration will drive some defense counsel onward.

It is at this point you can begin to expect improper questions. As give-and-take continues, his frustration will become more evident by the boldness of his challenge to the witness until finally, at the propitious moment, the witness can deal a telling blow by blurting out an answer that does very serious harm. If defense counsel becomes outraged and presses on in an effort, now, to browbeat the witness, the time has come for you to step in with well-taken objections. A good judge watching the development of this scene will sustain your objections and bring this matter to an end. The ending will be very pleasant—to you. This is a nice gambit but you can only utilize it with a good witness—and one you have carefully prepared.

An illustration of the manner in which a witness can handle himself well is this cross-examination of the pastor of a church. His church had been damaged by the construction of a new building on the one side and shortly thereafter another new building across the street. The pastor did an excellent job of handling himself on the witness stand and at the end of his interrogation was quite effective with some of his remarks as you can see:

BY DEFENSE COUNSEL:

Q. You were called to the church, you said, in the Fall?

A. That's right.

Q. Do I understand that before responding to that invitation you made an examination of the physical structure of the church?

A. And this is purely a pastoral lay type of visit, and you certainly do examine the building, walk through it with the council and make observations, yes.

Q. In the company of some of the members of the congregation you made this inspection, I gather?

A. Yes.

Q. And you were shown the office which would serve you as a pastor?

A. Yes.

Q. Did you examine that office and did you look for cracks around the windows, and so forth, and the doors?

A. I did not look under the drapes, and so on; but I certainly looked at the walls.

Q. And there were cracks in that area, were there not, of some substance?

A. The hairline cracks that one would expect in an old building.

Q. What do you mean by "hairline cracks"?

A. A paint type of crack.

Q. In October, the second window from the left of the pastor's office on the back wall, were there two cracks going up to the ceiling from the top right-hand corner of the window?

A. I could not specify a location of any crack, and the ones I was referring would be the same kinds that would be in my home, the kind of plaster that is just common to any older building.

Q. Do you remember that there were two cracks below and to the right of the same window?

A. I testified only to there being the kind of paint hairline cracks that one would normally see in an old building, that is all.

Q. In the pastor's office were there a great many such cracks or a scattered one or two or—

A. Very scattered.

Q. Very scattered?

A. Yes.

Q. Where was the secretary's office in relation to your office?

A. Outside of my door, outside of the door toward the south.

Q. Did you make any inspection of that area?

A. Other than the janitor having missed a few cobwebs, it was generally in pretty good condition.

Q. Do you remember observing two cracks on the front wall to the right of the steps by the basement?

A. No, sir. I cannot testify to that.

Q. You can't testify one way or the other as to whether they were there or were not there?

A. That's right.

Q. They were not called to your attention and you don't remember seeing them?

A. No, we didn't make a crack inspection.

Q. Incidently, when we were there on Monday we went first to the nave and observed it and observed the sanctuary, and then if you remember we went into the chapel. Has that chapel been renovated recently?

A. Yes. We repainted the walls and put in new light fixtures and removed a small library shelving in the right-rear corner.

Q. We did observe considerable activity in the church to the rear of the sanctuary and as you go into Carol Street to the right of the chapel. What is being done in that area?

A. The remodeling of the offices, repair and remodeling.

Q. This has nothing to do, actually, with efforts to repair damage done to the church either as a result of the construction of the Telephone Building or the Jones Building, does it?

A. There has been damage, you understand.

Q. You are not answering my question, Reverend.

THE COURT: He is attempting to. You may proceed with the answer.

THE WITNESS: Will you state the question, please?

BY DEFENSE COUNSEL:

Q. I will try to put it a little more directly.

To the right of the chapel and to the rear of the church, that would be the western side, what is the work which has been undertaken by the church?

A. Repair and renovation.

Q. And for what purpose? What is the reason you are doing this work?

A. There are two reasons; one, to repair some of the damage caused in the area and also to expand the office area to give us some storage space above the office area.

Q. Were there cracks in the floor of the basement when you first inspected the church?

A. The cracks in the basement were infinitesimal. I am sure there may have been some cracks small and not noticeable to my lay inspection of the basement.

Q. I am sure you recognize the view photographed in this (indicating) Defendant's Exhibit A, do you not?

A. Yes, I do.

Q. You observed this (indicating) separation of these coping stones from the concrete immediately adjacent—

A. Yes, a cement skirt.

Q. A cement skirt, you call it. That is a good phrase. Do you remember looking up that alleyway there in the Fall when you were about to come to the church?

A. Oh, yes.

Q. Did it look about like that?

A. This damage was not present when I was called, no.

Q. The coping stone wasn't separated at all?

A. It could have been some, but it was not the dramatic separation that you have (indicating) here.

Q. You don't recall it was separated to the extent that it appears to be shown in this photograph?

A. The separations have always been because this is a soft ground (indicating) here and it naturally was leaning.

Q. And there was evidence of separation in that area when you first came to the church but not as severe, according to your recollection, as shown in this photograph?

A. That's right.

Q. In September or October did you examine the front exterior of the church?

A. Again as I took the walking tour with the council I did.

Q. Did you observe the sidewalk in front of the door to the chapel

A. I suppose as a general observation I would have.

Q. Did you observe that the sidewalk in that area had settled about one inch?

A. I did not.

Q. Do you have a recollection of having looked and it had settled or had not settled?

A. I could not testify either to its having settled or not.

Q. Did you see a crack extending from the roof to the top left corner of the window on the front exterior?

A. I cannot testify to that observation.

Q. You cannot say that it was there, you cannot say that it was not there?

A. That's right.

Q. On the exterior facing Roan Way did you observe that the retaining wall had settled and pulled away from the concrete behind it? I think by "retaining wall" I am referring to those coping stones that are shown in that photograph.

A. I must repeat, my visit was a peripheral one and perhaps to see that there was a church there and it was in good condition, was my observation, and I did not make these scrutinies.

Q. You already told me that you remember seeing some degree of separation in the coping stones from the concrete skirt immediately adjacent to the building. It is your recollection it wasn't as severe as that?

A. I said it could because it is a natural place for this kind of separation to appear. It is only dirt.

Q. Was there ever any kind of break or fracture in the north wall of the church near the northwest corner which would be right outside your then location of your office?

A. Again, I have to repeat, my observation was not to look for any specific problems. I was looking at education areas, I was looking at office areas, I was looking at the general condition of the nave, the janitorial type of commitment; that was my observation and not toward specific fracturing of walls, sidewalks or stress areas.

Q. I want to make that plain, because in response to Mr. DeMay's question you had said that you made an examination of the church and you found it in very satisfactory condition, if I remember your phrase properly.

A. Absolutely. This church has been known for its having had excellent property committees and having been maintained to the best of the ability of the committee, a fine standard of care of the facility and excellent repair; and this is the only way a building of this age can be maintained. I was impressed with the property committee's attention to detail. I was also observant to the kind of janitorial care that had kept it in what I considered satisfactory condition.

Q. I appreciate that and I am not quarreling with that, but I was trying to find out, and I think I have found out, what you looked for, what you actually observed with respect to the physical condition of the church; and your answer has been that you were primarily interested in whether it served satisfactorily the purpose for which the church as a church was intended. Is that a fair statement or not?

A. That is correct. And that there were no obvious degenerate kind of lacked areas of control or repair.

Q. Forgive me if I seem to be stating what must be obvious; but the church was something short of 80 years old and there were many symptoms, if I can use the word, which would indicate the passage of time and the use of the church, and so forth, and its exposure to the elements and all other circumstances, isn't that right?

A. Being an antique lover I know exactly what you are talking about.

Q. Am I right or am I wrong?

A. She held up very well under all of my observations.

Q. But she was no longer a spring chicken, was she?

A. But she was a healthy chicken. She has been wounded very badly.

Q. When you responded to the call of the church she was a young lady of some 79 years of age, correct?

A. That's right.

Q. Don't you think I should quit at that point?

A. Are you asking me? Repeat your question.

Q. I will withdraw the question.

THE COURT: I think he was asking you if he should quit at that point.

DEFENSE COUNSEL: Don't you think I should quit my examination at this point?

THE COURT: That will do.

The contrary situation sometimes occurs—the witness who becomes so tongue-tied under cross-examination that he forgets his own name much less the vital facts to which he has just testified on direct examination. Now you must be on your toes.

### What to Do When Your Witness
### Is in Serious Trouble

With your witness in serious trouble you must make every effort to shield and protect him by prompt, legitimate objections. It's true that a jury does not like objections from plaintiff's counsel, but this is no time for platitudes. You must be absolutely alert, tense even, listening to every word defense counsel speaks, grasp the meaning of his question instantly, be on your feet before the question is completed and state your objection before the witness can even begin to answer. If you're going to object, do it fast.

I feel so strongly about this that during "delicate" cross examination I constantly stand in front of the counsel table, by the witness, or by the jury and both watch and listen to defense counsel. Experience has taught me to recognize the import of a question before it is completely uttered, and I have only to turn to the judge and make the objection on the instant. If the judge sustains the objections, you accomplish two purposes—you protect the witness and you disconcert defense counsel—sometimes to the point where he gives up the chase, feeling that he is being embarrassed before the jury. So much to the good.

You will note that I referred to the judge "sustaining your objections." That will happen if you know what you are doing. The Court most assuredly will not sustain the objection if it is poorly taken. Which leads to another subject.

### Do You Really Know the Rules?

It is pathetic, but true, that many attorneys try a case with a bare minimum knowledge of the Rules of Evidence. They try to rely on that sad, old generality that a question is "irrelevant, incompetent and immaterial." It's a poor objection to begin with and quite embarrassing when a savvy judge begins to inquire "Why is it irrelevant?" "Wherein is it incompetent?" "How can this be immaterial?" Stay away from this foolishness. If you have a valid objection make it specifically and to the point. To do so you must know the Rules by heart—in all of their many forms and varieties. A Handbook on Evidence should be on the desk of every lawyer and it is the kind of book that should be reviewed periodically solely for the purpose of refreshing your mind on the fine points of evidence.

## Some Types of Improper Questions

It's impossible to anticipate what defense counsel may ask but, almost always, improper questions fall into categories. Some of these are as follows:

1. The question that calls for hearsay. An old standby, it crops up in every trial: "Didn't Jane Doe tell you that.....?"

2. The question that assumes a fact not in evidence. Do you recall the old classic: "When did you stop beating your wife?"

3. The question that misstates a previous answer of the witness: "Mr. Jones, you previously stated that Joe Smith was going 35 miles per hour. Now, what was the.....?"

4. The question that calls for an opinion when you have not called the witness as an expert.

5. The question that requires the witness to "assume" facts: "Mr. Jones, assuming that....." If defense counsel offers the question subject to his proving the assumed fact later, that may be all right. Just don't you forget about it later—your opponent may be hoping that you will.

6. A question that goes beyond the scope of direct examination. If the subject is an automobile accident that occurred on June 25th, there is hardly any reason to cross-examine about a burglary of which the witness has some knowledge that occurred on May 16th.

7. Questions that attack the witness on the basis of some happening in the remote past.

These are typical of the things about which you must be alert and ready. Listening to the question is crucial, but it is a waste of time to know that "there is something wrong" without knowing what rule of evidence is being violated. Know those rules and review them constantly.

## When to Move for a Mistrial

This question goes in the category of "The Hundred Toughest Questions You'll Ever be Asked." What to do? Your case has gone in well, defense counsel has pulled a serious boner. You are prejudiced. Now what.

The Court can instruct the jury to ignore the question and answer—but will they? It helps a little if he criticizes defense counsel. If you make the motion, it's likely to be granted and weeks of work—in preparation and trial time—will go down the drain. If you don't make the motion, the jury is likely to remember the damaging testimony and return a defense verdict or a low verdict.

I can only recommend that if the case has gone in well, if you have a good jury, if the court cautions the jury and chides the defense counsel, if the statements are not terribly prejudicial then don't make the motion and take your chances. If any of the "ifs" mentioned above do not exist, then do make the motion, try to get an order that defendant will pay some of your expenses and try again another day. It's a tough decision. Your primary job is to protect the interests of your client and this duty may well demand that you take the mistrial. I strongly urge that if you decide to proceed with the trial be certain that your client understands the risk and consents to your decision to proceed.

## LET'S LOOK AT YOUR CROSS EXAMINATION

The time comes in every trial when it is your turn to examine the witnesses for the defendant. Since they will have testified to something adverse to your position it behooves you to decide quickly whether that "something" is important enough to justify any questioning and, if so, how you are going to approach the witness.

I suggest that you refrain from making the cross-examination a personal duel between you and the witness. If you are highly skilled—and feeling vindictive—you might proceed to tear up the witness for the personal gratification that it might give you (though the contest is an unequal one), but you do so at the jeopardy of antagonizing the jury. They may very well applaud what you have done to the witness and hate you for doing it. Your primary purpose on cross-examination is to get the witness to modify or recant his direct-examination testimony or to show that the witness is biased, prejudiced, ignorant or unobservant. You can do this without humiliating the witness or stripping him of whatever personal pride he has.

I once made such a fool of a doctor on cross-examination that when I paused for a moment and walked over to the counsel table he suddenly bolted from the witness stand and ran out of the courtroom. He was a nice man—just not very smart. It wasn't necessary for me to drive him to this length. It so happened that I was on close terms with the judge who was hearing the case and he took the occasion to call me into chambers and criticized me for what I had done, although acknowledging its effectiveness.

On another occasion, I utilized a vindictive attack on my client by defense counsel to great advantage. The plaintiff, a pleasant but not very intelligent young man, was cross-examined for nearly two hours; it was a terrible ordeal. Defense counsel, a tall, distinguished, brilliant man, used a prior statement, a deposition and a hospital record to great advantage and the plaintiff stammered, paused, couldn't answer, forgot, fidgeted, and did everything but break down and cry. The following neutralizing technique worked in this situation. I waited until my closing address. At that time I pointed to the defense attorney and told the jury about his fine education, his years of experience, his acclaim as one of the leaders of the Bar and his membership in the prestigious Academy of Trial Lawyers. Then I pointed to the plaintiff and told the jury of his eighth-grade education, his menial employment, and the fact that the only clubs he belonged to were the American Legion and the Knights of Columbus. At this point I stated that if this case was to be decided solely on the basis of the cross-examination of this plaintiff by this defense attorney, there was no need for the jury even to leave the courtroom—they could return a defense verdict right then and there. On the other hand, if they wanted to take the time to analyze the facts of the case, then.....I won that case. I so doing I learned the unforgettable lesson that you can go too far in cross-examination.

### The Best Is Sometimes None at All

It may come as a surprise—even sound like heresy—but there is no law that requires you to cross-examine every witness. In many cases there is no reason for it and no point to it. This usually applies to witnesses who are called to establish facts that are not, and probably cannot be, controverted. A good example is a medical records librarian who identified a hospital record and testified to the manner in which it was maintained in her department. What can one possibly gain by getting her to admit that she was convicted of embezzlement five years before and transferred from the business office of the hospital to the medical records room? This is a waste of time and effort.

The same rule applies to nearly all witnesses who merely identify records or testify from them. Leave them alone—unless of course their work is crucial to the case. There are other witnesses who are merely going to testify to one or two important, but not critical, facts. Pass them by with the confident statement "I have no questions of this witness, your Honor." In so doing you will save time, avoid nit-picking, secure the gratitude of the Court and possibly create some interest in the jury as to when you are going to cross-examine and whom you are going to pick on. If you really want to highlight and dramatize your cross-examination of a witness this is a good way to do it.

### Choose the Witness You Want to Examine

Inevitably there are certain vital witnesses in every case. The defendant is one, eye-witnesses and corroborative witnesses are others, an expert is one. These persons have to be cross-examined. However, they need not all be cross-examined in the same way nor at the same length. This is a time when, once again, you have to watch and listen. Some of these persons are going to be weak, uncertain or very obviously telling a tale that doesn't quite ring true. These are the ones you will want to go after, on the facts. Others will be solid citizens, very self-righteous about telling "the truth" and very sure they know exactly where the truth lies. These persons can be examined on the basis of their self-interest, prejudice (a term they will surely disavow), powers of observation or the basis for their opinions. Another witness might be one whose background may be inquired into for the purpose of attacking his credibility.

For example, in a recent case six or seven witnesses testified for the other side. I asked hardly a question on cross-examination until counsel called a psychologist as an expert. His opinion hurt, and his testimony was so crucial that I had to cross-examine him. There was no way to attack his qualifications. His opinion was firm and definite—not likely to be shaken. He made a good presentation and seemed quite sure of himself. The central issue in the case concerned the mental capacity of a young black man and, his behavioral problems at a home and school for delinquent children. I noted that the doctor's testimony and opinions were entirely based on various records kept at the Youth Center—I.Q. tests, social records, scholastic records, background investigations, reports of various incidents at the school, and so forth. Curiously he had never interviewed the young man or his teachers nor visited the school. The best I could do therefore was to inquire into the basis for the doctor's opinion. It went like this:

BY MR. DeMAY:

Q. Dr. Jones, sir, as I listened to Mr. Brown direct his questions to you and you expressed your opinions, one of the things that impressed me is that there was constant reference to John Smith having set a fire previous to the accident of April 1. Now, do I take it correctly that that is one of the important bases for the opinions that you have expressed?

A. It is one but not the total by any means.

Q. I understand, but it is one?

A. Certainly.

Q. So therefore I take it that you have made inquiry into the circumstances under which that fire was set?

A. No.

Q. You have not?

A. No.

Q. What date was it that that fire was set?

A. I don't remember the specific date.

Q. Where was the fire set?

A. I don't know where the fire was set.

Q. Under what circumstances was the fire set?

A. I don't know under what circumstances the fire was set.

Q. Was it a big fire or a little fire?

A. I don't know that either.

Q. A paper fire or a wood fire?

A. I don't know that either.

Q. In a cottage, in the school or outside on the grounds?

A. I don't know that either.

Q. Dr. Jones, don't you think that you ought to have made inquiry about the circumstances if you are going to rely upon that as one fact among others on which you base your opinion?

A. The assumption that I made was that this was a fire that was not set for a good purpose.

Q. How do you know that, sir?

A. Because it was indicated on his form. In his folder it was listed. I assumed that if he was setting a fire to cook some soup that they would not put that sort of thing in his folder, that they would put something in his folder that had significance.

Q. Did you make inquiry of the person who made the entry in the file?

A. No.

Q. You did not?

A. No, I did not.

Q. Reference has been made to various so-called incidents in which John Smith has been involved, and counsel has included them in the various questions that he has asked of you. Now, what are those incidents that you deem to be appropriate as forming a basis and foundation for your opinions?

A. There were a number of incidents in there from which I gained a general impression. I don't have at my finger tips and could not remember all that is contained in the 228 pages that are in there.

Q. Well, Doctor, did you make notes as you went through those 228 pages as to what was important and what was not?

A. I made notes regarding description of John Smith's behavior regarding some of my impressions, yes.

Q. I want to go back to the incident, sir. Can you tell the members of this jury how many incidents are reflected in that file that's before you.

A. No way could I do that. Could you tell me how many there are?

Q. Let me ask you this, Doctor: Do you know the details of any of the incidents that are reflected in that report.

A. Only as they are described in the reports.

Q. But you can't even tell us how many there are, nor can you tell us what those incidents are?

A. No.

Q. Have you ever talked to any of the persons who made the entries in there with regard to the details of these various incidents?

A. No.

Q. And yet you say that you rely, in part at least, upon the reporting of those incidents as the basis for your opinion?

A. I can only assume that—

Q. Is that correct, Dr. Jones? You rely in part upon those various incidents as forming the basis and foundation of your opinion?

A. Of course. I can only assume that the people reported the incidents truthfully and honestly and accurately.

Q. In detail, Doctor?

A. To the detail that they put them in the report.

Q. Do you not feel that the details and circumstances of these incidents are important in understanding John Smith's role in them?

A. When they reach the level in terms of numbers and quality that are contained in this report, they take on a less significant role.

Q. You say in terms of numbers and quality. Let's get back to numbers and I'll ask you again.

A. I don't know the numbers, no.

Q. You are the expert. How many incidents are in that folder that you have personally reviewed, sir?

A. I don't know. Do you know?

Q. Doctor, I'm not expressing the opinions, sir. I have an opinion, but I'm not permitted to testify. Let me ask you, Dr. Jones, when did you get involved in this case?

A. I got involved in this case when Mr. Brown asked me if I would review the file.

Q. When was that, sir?

A. I don't know the specific date. I'd have to refer to—

Q. Approximately?

A. Two months ago.

Q. That would be near the first of the year?

A. Two months ago, with standard deviation of fifteen days.

Q. All right. Approximately the first of this year; is that correct?

A. With the standard deviation of fifteen days, yes.

Q. Now, having two months, did you ever call John Smith to your office and personally interview him about, No. 1, background, his attitude, his feelings, his emotions, the data in that file?

A. No. I had to assume that what was in the file was accurate.

Q. But you did not call Mr. Smith to your office in the last two months to personally interview him?

A. No. That's what I said.

Q. Did you have occasion in the past two months to go out to the school and observe the school, observe the students and the teachers, at any time?

A. No.

Q. Did you have occasion in the past two months knowing that you were going to appear here for a jury and express opinions to talk to Mr. White, who is the principal of that school?

A. No.

Q. You did not feel, sir, that having a conversation with the principal and observing the teachers and students, that you would have a better understanding of what goes on there and the relationship that exists between the teachers and the students?

A. There is no question that I would, but to be able to make the statements that I made to those opinions, I do not feel that I needed to do that.

Q. You made the statement, I believe—please correct me if I am wrong—that in evaluating the ability of a young man to function, emotional factors are every bit as important as his tested IQ. Is that an approximately correct statement?

A. Yes.

Q. Now, in trying to determine the emotional factors that existed in this young man, did you ever in the past two months sit down with any of the teachers or social workers and go over with them in detail what kind of a boy this was?

A. No. My testimony is based on my having read the file and nothing else.

Q. Had you talked to these men, would you have an even deeper grasp and understanding of what this boy was like?

A. There is no question that I would have, but to make the statements that I made I did not feel that I needed to do that.

Q. You certainly did not?

A. Pardon me?

Q. You did not do it?

A. That's what I said.

Q. You have also indicated, by the way, that 100 as an IQ is in the middle of what is considered normal range. I think that was the statement that you made. Is that right?

A. That's what I said.

Q. Incidentally, do you remember what kind of an IQ test was given to this boy?

A. No. I would assume it was one of the individual intelligence tests.

Q. You assume that, sir. If you went through the file, do you know whether or not you could find specifically what kind of an IQ test was given to this boy?

A. I would think, so.

Q. But you made no effort to ascertain what that test was?

A. Right at this particular moment I don't remember, no.

Q. Does it make a difference, Doctor Jones?

A. It can.

Q. Because certain tests are usually—or let me put it this way: certain tests have been criticized when they have been given to young black men coming out of a ghetto environment?

A. Right.

Q. Isn't that right?

A. Yes.

Q. And isn't that because the fact that they are highly verbal tests that measure one's intelligence to a great extent upon one's prior educational background?

A. That's correct.

Q. Isn't that right?

A. Yes.

Q. And we have decided that these young men coming out of the ghetto don't have the capacity to verbalize and therefore do poorly on this type of IQ test, right?

A. That's correct.

Q. Whereas in point of fact they can be pretty smart?

A. They can be higher than their tested IQ's. There is no question about that.

Q. Higher than their tested IQ's?

A. Yes.

Q. Is one of the types of tests that has been criticized the Binet IQ test?

A. Yes.

Q. It has been. Do you know whether or not this boy was given a Binet IQ test?

A. I testified a few minutes ago that I was not specifically sure that that was the one that had been given to him.

MR. DeMAY: I think that's all I have. Thank you very much.

### Just What Do You Want from the Witness?

Your cross-examination must be purposeful. Either you are going to try to attack the credibility of a witness or you are going to try to get him to admit something of value to your case. The important thing is that you know what you are after. There is no point to your asking a lot of questions in a meandering sort of way in the naive hope that you will literally stumble onto something important. That rarely happens. You simply antagonize the jury and the judge since it becomes readily apparent that you don't know what you are doing or where you are going and that you are wasting everyone's time and, possibly, badgering the witness for no good reason. Rather than do this, don't cross-examine at all!

What you should do is to make up a small outline—it need only be a few "words and phrases"—that you want to interrogate this witness about and then stick with it. For example if a witness has testified about the speed of your client's car, you may want to examine him about his location when he saw the car, the length of time he had it in view and his ability to judge the speed of a moving vehicle. If the witness testifies to an expert opinion, you may simply cross-examine on the basis of his experience with the type of problem involved in the case. Where a person tells the jury that the plaintiff is, in essence, a malingerer cross-examine on the basis of his known antagonism to the plaintiff or the fact that he has had so few contacts with the plaintiff that he is in no position to pass judgment. The important thing is that you know what you want from the witness— and get it. Don't permit yourself to spend a lot of time on miscellany. Usually the facts that you want brought out are pretty obvious. Your job is to concentrate on developing only those facts.

Granted it is difficult, on occasion, to decide what you do want from a witness that you might be able to get him to admit. The last portion of that sentence is the crux of the problem—"things that he will admit." It is pretty clear that as to the key aspects of his testimony the witness is not going to recant. Thus, if a witness says that a traffic light was red, you are not going to get him to admit that it was really green. You can forget that approach. However, if he went on to testify in general, about seeing the accident happen and hurrying to the scene you might well cross-examine on the basis of the position of the vehicle after the accident or the precise parts of each vehicle that were damaged.

Again, suppose your case involves a claim for brain damage with its multifarious problems and the defendant calls a former school teacher to prove that the plaintiff always did poorly in school as showing that your client's loss of gray matter is no big thing. You can't attack the teacher directly—she won't recant her positive testimony on direct examination—

but you can develop the fact that your client was gregarious, full of fun, helpful and in short, the life of the class, as contrasted with his present moody, morose, solitary life-style. This approach is very effective.

It is my observation that you can do much better by "using" the defendant's witnesses to improve your case, rather than trying to destroy their testimony. Medical doctors are excellent subjects for this purpose. Assume for a moment that the defense calls a doctor to testify on the question of causation—that your client's condition did not result from the accident. If he has the necessary qualifications, if he has examined both the records and the client, there isn't much hope that you can successfully challenge his opinion. What you can do is to bring the doctor before the jury and with medical charts or anatomical models have him describe the nature of the injury, the type of operation and how it was done, his prognosis, his comments on the pain associated with the injury, the diagnostic tests or the therapeutic measures, and limitations which will exist on the activities of the plaintiff due to the injuries.

Cross-examination like this is wonderful. It makes the doctor your witness before the jury—reinforcing all that your own doctor has said, taking away the influence of his opinion on the causation question and, actually, making him your friend in court. This tactic, while not dramatic, represents cross-examination at its best. It can be done very easily because if you compare the report of your doctor and the defendant's doctor you will note that they are in reasonable agreement as to everything except one or two salient points. Your job is to emphasize the areas of agreement and to ignore argumentative issues.

In conclusion, the essence of good cross-examination is to decide, in advance of trial, if possible, or, most likely, during the direct examination exactly how you are going to handle the witness. Be sure to jot down a few notes as an outline, and then go about the business of getting this information promptly and directly.

### Get What You Need and Stop

When your cross-examination has placed before the jury and in the record all of the facts or opinions that you want from a witness then stop! Stop immediately! There is absolutely no point in going on. You have received the testimony that you wanted and to go further is to jeopardize your case. This is what the good trial lawyers mean when they make bitter jokes about that "one question too many." They are referring to the cases where the cross-examination was going so well that they began to fool around with the witness—asking questions that were completely beyond their initial outline and plan. The denouement comes suddenly—always unexpectedly. In answer to that "one question too many" the witness can deal a stinging blow which, if it doesn't seriously hurt your cause, will certainly do it no good. Don't let yourself be tempted to go on just because you have been quite successful with a witness. Get what you need—stop!

### Beware of "How" and "Why" Questions

In cross-examination you must be the boss—don't ever let a witness get ahead of you. You control the questioning, choosing the subject matter and the approach. Above all you control the questions themselves and the manner in which they are asked. Every lawyer will use his own manner of asking the questions—whether loud or soft, challenging or pleading, slow or fast. This has to be a personal matter. As to the questions themselves, however, a few words can be said. The best way to control the witness is to ask questions that require a "Yes" or "No" answer because in so doing you will be stating the fact and the witness is called upon solely to admit or deny its truth. This doesn't give him much leeway for mischief.

Many years ago I was taught a lesson in this regard. At a new construction site a young boy had climbed and fallen from a wall sustaining injuries. I asked the defendant's foreman "how high was that wall?" He promptly replied "High enough that a kid that age should have known to stay off it." That hurt. It would have been better to ask him "Isn't it true that this wall was approximately twenty feet high?" Always, try to avoid these "how" and "why" questions. By their very nature they shift control of the interrogation to the witness. Just imagine what any defendant doctor could do with a question "Why did you perform this prostatectomy by the supra-pubic approach rather than a transurethral resection?" He would first smile (at you), second, take a deep breath, and third, launch into such a devastating answer as to blow both you and your client right out of the courtroom.

Part of the problem is that once a witness is turned loose with a question like this you can't stop him. There is no valid objection you can make to shut him off. Like Pandora's Box, once it's opened there is nothing but trouble. Avoid this headache—stick to the "Yes" and "No" questions—"Were you driving at a speed of 35 miles per hour?" "Did the Plaintiff tell you to sell the land?" "Doctor, aren't there four standard techniques for removing a prostate gland?" "After the snowfall did you shovel the snow from your sidewalk?" "Yes" and "No", "No" and "Yes"—that's all you really want as answers on cross-examination.

### Should You Let the Witness Explain an Answer?

Not voluntarily. Sometimes the judge will insist on the right of the witness to explain his answer and on occasion the witness will put you in an embarrassing position before the jury if you refuse. There is nothing you can do about these things. Insofar as it is in your power, though, don't let the witness explain. Truthfully what he wants to do is ramble, justify or avoid a direct answer. You can tell him that he can explain on redirect examination if his attorney thinks it is important; tell him that he must answer "Yes" or "No" or ask him why he is reluctant to answer positively. If necessary, withdraw the question for a few minutes and start on another subject. Do anything, but don't let the witness start "explaining" his answers. Once successful with this tactic the witness will want to "explain" every sensitive answer and the cross-examination will become a futile waste of time.

### What To Do if the Witness Breaks Down?

This does happen from time to time and it poses serious problems. Jurors take a very dim view of an attorney who has been so effective that a witness suffers public humiliation. When a man starts crying on the witness stand you had better do something. The best thing to do is to ask for an immediate recess and get him out of the courtroom. As an alternative offer him a glass of water and give him a few moments to collect himself. Perhaps you can begin again with a change of subject, or you might consider stopping the cross-examination at this point. It is also appropriate to say a few words of explanation—not apology—to the judge and witness, for the benefit of the jury. You might point out that the search for truth can lead to personal hurt or that cross-examination is an effective tool but that witnesses suffer from it. Try to say something that will let the jury know that you had to ask the questions, but you're sorry to have so embarrassed the witness.

These same rules apply in general to a woman on the witness stand, but not quite to the same extent. Jurors are not shocked or surprised when a woman cries a little. Treat her with compassion and sympathy and you will be all right.

Children and elderly people are in a special category. Never, never push one to the point of emotional collapse. Never, never. If you do, the jurors will execute retribution in a most awful manner—a defense verdict in a matter of minutes even if you have the most meritorious of claims. A jury will simply not forgive you if you make a child or a grandmother cry.

Cross-examination is a vital part of every trial. It can be effective and, to be frank, it can be fun. Pick and choose the witnesses you want to examine, know what you are after and when you get it, stop. It will add significantly to your chances of success in the trial of a lawsuit.

# CHAPTER 12

# How to Deliver the
# Closing Address

In your opening you were not permitted to comment on the evidence, and the trial itself consisted of colloquy between yourself and the several witnesses. The Closing Address is your only chance to discuss the evidence, the witnesses, and any other matter you deem pertinent, with the jury. It represents your best opportunity to persuade them that your cause is the just one.

Fortunately, the burden is entirely on you. No longer are you required to "speak" to the jury through the mouths of others; on this occasion the ideas, the words, the gestures and the manner of presentation are yours. This is your chance to win the case on your own abilities.

There are very few legal restraints on what you can say or do. It is more than a test of oratory; it is a test of your ability to summarize the trial, to select those portions of it that are so significant that the attention of the jury should be specifically directed to them, to argue the merits of your position, and to persuade the jury to return a verdict in your favor.

In so doing you are permitted to be passionate and inflammatory, coldly analytical, biased or critical, sarcastic, or whatever you like. Your only goal is one of persuasion and in accomplishing that goal you may adopt any technique or approach with which you are most comfortable and which you have found to be most successful.

There are several things to be considered as you begin to prepare your closing. Let us analyze some of them.

## WHO GOES FIRST?

The answer to this question can make quite a difference in your preparation. If you are going to speak first, your speech can logically be separated into an introduction, followed by a discussion of liability, then injuries, and finally damages. If you are going to speak second, however, you should spend some time at the beginning of your speech rebutting the argument of defense counsel. This is going to use up valuable time and raises the question: should you plan to lengthen the amount of time you intend to speak or should you shorten the time allotted to one of the other elements of your speech? In addition, your rebuttal will inevitably touch upon matters you had previously planned to discuss in detail relating to liability or medical. To what extent shall you go into these matters on rebuttal? What kind of adjustment will this require in your affirmative discussion of them?

Another matter to be considered is the fact that the attorney who speaks first will be facing a relatively fresh, attentive jury; the second speaker may find the jurors both tired and a little bored. If you are that second man, be sure to ask for a recess before you begin to speak. This will enable the jurors to get refreshed and to be revived a little before you begin.

Your introductory remarks might well change depending on the sequence of your speech. You will note that the first speaker nearly always begins with a few jokes and he will express his thanks to the jurors for their attention during the trial. This is obviously designed to get the jurors to relax and to put them at their ease. If you follow this man, there is hardly any reason for you to adopt the same technique—the jurors are already at ease, perhaps too much so. You should begin by saying or doing something that will catch their attention and waken them. This would be a good time to begin by raising your voice and describing, graphically, the injuries your client sustained. In the alternative you might use your model, skeleton or other large exhibit and begin by discussing it with the jurors. Try anything that will force them to do something more than merely sit back and listen.

## HOW MUCH TIME SHOULD YOU TAKE?

In the average case of a four- or five-day trial I recommend a closing speech of about 45 minutes. It is the opinion of one of our older and better local judges that "if you haven't convinced them in 30 minutes you're not going to convince them at all." I don't agree. That is entirely too short a period of time.

The plaintiff's attorney has to touch all bases—liability, injuries and damages—and it simply cannot be done in 30 minutes. In fact, if there is any serious problem that requires extended discussion, or, if there are a multiplicity of witnesses or issues, then it is both easy and necessary to extend your speech to an hour.

The closing address is too important for you to rush through it. It would be better, really, if you not think of it as a lecture or speech, but rather as a highly effective and dynamic tool or device that, alone, can enable you to win a case.

A bitter defense attorney once said to me about a plaintiff's lawyer who had won the case: "He doesn't care what the facts are so long as he can talk to that jury." While that is clearly an extreme statement it illustrates the power of an effective closing address.

It takes time to develop and utilize that power. Don't hurry.

## HAVE AN OUTLINE AND STICK TO IT

A good closing address is rarely spontaneous—it is planned. That is true of any good speech from the Gettysburg Address to the State of the Union Message. There is no other way. While you should plan your closing it is not wise to write it because of two reasons: First, being an unskilled orator you will inevitably begin to read it; and second, you will not be standing still, as at a podium, but will be moving around showing exhibits, demonstrating, and writing on the blackboard. You might give a lecture but you will not be giving a speech. However, you can, and must, take the time to prepare an outline.

On the night before you are to close to the jury go off by yourself for a few hours and think over the trial. Make notes about the key witnesses and the critical portions of their testimony.

If you did well on cross-examination you may want to remind the jurors about it, so jot down the names of those persons and make short notes of the revealing answers.

Recollect the testimony of your doctors and highlight their most serious comments.

Compute and re-compute your items of damage and loss so that you are positive they are complete and completely accurate. You don't want to give the defense attorney a chance to interrupt and embarrass you by pointing out that you can't add.

After you have made these notes begin to work up an outline that will pull everything together, and put them in the order in which you want to present them. Be sure to put comments in your outline pertaining to things you want to do—"Pass around hospital record—Exhibit 2," "Use Damage Chart here," "Demonstrate with client," "Put on blackboard."

When you have finished you will have a document that will do wonders toward keeping your thoughts well organized and your closing on course.

It is so easy, in the midst of a fiery argument, to get so emotional and excited that you simply forget what your next point is to be. I'm sure you have seen that happen. When it does occur the speaker falters, hesitates, and becomes confused. That is where the outline helps. As soon as you realize that you are lost you can take a quick glance at your notes, pause a moment to reflect, and then you are off on your next point. Everything is nicely tied together because of your advance planning and that irreplaceable piece of paper before you.

## REBUTTING DEFENDANT'S ARGUMENT

This part of your closing will have to be spontaneous. There is no way you can plan in advance to meet something you have not heard and your response will depend as much on how things are said as well as what is said. You will have to listen carefully to what the defense attorney is saying and I assure you that somewhere in his speech he will make a comment or remark that you can seize on to launch into an attack on his argument. Sometimes he will suggest that your client is lying or is greedy and you can begin with that; at other times he will challenge the credibility of one of your witnesses while relying too much on one of his own and you might use that as a starting point.

On one such occasion I began my closing by writing the name of the plaintiff and of the defense witness, whose virtues had just been extolled, on the blackboard in big letters. Then I told the jury that I agreed that one of them was not telling the complete truth and that I would gamble the whole case on the veracity of the plaintiff. This is a dramatic and effective gesture in the right case, but I suggest that you use it sparingly. Nonetheless, it illustrates the principle of which I speak—to seize something in the defendant's closing that will give you an effective means to destroy or damage his argument. Another illustration of this technique would be the following:

The defense attorney was an older man—tall, thin and almost pontifical in his attitude. He fairly exuded the belief that the plaintiff was lying and, in the manner of a schoolmaster, he lectured the jury on the virtues of truth and honesty and the correlative evils of lies, greed and the deliberate distortion of the truth to gain material ends. He quoted extensively from the Bible and especially St. Paul who was his favorite source of aphorisms. It was quite effective since some genuine doubt could exist in the minds of the jurors about the plaintiff's truthfulness and the correctness of his recollection. What to do? I promptly told the jury at some length that, like St. Paul and the defense attorney, I too loved truth; like St. Paul I, too, deplored anyone who would distort the truth to gain money. Then, standing before the blackboard with chalk in my hand, I reminded them that, nonetheless, St. Paul said that there were only three great virtues, Faith, Hope and—here, I wrote in giant letters—CHARITY. The jury laughed, the thrust of the argument of defense counsel was blunted, and I could go on, now, to a sensible discussion of the case.

This is the kind of thing that I am suggesting you try. You only have so much time before that jury. Don't waste precious minutes in a detailed rebuttal of defendant's argument. You can't do a good job, it's too defensive, it looks bad, and the jurors get tired. Instead, try to strike at the general theme, tenor, approach or attitude of the defense attorney. Talk about this for no more than five minutes or so and then be rid of it. There is too much to discuss in your own case without wasting time on the defendant's case.

## TRY TO BE INTERESTING, DRAMATIC OR HUMOROUS

Each of us has something going for him. It can be wit, sincerity, logic, a charming manner or good looks. Whatever you have—use it now. Don't worry about the qualities you lack—we can't all make people laugh—and don't imitate others. Concentrate on your particular God—given talents and use them.

Your job, now, is to capture and hold the attention of that jury and to win them to your way of thinking. Do this by emphasizing those qualities you exhibit best—whether it be a flair for drama, good-natured joking with the jury, or using the blackboard and charts to overwhelm them with the logic of your position.

Get loud if you want, or pound the table. Just remember that you are making a closing and not giving a speech. If speech-making was all there was to it, you would probably do better to type up the speech in twelve copies, hand them to the jurors and allow them thirty minutes to read it. I have heard fine plaintiffs' attorneys close to a jury by talking to them for thirty minutes about everything in the world except the facts of the case, then spend ten minutes demonstrating on a blackboard why the jury must return a plaintiff's verdict. These are successful men.

What these men know and what I am trying to point out is that a trial is, for most people, an "experience," and your closing should be a remembered aspect of it.

Don't be dull. Don't be boring or disinterested. Let there be an attitude of excitement, enthusiasm and confidence about you so that the jurors want to watch and listen to you and will be influenced by what you have to say.

## USE THE BLACKBOARD

In this instance these words have to be a command and not a request.

I'm sure that every defense attorney would say that if there was one tool he would want to take away from the plaintiff's attorney it would be the blackboard.

You can use it to dramatize certain points in your closing, you can use it to list important facts or witnesses, you certainly want to use it to itemize some or all of your elements of damages.

This tool is so flexible—you can erase, underline, cross-out, all for effect, and you can print in large letters or write in small ones.

Above all it is there to imprint its visual message on the minds of the jurors. It is so valuable that if you leave writing on it when you conclude, I am sure that the defense attorney will ask that the board be erased before the judge begins his charge. He doesn't want that jury constantly looking at what you have written.

In addition to its other advantages, your use of the blackboard will be a welcome respite for the jurors from the steady drone of your voice. The few moments you spend writing will enable them to stretch, relax their attention and take a "mental break." When you turn to them again you will now have the strong influence of a visual aid lending its support to your spoken word.

A blackboard is a truly vital tool which must be utilized in your closing address.


## TALK ABOUT THE HIGHLIGHTS OF YOUR CASE

When you begin to think of what you intend to say to the jury about your proof, bear in mind that there is no reason to recapitulate the case in detail. You must realize that the jurors will remember most of what was said and done. To think, or act, otherwise will be to insult their intelligence.

Your job is two-fold: to summarize and pull together all of your testimony in a clear and concise manner, and to point out specific aspects of the case that you think should be remembered.

It might be helpful to point out how the testimony of each witness has supported and corroborated that of the others and the manner in which the documentary evidence supports all of them. This is also the time to stress the fine character, background or experience of some of your witnesses.

If you used an expert engineer, for example, don't spend a lot of time talking about what he said—the jurors will remember that—but talk about the first landing on the moon and the fact that he was one of the principals guiding that effort. If I had Dr. Jonas Salk as a witness, I would only mention his opinion, so far as testimony is concerned, and would spend a lot of time discussing the fact that he was the developer of the polio vaccine.

After you have argued the main elements of your case, and if you have done well on cross-examination, you might spend a few minutes reminding the jury about how poorly the defense witnesses performed. I say "a few minutes" and I mean that. Don't permit yourself to become so enamored of your success on cross-examination that you forget that it is your case-in-chief that you are supposed to be talking about.

## SHOULD YOU IGNORE DAMAGING TESTIMONY?

There are conflicting opinions about how to handle damaging testimony. One school argues that you should meet it head-on, since it is there for all to see, and try to rebut it with argument. The other group chooses to ignore it on the theory that it cannot be effectively argued away and to mention it at all merely reinforces it. I believe that the latter course is best.

Damaging testimony springs either from the cross-examination of your witness or direct examination of a defense witness. The latter is easier to handle. After all, in every case some conflict is inevitable and is expected by the jury.

If your witness says a traffic light was red and a defense witness says the light was green, there is not much point in arguing about the testimony of the defense witness. It takes too much time to discuss his physical location, powers of observation and the like. You did all of that on cross-examination and the jury will remember it. Emphasize the positive in the short time available to you and talk about the testimony of your own witness.

In like manner, if your doctor gave you medical causation and the defendant's doctor did not, then ignore their doctor. Talk about your witness—what he said, his excellent background and experience and, possibly, the fact that he had more contact with the plaintiff than the other doctor did, or that he carefully examined certain charts and records that the other doctor never bothered to study. Simply ignore the negative testimony of the defense.

A much more difficult problem confronts you when the damaging testimony has been elicited on cross-examination of a principal witness of yours. It hurts and there isn't too much you can say about it. What is the point, therefore, in bringing it up? It's a great deal like scratching poison ivy—it only makes things worse.

Certainly, it goes without saying, that if you can think of a good, effective way to rebut the effects of damaging testimony, then by all means do so. My point is that unless your rebuttal is going to be completely effective—and it rarely can be—then it is a complete waste. There are several approaches you might consider, such as attacking the defense attorney for the way in which he cross-examined the witness, or searching for support from the testimony of other witnesses, or trying to find some chart, document or record that will substantiate the testimony of your witness on direct examination. However, these things have to be very strong or you will simply be wasting your time and further damaging your case.

The very best approach is to face up to the unhappy fact that your witness has been hurt, your case has been damaged, and you have to forge ahead completely ignoring this fact, emphasizing the positive, and hope that the jury will be more impressed by the other facts and testimony.

This is extremely difficult for any attorney to do. It takes nerve and self-control. The temptation to talk about the damaging testimony—to try to explain it away—is almost irresistible.

Don't succumb to the temptation. Ignore it. Don't mention those damning statements. I am certain that in your case-in-chief there is much good for you to talk about. Use your time and ability to discuss those facts. Have the nerve to ignore damaging testimony.

## SPEND PLENTY OF TIME ON DAMAGES

Most attorneys spend too much time on liability and not nearly enough on damages. Granted that liability will determine whether or not you receive a verdict at all, it hardly does much good if you receive a low one. The only way you can be assured of a satisfactory amount is to argue at length about the damages. Whether your liability case is easy or tough you must set aside a substantial amount of time in your closing to go over the medical testimony, discuss pain, suffering and inconvenience, detail the specific losses your client has incurred to date and may incur in the future and, where permissible, to argue the amount of the award the jury should return.

With regard to that latter item—arguing the amount of the award, jurisdictions vary in their rules permitting and regulating it. In Pennsylvania, the attorneys are not permitted to argue any sum as an appropriate verdict in the case or to assign a value to pain, suffering and inconvenience, or to future disability. Obviously this restriction severely handicaps the plaintiff's attorney in his attempt to translate a client's injury, pain, or disability into terms of money. The jury is left groping and must literally pull a figure "out of the blue."

If your jurisdiction permits such argument, make the most of it. The figure that you suggest must always be on the high side of reasonableness. In a sense you are negotiating with the jury. They understand that your appraisal will be influenced by your obvious interest in the case and will, therefore, discount any figure you give them because of that fact. Nonetheless, they are looking to you for some guidance and help so be sure to give it to them.

Above all, give them a figure that you can justify. Don't ask for $100,000.00 for a simple arm fracture that healed promptly and without complications. Such antics antagonize ordinary people. If you're uncertain about the value to place on a case, consult with other plaintiffs' attorneys or check the records to see what the verdicts have been in your area for similar injuries.

If, as in Pennsylvania, for example, you cannot argue a specific sum, then the burden of going into detail with regard to damages is even greater. It is only by virtue of a clear and detailed understanding of the injuries and losses that your jury can hope to return a fair verdict.

### Review Medical Testimony Carefully

Most jurors have a poor knowledge of their own bodies. I would hope that your doctor would have carefully explained the injury to the jurors, demonstrated to them with medical charts and skeletal models, and discussed future problems that the plaintiff will, or is likely, to face. Unfortunately, despite your efforts, he probably couched some of his testimony in medical jargon and presumed at least a minimal medical understanding of the human body. That's where the problem comes—the jurors did not understand the technical words and the presumption of knowledge is erroneous. You could not do much to straighten the matter out during direct examination, but now is your chance.

Go back over that medical testimony in the greatest detail, and simplest language, possible. You can do the demonstrating now and make that jury very much aware of just how much damage has been done to your client. You might discuss how an injury to one part of the body can affect other parts of the body and how an injured organ, even though substantially corrected, can adversely affect your plaintiff for the rest of his life. This is your chance to explain all of the medical aspects of the case as you want them explained—in a clear, lucid, persuasive manner that will leave the jurors impressed with the precise extent to which your plaintiff was injured.

### How Do You Explain Pain to the Jury?

Every human being shies away from pain. We not only do not want to undergo it, we don't want to talk about it. That makes the subject of pain and suffering a little difficult to handle with a jury—but handle it you must because much of your damages will be based on that intangible.

When you do talk about pain you are always in danger of being too callous or too maudlin. The latter is the greater danger. You had better know your jury pretty well at this point. You can push the women to the point of tears, but if your men are engineers, farmers or accountants they will resent it. On the other hand if you are too casual, you will not be able to develop the natural empathy that women feel for one who is suffering.

My suggestion is to go ahead and get emotional up to the point that you approach the dramatic—then switch to a very detached manner of speaking even though the words you use are blood-curdling adjectives. It is interesting to watch a skilled plaintiff's attorney at work on this problem. He will have the women close to tears as he discusses the hospitalization, the operation, demonstrates the screws and clamps used by the orthopedist and the traction devices; then when he comes to the really serious part of the subject, the morphine that will have to be administered in the future, the progression from wheelchair to bed, the tragedy that stares the family in the face—he will talk directly to the men and in as unemotional a tone of voice as it is possible for him to use.

You can talk about pain being like stepping into the "fires of hell" but you had better not shout those words. Save your emotionalism for canes and crutches and things that are by their nature unemotional—mere objects. The flesh and blood will speak for themselves and do not require verbal "window dressing." Be sure, however, that you do speak of them—calmly, deliberately and at length.

### Demonstrate Your Client's Disability

While you are talking about your client's limp, inability to use his arm, or lengthy scar, demonstrate it. What better way to get the point across? If your client cannot hold tools in his hand be sure to have some in the courtroom and, with him standing before the jury, hand them to him and let him drop them on the floor. If he has hideous burn scars on his chest pull up his shirt and show them to the jury again. He has to live with them daily and the jury surely can look at them a second time to remind them of what he has to go through. Don't hesitate to do this—it is very effective. Of course, the defense attorney will object—he certanly doesn't want it done—but most judges will permit it.

On one such occasion, as I directed the plaintiff to hobble around the courtroom, even the judge exclaimed "that man is in terrible pain." He knew it all through the trial but the words never came out until that moment when, for the last time, he saw that man try to move. Jurors react the same way. They haven't quite realized that the trial is nearly over until you tell them so and ask them for the last time, and before their verdict, to look at a twisted leg, scarred face or an amputation site.

### Prepare a Chart of the Losses

If your client's losses are at all extensive, the best way to present them is by a large chart. This has to be prepared ahead of time and must be scrupulously accurate. If there is any argument about some amount, either leave it off the chart or use an acceptable, though lesser, sum. All printing must be large so that the jurors can easily see the words and figures. This chart should contain, separately listed, the hospital charges, past lost wages, future lost wages, life expectancy and degree of disability, if any, and finally, the words "Pain, Suffering and Inconvenience" with question marks in the space set aside for figures, or, if you are permitted, your estimate of the value. Such a chart is an excellent way to present your client's losses to the jury. At one glance they have all of the essential data before them. Where matters require elaboration or explanation you can place the chart on an easel and step to the blackboard to make a written analysis or explanation. Whatever else you may forget, don't forget this chart.

## PLACE YOUR CLIENT WHERE THE JURY CAN SEE HIM

It is the client who is going to receive the award of the jury, not the attorney. Too many lawyers forget this and permit the plaintiff to become lost among a number of spectators or to become hidden by a blackboard or easel. In your enthusiasm to explain things to the jury don't ignore the plaintiff. Let him and his family occupy conspicuous positions before the jury during the closing addresses and the charge of the court. They should sit in the front row of the spectators' seats and in such a position that they will not be shielded from view by any of the courtroom equipment or exhibits. This is the last chance the jury will have to look at the plaintiff, and his family, evaluate them and to meditate on what effect their verdict may have on that family unit. In a close case the very presence of the plaintiff, in full view of the jury, can be the factor which sways them to a favorable verdict.

## CONCLUDE POSITIVELY, STRONGLY AND CONFIDENTLY

If you lack faith in the merits of your case, you cannot ask the jury to have any. If you are not sure of your witnesses and their testimony, why should a jury rely on them? You must demonstrate to the jury that you believe in the plaintiff's case and that they must also. To do this you have to express a confident attitude and use language that is both positive and strong. I do not call for any display of arrogance—that can be deadly. You can be humble, quiet and soft-spoken and still let that jury know that you believe the plaintiff should win this case. This is no time for equivocation, self-doubt, or an attitude that while you would appreciate a favorable verdict you really don't deserve it. You must let the jury know, by act and word, that they should return a verdict for the plaintiff. Do this by adopting an attitude of self-confidence, by using positive language and by speaking in strong terms on behalf of your client and your case.

# CHAPTER 13

# Trial Briefs: Points For Charge; the Charge of the Court

A trial brief, or memorandum of law, should be one of the essential tools you carry with you into every courtroom. I realize there aren't many lawyers who enjoy writing a brief. To do so without a specific request from the court will strike many of them as performing work that is not needed. While I might agree that a trial brief is rarely requested I won't agree that it is rarely needed.

If you will think about it for a moment, I believe that you will have to agree that every case has some significant problem that is going to require a decision by the judge. Sometimes the key issue will be a procedural one, other times it will involve a matter of evidence, and, most frequently, it will involve substantive law. Your success will depend on how the judge rules on that issue.

Since this is true, and since you are working on a contingent fee basis in which your remuneration depends on a good result in the case, what reason is there for not submitting a brief on that issue, or at least, a memorandum of law? The answer is that, aside from weariness, there is no reason. The judge and his clerk will have to research the question and it is possible that they will come up with the wrong answer unless they receive help from you. It is my suggestion, therefore, that you always prepare a brief, or a memorandum, on anticipated legal problems.

## BRIEF OR MEMORANDUM

As a general rule, a brief should be prepared when you want to explain the legal basis for your lawsuit. It should discuss your theory of liability and should contain a lengthy statement of the facts that you intend to prove, the applicable law, and an argument in justification of your position. Obviously, almost as a matter of definition, such a brief need be prepared only when your case is either so complex as to pose unusual problems or so novel that the judge will not be immediately familiar with the law and the manner in which it has been applied. It is not a matter of the legal principles being something new, it is a question whether your judge is acquainted with those that apply in your case.

I call to mind that in my area nearly all Federal Employers' Liability Act cases were filed in Federal Court until a few years ago. Then a change occurred concerning the manner of selecting persons for jury service and immediately the plaintiffs' lawyers began to file such cases in the State Common Pleas Court. The judges simply were not familiar with either the statutory or the case law involved in these lawsuits and, as a result, a trial brief was required in every case. I think that much the same thing is true in airplane cases, which are relatively rare, anti-trust cases, and probably medical malpractice cases (in some jurisdictions), to name a few. The judges need help in these cases and it is in your best interest to provide that assistance by writing a trial brief.

A legal memorandum, of not more than two or three pages, should be prepared when you are concerned about one specific issue. (This is not to imply that you are allowed only one memorandum per trial.) Anytime you are aware of a legal problem that is going to arise in the courtroom, prepare a memorandum concerning it. You will notice that most of the time these will involve procedural and evidentiary matters.

Some good examples would be the instance in which you must have the testimony of a young child and the question of his capacity to testify arises; when you are trying to prove an official document from a foreign jurisdiction; when you plan to use testimony, such as hearsay statements, that is ordinarily prohibited; or when you decide to proceed in some unorthodox manner not contemplated by the Rules of Procedure. The judge has a right to be inquisitive concerning the legal basis for your intentions and it will do wonders for your cause to produce a good memorandum that will satisfy his curiosity. A judge is not going to let you proceed merely on your word that it is an acceptable way to try the case; he will let you go ahead if you can show him good precedent for your actions. A memorandum will provide the key to gaining his consent.

### Judges Appreciate Briefs and Memorandums

It is good for all of us to appreciate the fact that, completely aside from the legal justification for submitting a brief or memo, judges like a lawyer who has taken the time to prepare these things. They feel that it shows a sign of respect for the Court—an awareness that the judge is a human being and that there are so many demands on his time that he is limited in the effort that he can devote to the peculiarities of an individual case. If you are the one who is asking him to permit something unorthodox, or to consider an unusual approach to a case, then he rather expects, and certainly appreciates, anything you can do to make his decision easier. Your brief is a big step in that direction.

In addition, the average judge feels that the lawyer who submits a brief, or memorandum, is a lawyer who is prepared. He gives the impression of confidence and knowing what he is doing. The judge will have respect for such an attorney and will be more careful in his deliberations and rulings than he will be with someone who, rather flippantly, and on the basis of a bare assertion, requests the right to do something that is not ordinarily permitted.

## THE CHARGE OF THE COURT

A Charge is a duty of the Court and one in which the lawyer does not play too much of an active role. The substance of the Charge, and its organization, are entirely discretionary with the Court except that there are certain fundamental matters as to which he must charge the jury and of which he is aware. The attorney must realize, however, that there are certain things he must do, and that while his role in the Charge is minor it is essential. It should never be forgotten that when the Court begins to charge the jury they will be more attentive than they were at any time during the trial, with the possible exception of plaintiff's opening address. This will be the first time the judge will have spoken to them at length. They are anxious to listen and willing to be impressed. What he says, therefore, is going to have great bearing on the outcome of the case. It behooves you to make every effort to insure that he says as much as possible in favor of your client.

### Prepare Points For Charge

The only way in which you can have some influence on the charge of the Court is by submitting Points For Charge. These will be your suggestions concerning the several matters that he must tell the jury. Since the charge will be a statement of the legal principles which the jury must apply to the facts, your points will concern themselves with legal matters. It is inappropriate and a waste of time, to include statements of fact. The judge is not going to include them in his charge and may well become annoyed at your presenting them.

Points For Charge serve another purpose in addition to the immediate one of guiding the jury—they are also a vehicle for appeal in the event of an adverse verdict. This purpose is equally as important as the former. Your points will contain statements of every legal principle which you think applies in your case and if the judge refuses some of them the Appellate Court can be presented with a well-documented basis for granting a new trial. Accordingly, your thoughts have to be directed first to the jury, and then beyond them, to a higher court.

### Prepare Points During the Trial

There is a tremendous flurry of activity at the end of a trial and not much time in which to get everything done. In a matter of a very few hours you could be preparing for an argument on defendant's Motion For a Directed Verdict, and trying to complete a brief on that subject, preparing a closing address on the assumption that you are going to win the aforementioned argument, and trying to prepare Points For Charge. This is a great deal of work that has to be done quickly. Unfortunately, haste leads to errors.

You can alleviate this pressure, and save time, if you will work on your points throughout the trial. At the end of each day you have to take the time to review the testimony of that day and get witnesses ready for the next day. While you are doing this jot down several notes on matters which occurred that day and legal principles which you think should be included in your points for charge. Many of those points will begin with a factual statement and it is a big help to make a note, each day, of the salient facts that were proved and who testified to them. In this way, when the time comes to prepare your points, you will have readily available the pertinent facts and the legal principles which, when combined, will make up your points. It should be obvious that this method of preparation is far superior to your waiting to the end of case and then trying to remember all of the important legal principles you want presented to the jury. The latter course leads to shoddy workmanship because you are relying too much on your memory and, if you are rushed, you will forget.

### Be Timely and Specific

The rules of every court contain a provision relating to the time for filing Points For Charge. In this, as in most other parts of a lawsuit, there is a limitation which must be adhered to. Thus, Rule 51 of the Federal Rules of Civil Procedure specifically directs that requests for charge be filed "at the close of the evidence," or earlier if the court so directs. It also requires the court to rule on the requests prior to closing arguments. Our Pennsylvania Rules of Civil Procedure (Rule 226) direct that the Points For Charge be filed before the closing addresses are begun. Your court probably has a similar rule. While it is true that most judges are reasonable enough that they will accept your points anytime before they begin actual work on the charge, nonetheless, you had better know your judge very well before you rely on this kindness. Certainly an appellate court will look only at the Rules and will insist on your compliance with them.

Your Points For Charge should be very specific and each should express only one legal principle. This makes it easier for the judge to rule and lends clarity to the point if he reads it to the jury. If you combine two or three legal rules in one point, there is apt to be some confusion or misunderstanding.

Finally, be sure to have a citation of authority at the end of each point. This gives credibility to your points and will incline the judge to use them since he knows they are based on good precedent. When you have no authority for some of your points, list those together at the end of your document. You might lack citations either because there is no law on the subject or because you were too rushed to locate it. In either event, by placing them together, the judge will understand that these are expressions of what you believe the law to be or ought to be. He will appreciate it and will look with interest at what you have written since he knows it is not an attempt to deceive him in any way.

### Don't Bother with Routine Matters

Don't belabor a judge with points that relate to matters upon which he must charge in every case. You know that a good 70 percent of his charge is perfectly routine, that he has it all written down, and has given it so many times that he probably has it memorized. Don't waste your time, and his, by mentioning these things. You have enough work to do without unnecessarily adding to your burden. Concentrate on those matters that are specific to your fact situation. Every case has them. Even in a routine, run-of-the-mill lawsuit there will be facts which justify your asking the judge to present the law in a slightly different manner from what he might ordinarily do. You may not need many points in a case like this, but the few you do submit could make an important difference in the outcome of the case. Where the case is more involved and includes novel or infrequently used legal principles you are going to need numerous points. Don't waste your time on miscellany.

### Make Certain the Judge Rules on Each Point

Since your Points For Charge are going to be filed as part of the pleadings in the case, you must be sure to go over them in detail with the judge. Usually this is done in chambers as a matter of convenience. It is a good opportunity to argue with the judge about the applicability of your points and, where appropriate, to make minor changes. Sometimes the judge will simply object to the way you have phrased certain statements and you can make them acceptable by changing a word or two or by inserting or deleting a clause. With these minor changes the judge may well agree to use the point in a manner that will still work to your advantage.

Another benefit to be gained by this conference is the opportunity to trade-off with defense counsel. On occasion you will find that the defense attorney is quite insistent that the judge include certain points which, to you, don't seem all that important. This is the time to agree with him on the condition that he is equally cooperative regarding some of your points. It is a matter of your good judgment whether such an exchange works to your benefit or not.

The most important feature of this conference is for the judge to rule on each and every one of your points. He should write on the original, or dictate to the court reporter as part of the record, his decision to grant, refuse, grant as modified, or to incorporate in his general charge, each of your points. If you do not insist on this, you could be in trouble trying to use a particular one as a basis for appeal.

Be on your guard when a judge tells you that he is going to incorporate your essential points in his general charge. Sometimes they will be so disguised that you can't even recognize them, and other times the judge will simply forget to do it. You are going to have to listen very carefully to make sure that he does what he said he would do. This is not to imply impropriety on the part of the judge—it is just that his ideas and yours may be radically different on the subject of whether your points were really touched upon in the general charge.

### Listen Intently to the Charge and Make Notes

During the Court's charge you have no other duty than to listen and make an occasional note. If, in your jurisdiction, as in Pennsylvania, the judge must summarize the facts and contentions of each side you must be sure that he does so in a balanced and equitable manner. If he leaves out something that is vital to your position, make a note to call his attention to it after he finishes.

You will also be listening to make certain that he does cover all of that routine "boilerplate." Since it is routine it always deals with fundamental matters, and because it is routine it is possible for the judge to forget some essential item such as defining "burden of proof," "negligence" or discussing "credibility of witnesses." If the judge does forget, and you also miss it, you have a very unwelcome problem on your hands. An appellate court will have no hesitancy in reversing a favorable verdict where the trial judge has committed fundamental error. This doesn't happen often but your job is to make sure it does not happen at all.

Finally, you must be attentive to ascertain whether, in fact, he has incorporated into his charge those various points of yours that he said would be there. You had better remember what they were and if they are not included in the charge in satisfactory manner, make a note to call this to the attention of the judge.

## Put All of Your Objections on the Record

At the end of his charge the judge will ask counsel, on the record, for any additions or corrections they may have. This is a "now or never" situation because if you keep silent you will be in a poor position to complain about the charge on appeal. Don't ever depend on that ephemeral "fundamental error" to compensate for your mistakes at this point. Most cases do not have such error and if you have not entered formal objections, on the record, they will not be considered on appeal.

At this time you must consult your notes and then take specific exception to those portions of the charge to which you object. You should also ask for correction of those parts of the charge which, while technically correct, may have been laboriously worded or somehow misleading. Third, you should again ask for a charge on those points of yours that were supposed to have been mentioned but which were not. Finally, you should seek correction or clarification of any factual statements by the judge which seem to be wrong or incomplete. Usually, you will not get very far in this regard but you, at least, have to explain why the ignored facts are important and why they should be specifically mentioned to the jury. Sometimes the judge will agree with you and will tell the jury the additional facts. Certainly, if you keep silent, the judge will never change his statement of the facts, so you have nothing to lose by bringing it up at this point.

## Should You Leave the Judge in Error?

This question should really be asked in two parts: What do you do when the error is in your favor? What do you do when the error is against you?

Certainly in the first instance you stand a good chance of winning the verdict and losing the appeal. That can be heartbreaking, especially when you have tried the case very well and it has gone in smoothly. You can't let that error stand. You must do everything in your power to convince the judge that he is wrong and to correct the charge. In this endeavor you will be enthusiastically joined by the defense attorney. Between the two of you there is a good chance that the judge will acknowledge his mistake and you will get the matter clarified.

Some lawyers will disagree with this approach. They prefer to adopt the attitude of allowing the error in the record and securing a favorable verdict. The theory is that the defendant will appeal and while that appeal is pending you can negotiate a favorable settlement. At first glance that sounds plausible, but things don't really work out that way. If, as I am assuming, the error is obvious, the defendant is going to get a new trial. He is under no great pressure to give you a favorable settlement. In addition you are going to have to invest a lot of time, and some money, in reviewing a transcript and writing an appeals brief. To what avail? When the new trial is granted you have to re-try the case and the second trial may not be quite as smooth as the first one was. I simply cannot see any real gain in this approach. If the case has been well-tried, you simply do not want an erroneous charge no matter how favorable it may be.

The second situation—where the error is against you—poses a different problem. Many lawyers will argue that you now have the best of all possible words. If the verdict is a good one, fine; if it is a bad one you now have a solid basis for appeal. They consider this situation a true gift.

At the risk of being accused of altruism, I simply do not like, and cannot recommend, your permitting serious error to remain in a case. I would rather make the objection (which, of course, is required) and then strenuously point out to the judge where and why he is wrong. I think that, at the least, you should give him a clear opportunity to correct his charge. If he refuses, then you will have done all that you can. The problem is his. But to merely take the exception and then remain silent strikes me as taking advantage to a certain degree. Certainly we all have to make several such decisions in a trial—when to speak out and when to remain silent. These decisions do not, technically, involve either legality, ethics or morality but rather a broad concept of justice—perhaps, even, a personal standard of conduct. Whatever it is, you have to make the decision. I vote against it.

### Questions of the Jury

From time to time a jury is going to send down a question to the judge. Unless it is completely irrelevant (When do we eat? Can I call home?) the judge should summon counsel, read the question, and discuss an appropriate answer. Whatever the resolution may be you must make the question, the judge's response, and your objection, if any, a part of the record.

Insofar as the answer to the question is concerned there is no objection to repeating a small portion of the charge relating to one matter of law—i.e., a definition of negligence. Where, however, the question relates to both fact and law or deals in generalities, as it often does, you dare not let the judge give a very narrow response. You should make certain that he gives a complete charge encompassing all aspects of the question. For example, if your plaintiff is a five-year-old child and the question asks for additional charge on the subject of contributory negligence, you should not let the judge define that phrase without going further and explaining the presumption against contributory negligence in a child of that age. In many such instances it would be prejudical for a judge to repeat and re-emphasize one portion of his charge without mentioning other parts of the charge that relate to the same subject. You must be prepared to argue very vigorously about this matter and to try to convince the judge to say nothing at all or to give a complete charge on the subject. Of course if the question is: "Is there any limit to the amount we can award the plaintiff?" make sure the judge says "No."

# PART III
# Settlement

# CHAPTER 14

# Some Thoughts About
# the Benefits of Settlement

The only purpose of the preparation and trial of a lawsuit is to secure a monetary award for your plaintiff. Unfortunately you soon learn that if every case is tried to verdict, the result will be that some plaintiffs receive an amount which a jury believes is adequate to compensate them for their losses and some receive nothing. Perhaps that is the way every case should be handled. It doesn't take very long, however, before the intelligent attorney begins to worry about this "all or nothing at all" approach. He realizes that most of his cases are not clear-cut in terms of liability and damages—that some are sufficiently questionable that it will be very difficult for a jury to decide in favor of a monetary award for plaintiff or a defense verdict. He knows that his clients are rarely completely right or completely wrong.

Consequently, the lawyer will begin to ponder the desirability of compromise which has to be in the mind of every person who deals with serious conflicts among people. Compromise, in a lawsuit, is a settlement. It is an ideal way to resolve the differences between the parties and to help the plaintiff; it is essential to our judicial system, and it is beneficial to the plaintiff's attorney. You would be wise to think about the fact that as a result of every settlement your client will leave your office with something in his pocket; if you try every case, some of your clients will leave penniless. In addition, with regard to its advantages to you, may I remind you that in the introduction to this book I called your attention to the fact that while you may love a trial, your partners and your wife love settlements. Trials are fun and bring fame, settlements pay the bills.

The entire concept of settlement as a compromise has been both widely praised and condemned and I'm sure you are familiar with numerous aphorisms both pro and con. To my mind the condemnation is so much talk. There can be no legitimate argument against compromise; there can be some legitimate dispute about whether a particular case should have been settled—and the answer to that can never be known. It will always be a matter for speculation.

Your decision is not whether to settle some of your cases—you must; the problem is how to arrive at a proper settlement. That is the problem I will try to help you resolve in this section of the book.

## THE SETTLEMENT LAWYER VERSUS THE TRIAL LAWYER

You will find that within the Plaintiff's Bar there are always arguments going on about whether cases should be settled or tried and the attorneys do tend to be identified as preferring one technique or the other. As with the others you also are going to develop a preference for settlement to trial or vice versa. It's an inevitable development based on your personal attitude, experience, ability and results with each mode of handling a case. However, whatever you do today does not dictate that you continue with that approach tomorrow. You can change if an examination of your results indicates that you should. Leave aside the critical remarks. We all know that the man who tries a lot of cases will have a long string of losses—and clients who are worse off for having been represented by him; in like manner the attorney who habitually settles his cases cannot do his client justice. You must survey your own practice—and attitude—to determine whether you have become one-sided in your approach to your cases. There are some legitimate comments one can make with regard to both types of attorneys—the one who tries too often and the one who settles too many cases:

1. The attorney who habitually tries his cases to verdict is a frequent loser;

2. The lawyer who consistently gets large verdicts is a person who picks and chooses his cases very carefully, tries them infrequently, and always has one eye on who the defense attorney will be;

3. The attorney who settles at any price gets just that—whatever pittance the defendant will give him;

4.    The habitual settler is habitually unprepared. Why prepare a case when you know in advance that you are going to settle it?

5.    The "trial man" is too careless of his client's interests; the "settlement lawyer" is too cautious to do his client much good.

Your job is to chart a course between these extremes.

If there is one perfect time in which all of the varied talents and skills involved in both trial and settlement are brought to fruition, it is in a settlement at trial. At this time the plaintiff's attorney has prepared, he is in the courtroom, he has seen himself and his witnesses tested by defense counsel, he has made appropriate adjustments in his appraisal of the case and, finally, he has forced the defendant to come up with an offer that satisfies him. That is the work of a good settlement lawyer at trial or a good trial lawyer who knows when to settle. Unfortunately, every case cannot wait for this propitious moment.

## SETTLEMENT IS DEPENDENT ON TRIAL

Verdicts make settlements possible. That is an axiom of trial practice. If, in your jurisdiction, the highest verdict ever returned for the type of case you are handling is $25,000.00, no defendant will pay $26,000.00. You will be limited, in appraising your case, to what others have done before you at trial. Whether you want to break through this barrier and raise the verdict range is one of the things you must decide before you think seriously of settlement. If you have the proper case, and the clients consent, then, by all means, try to do it. If you are successful, it will decidedly increase settlements for that type of case; if you fail, no great harm is done as far as future settlements are concerned.

As a rule of thumb you should settle most cases in which the liability is good and the injuries and damages are generally irrefutable. There is no advantage to a defendant in forcing you to trial in this type of case and they will want to talk settlement. More important, they have very little pressure that they can apply to make you settle. If you can control yourself and not make an exorbitant demand, the case will settle. On the other hand, if you want a large verdict this is the kind of case in which you will get it if you go to trial. Your client may be interested only in the financial considerations, but you may also be interested in enhancing your reputation, in securing new clients by the publicity that may follow a good verdict, or in establishing a higher verdict and settlement range for this type of case. These are all legitimate reasons for a trial.

There is just one word of caution: Your client must know of the risk involved. Make him sign a document acknowledging the offer, admitting his awareness of the dangers and hazards involved, and agreeing to a trial of the lawsuit. Even excellent cases are sometimes lost and there should be no need for client-complaint after the verdict.

Another type of case that settles easily is the one in which the liability may not be very strong—just enough to get you past a non-suit and to a jury—but the injuries are severe and the losses substantial. In this situation the defendant must recognize that since the jury is certain to get the case their normal sympathy for a badly-injured plaintiff will lead them to find in his favor. It is in these situations that we often find the "runaway" verdict—one the defendant never expected. Most defendants would rather not take the chance; but before they come up with their final offer you can expect several earlier proposals, and they will belabor you mightily with caustic comments about your proof on liability. Most of these cases will not settle until the day of trial or, possibly, during that period between pre-trial and trial.

The "gray" area is composed of that very large number of cases in which liability is not clear, the extent of the injuries and their causation is in dispute, and the amount of the plaintiff's damages or losses is not great. These are the cases that make up the bulk of our trials. They can be settled if you are diligent, patient and skilled at the art of settlement. It is in this area that outside influences come to bear—your personal relations with the defendant company and defense attorney, the general policy of the defendant, the attitude of the claims manager, the time of the year (many companies like to try to clear their books at year's end), the general economic situation, and the kind of verdicts the current jury panel is returning. Some of these things are beyond your control, but many are not.

If you really want to settle a case of this kind, it can be done, but if you are going to go to trial, it will be this type of case you will most often bring to the courtroom. Your decision should be based on an appraisal of just how strong your case is. If the witnesses are knowledgeable and make a good impression—even though their testimony will be contested—try it. If the plaintiff is weak or your doctor cannot give you a good definite opinion on causation, settle it. Where the injury is clear, though not a disabling type, you might consider trying the case; where you have a strong suspicion of malingering on the part of your plaintiff, you will naturally lean toward settlement.

The case that most assuredly will not settle—except for nuisance value—is the one in which all of the liability facts are in dispute and the injury is minor. Where is the incentive for the defendant to make an offer? There is none. He has everything to gain and nothing to lose by forcing you to trial. My only question is—why are you handling this case? It had an uncertain past and has no future. If it is one of those cases that looked reasonable at the beginning, but faded after investigation and discovery, you have no choice but to try it. Chalk one up to experience and do your best to avoid this kind of case in the future.

## SETTLEMENT IS HARD WORK TOO

There are many long hours ahead of you between the time you open a file to begin its study for the purpose of determining your demand and the time you close that file with a check in your hand.

It is well to remember that up to the moment of trial the defendant is really not under any compulsion to settle with you. There are no court-supervised time limitations regarding settlement. If you want the case settled, all of the impetus must come from you.

There are many chores that must be constantly attended to if you are to effect a settlement:

(1)    You are the one who has to initiate the negotiations;

(2)    You are the one to make the telephone calls and the seemingly endless follow-up calls;

(3)    You have to collect the bills and medical reports and send them to the defendant;

(4)    You must keep pressuring your local claims people to put pressure on that faceless, anonymous individual in the home office whose decision is holding up the settlement;

(5)    You have to try to satisfy that person with wage records, tax returns, death certificates, and other documents; and

(6)    You must keep your client informed with what you are trying to accomplish.

This work cannot be done quickly because there are too many people involved. If your case has any substantial value, it will have to go beyond an adjuster or supervisor. Your demand will be reviewed by a committee or the claims manager. If the demand is beyond their authority, the file has to go to the home office. There it is sure to get lost—at least once.

Merely getting the attention of the local people is job enough. The average insurance adjuster carries a back-breaking case load. He has a difficult time keeping abreast of his cases. Yet, you must force him to single out your case for his attention and to negotiate with you. That takes patience, but it brings results.

The settlement process is very hard work. Insurance companies are not in the business of giving away money—they have to be convinced that they should pay you anything. Then the individual persons want their files protected by demanding documentary proof concerning the various elements of your claim.

## SETTLEMENT—THE LIFE BLOOD OF YOUR PRACTICE

The Plaintiff's attorney would starve if it were not for settlements. You will not try to verdict six cases per year on the average and most of those will not be cases of great value. The variables, consisting of the number of cases you have, the number of trial weeks your court has scheduled, the availability of defense counsel and the number of unavoidable continuances, all militate against your trying many cases to conclusion. Even of those six cases you may find that two of them result in a defense verdict. (If there are more than that, you had better re-examine the kind of cases you are trying or your courtroom tactics.)

The net result is that if you are going to serve your clients and earn a living for yourself, it must be through settlements. As a guess, and I have seen no statistics on the subject, settlements will account for 60 percent of your total fees and 80 percent of the number of cases you close in a year. Since your settlements are so obviously important, vital, even—it behooves you to handle them with the greatest care and to get the last penny out of each case.

## A FEW STATISTICS

It seems to me that anyone who examines the statistical data regarding the number of cases tried or settled has to be impressed by the vast preponderance of the settlements. A few facts can resolve a lot of argument. Let me just mention some statistics from this area which you might use as a guide for yourself, your fellow lawyers and your court.

To place things in perspective, Allegheny County, Pennsylvania, is the ninth largest county in the United States, with a population of about 1,600,000 people. We have a magnificent Bench composed of judges who are generally in the 50-60 age category. Many are former trial lawyers. They are a hard-working, aggressive group of men as evidenced by the fact that the Civil Division disposed of 3,345 cases which were "at issue" in 1972; 3,530 such cases in 1973; 3,338 in 1974 and 3,426 in 1975. It is interesting to note that the disposition time from the date of filing of a lawsuit to the date it is closed has decreased from 15.5 months in 1972 to 13.9 months in 1974 and 13.5 months in 1975.

A more accurate measure is the disposition time measured from the date a case is placed "at issue." After a case is filed the attorneys must place it "at issue" when they believe it is ready for conciliation and trial. The minimum time in which to do this is 60 days after the date of service of the complaint. Our records reveal that from the issue date to the closing date the elapsed time has decreased from 10.9 months in 1972 to 9.9 months in 1973 and 9.4 months in 1974, but up to 10.2 months in 1975. The cases move quickly. I have had cases appear on a trial list within six months of the filing date and have had to ask for a continuance because my plaintiff had not completed his medical treatment and the doctors could not give me a firm prognosis.

The key to the success of our courts is settlement, which they stress at every stage of a lawsuit. Six times a year the entire Civil Division devotes a week to "mass conciliation" in which every judge will take a group of cases and work with the lawyers to try to settle them. Twenty-five percent of our cases are settled at these conciliation hearings. In addition we have two judges routinely assigned as Calendar Control Judges. They run the trial list. Every single case that appears on the trial list is conciliated by one of these judges before the attorneys are permitted to select a jury. Finally, when a case is sent out to a courtroom, the first duty of the trial judge is to get the attorneys into his chambers and try to settle the case. He will continue that effort throughout the trial. This system works.

Let's look at a few statistics relating solely to trespass cases. On December 31, 1972, there were 3,376 trespass cases pending in our Common Pleas Court. How many were tried to verdict during the year 1973? Answer: a paltry 163. As a matter of curiosity there were 96 plaintiffs' verdicts and 67 defense verdicts. The ratio is about 3 plaintiffs' verdicts out of every 5 cases tried. And settlements? Without court assistance there were 1,018; there were 698 of them at the pre-trial conciliation conferences; the calendar control judges settled 523; the trial judges 220, and 183 more were reported settled to the Assignment Room or the Calendar Division at some other stage of proceeding. The total of these settlements is 2,642. The ratio of settlements to verdicts is 16 to 1.

In the year 1974, the figures are about the same. There were 171 cases tried to verdict, only 8 more than the previous year. The plaintiffs fared slightly better, securing 64 percent of the verdicts. The actual figures were 109 plaintiffs' verdicts and 62 defense verdicts. Once again the settlements far outstripped the verdicts. There were 969 trespass cases settled without court help; 479 in pre-trial conciliation; the calendar control judges managed to settle 392 cases from the trial lists; the trial judges settled 191 cases during trial; and, finally, 155 cases were reported settled to the Assignment Room or the Calendar Control Division. The total settlements amounted to 2,186 cases. The ratio of settlements to verdicts is about 13 to 1.

Finally, in the year 1975 there were only 146 cases tried to verdict by a jury and of these plaintiffs' verdicts numbered only 86, or 59 percent of the total. It would appear that the number of plaintiffs' verdicts went down about 5 percent from the previous year. Settlement figures, restricted to the categories previously mentioned, show that 2223 cases were settled; of these 303 were settled by Trial Judges; 526 were settled by Calendar Control Judges; 347 at Pretrial Conciliation Conferences; 932 without Court help; and 115 were reported settled to the Assignment Room or Calendar Control Division. The ratio runs about 15 to 1.

There is no reason to believe that your jurisdiction is significantly different from mine. The statistics reveal that settlements overwhelmingly outnumber verdicts. The lesson for you and for me—indeed for every plaintiff's lawyer—is that we should develop our talent at settlements to the highest degree possible. It should not be treated in the cursory, offhanded manner that it frequently is. In this connection one final statistic might be mentioned. A study of the median verdict and the median settlement would show the following:

### AMOUNTS INVOLVED IN TRESPASS CASES

|                   | 1972       | 1973       | 1974       | 1975       |
|-------------------|------------|------------|------------|------------|
| Median Verdict    | $6,000.00  | $5,600.00  | $5,000.00  | $6,000.00  |
| Median Settlement | $3,500.00  | $3.750.00  | $4,500.00  | $5,500.00  |

The ordinary verdict seemed to be going down for awhile, and has now gone up while settlement values are steadily going up. This strikes me as a curiosity which I cannot explain. Neither can the Court. At the same time, the extremely high awards in both settlements and verdicts are steadily rising.

## SETTLEMENTS DEPEND ON VERDICTS

It might be logical to inquire why, if settlements are so numerous and obviously important, one must know so much about trials. The reason is crystal clear and beyond argument—all settlements depend on success at trial. If a defendant knows that you cannot try a case well, there will be no satisfactory settlement. If you cannot, or will not, try a lawsuit when necessary, you will never get a good settlement.

Finally, in general, the highest verdict in your area for a specific type of case will establish the outer limits of your settlement possibilities. Do not be deceived by the "median" figures I have cited. They are interesting, but encompass every type of trespass case and thus lose applicability in your specific instance. You must analyze your case carefully, find a similar one that went to verdict and then let that amount guide you in setting a settlement value on your case. As I mentioned earlier, it is an axiom of trial practice that verdicts, small in number though they may be, make settlements possible.

# CHAPTER 15

# Handling the Client

It frequently happens that the biggest problem in settlement is not in determining the proper settlement figure, or in getting that sum from the defendant—it is in getting your client to agree to that amount. The client can cause you more difficulties than all of the claim adjusters, supervisors, and managers combined. There is one thing of which you can be certain—your client will never underestimate the value of his case. Your principal chore will be to bring him down, not raise him up.

## YOU—NOT THE CLIENT—ARE THE EXPERT

If your client gives you trouble regarding your recommendation of a settlement figure, it is proper to ask diplomatically how many cases he has settled and for how many years he has been involved in settlement negotiations. There is no sense in procrastinating on this matter—you—not the client—are the expert!

You have to explain that a settlement involves just as many variables as a trial and each of these requires a judgment decision for proper analysis. The client wouldn't begin to tell you how to cross-examine a witness—or whether to do so at all; in the same way he is in a poor position to evaluate the medical data that you have and to balance it against the liability in the case. His appraisal of the witnesses is that they are all friends named Joe, Bill and Tom—your appraisal is that they are witnesses who are fair, poor and terrible. Thus you have to impress him with the fact that settlement involves a variety of factors and that it is a part of your work which requires its own expertise; that you have done this for years in many cases; and that he has neither the experience nor the talent to determine whether the settlement is proper or not. With this in mind, he will, hopefully, accept your recommendation.

## UNHAPPILY, EVERYONE UNDERSTANDS MONEY

The problem lawyers have is that we are dealing with our clients in terms of money—dollar bills—and everyone understands that. We can envy the medical doctors who (1) rarely have to tell their patients anything and (2) when they do, can use technical words and Latin phrases that leave the patient impressed but just as ignorant as he was before he asked the question. We don't have that "out." Would that we did.

To compound the problem every client suffers from what I call the "cash register syndrome"—every time they feel a twinge of pain, a cash register rings in their minds. When the time comes to discuss settlement they have managed to ring up quite a bit of money. Oddly the gross total always manages to be a nice round figure—like $50,000.00 or $85,000.00. These amounts just seem to have a pleasant sound to them. Clients will pull them "out of the blue" so to speak just because they give one a warm, happy, contented feeling. I have never had a client who presented me with a settlement figure of $11,218.00 or $43,785.57. Apparently neither sum is euphonious as one speaks it.

The best way to bring this type of client down to earth is to ask him to justify the figure. Tell him to explain to you why anyone would pay him such a sum in settlement of his case. He can't do it. When he comes up with a few ideas they will nearly always be vague and general and it is usually simple to pick them apart. At this point he begins to realize that the matter is not quite as easy as he thought it was.

## EXPLAIN THE CASE TO YOUR CLIENT

It is likely that, except for the first time you met him, you have not had a long conversation with your client regarding all of the facets of his case. Since that first meeting your encounters have been for a specific purpose—to answer interrogatories or to prepare for a deposition. Now is the time to go over the entire case with him and to take plenty of time in doing it. Just be sure of one thing—that his wife is there. There is no point in going over the case without the spouse, or the parents if a young adult is involved. If you don't talk with them, then when the client returns home he will be bombarded with questions he cannot answer and opinions he cannot rebut. By getting everyone together in your office at one time you have the opportunity to hear nearly every statement and argument that will be made and to answer and explain to the satisfaction of everyone. In this way a lot of argument and misunderstanding is avoided.

Four areas that you ought to include in your talk with the family are:

1. The liability side of the case;

2. The medical situation;

3. The witnesses; and

4. The jury verdicts and attitudes.

Let us consider these separately:

### 1. Liability Problems

The chances are that your client believes he ought to recover solely because he was in an accident. To be sure, he will have some concept of fault but he will have convinced himself long ago that the defendant was entirely responsible for what happened. It is now your duty to explain to him all that you have learned about the happening of the accident from your investigation and discovery techniques. For the first time your client will realize that things are not quite as one-sided as he has hitherto believed. He has always glossed over unpleasant details, when he has known of them, but now he has to realize that those details must alter his thinking quite substantially.

Second you have to tell him about the applicable law. This is a complete mystery to him. He will be very interested, but when you explain certain aspects of it he may be quite indignant. This is when you're going to hear angry comments that "The law is an ass," or "That's absurd." Take the time to explain why the law is framed in the manner it is, but if he persists you simply must tell him that you can't fight it—at least not on this day—and that you and he are stuck with the way things are, not as you might wish they were. Try to give him a good basic understanding of the applicable law and the manner in which it applies to his case.

### 2. The Analysis of the Medical Data

This is another area in which the average client is ignorant and worried. He doesn't know in detail what was done to him, or why, and he is deeply concerned that there may be some future complications. Explain the medical procedures as best you can, but be very careful about assuring him that his concern about future problems is imaginary or unnecessary. That is neither your job nor your duty. The most that you can say is that the prognosis of the doctors is so-and-so, that this is what they will testify to, that it is only an opinion and that it must be accepted by him, for settlement purposes, just as the jury must accept it at trial time. Tell him that if the doctors are wrong there is nothing you can do about it, but that at this moment you can only take their word and hope that they are correct.

Even if your client does not agree with the doctors or is not convinced that they are right, he will appreciate the fact that you and he have nothing else to rely on.

### 3.  Witness Problems

Now you are getting into an area where the client can understand you easily. He can appreciate the problem in a medical malpractice case, for example, in which you have only one expert witness and the defendant plans to call three such persons. He can realize the implication of the fact that his witnesses are all immediate members of his family whose bias is obvious and the defendant's witnesses are strangers. He knows what you mean when you tell him that Joe Jones, a key witness, is not very smart, is quite unsure of himself, and will probably be tongue-tied on the witness stand.

These things will mean more to your client than anything else you tell him because the judgments involved are the kind he makes every day. He knows that some people are knowledgeable while others have empty heads. Prejudice and bias are commonplace concepts to him. He will respect a signed statement of a witness over the verbal comments of others. Judgments based on the education, experience, training, responsibility, authority and occupation of a witness are familiar to him. But he will not have really thought about these facts until you take the time to go over them with him and point out that they have an effect upon your thoughts regarding settlement.

### 4.  Jury Verdicts and Attitudes

Here again you deal with a subject that the client can easily comprehend. If he thinks his case is worth $25,000.00 and you tell him that the highest verdict in your jurisdiction was $10,000.00 for a similar case— that statement has meaning to him. He knows that he has overestimated the value of his claim. You must make him realize that the jurors will not view the case in the same subjective manner that he does.

To illustrate this point you might ask him what amount of money he thinks his sister would award if she were on the jury and the plaintiff was his neighbor. Would she return the kind of verdict that he is thinking about? This might elicit some amusing comments about his sister, but the client will know what you are driving at.

Another topic that should be discussed is the attitude the jurors may take with regard to the wealth, position or notoriety of the plaintiff. A rich plaintiff can suffer as much as a poor one, but he does not evoke the same kind of sympathy from a jury because of his wealth. A young man who flaunts the fact that he is a hippie and is not about to change will antagonize some jurors and may get a lower verdict than his collegiate brother. These factors affect settlement and the plaintiff should be apprised of that fact.

The type of defendant will also influence settlement. Where a parishoner sues his church, despite the fact that there is a valid cause of action, the recovery may be lower than if the defendant is a business corporation. By how much must you adjust your demand when a minister or nun is the defendant? They may be the worst drivers in the world, but no jury will return an objective verdict against them. The same consideration applies where you have brother suing brother or one friend trying to recover against another. These are legitimate and difficult factors affecting a jury's attitude which your client must understand when the two of you discuss settlement.

## EXPLAIN THE ADVANTAGES OF SETTLEMENT

There is no denying that "a bird in the hand is worth two in the bush." A settlement insures the fact that your client will get some reasonable compensation. If he elects to go to trial he stands a chance of getting nothing or less than the offer. The more dependent your client is on a successful conclusion of his case, the more strongly you should urge him to settle. If he and his family are in serious need of money, they are certainly in no position to take a chance on a trial when you have a respectable offer to submit to them. Insist on this especially when the husband and father (and it is usually he) talks pretentiously about "rolling the dice." You should put a stop to that nonsense in a hurry.

If your client does not urgently need the settlement, you can be a little more lenient about his willingness to reject an offer. It is always possible that your appraisal of the case is too low and if the client feels strongly that he wants the case tried, then accommodate him.

A second advantage to settlement is that the money is paid forthwith while your anticipated trial date may be many months away. It is possible that your client could use that money now for college, marriage or a present business opportunity. This is entitled to some weight. You should tell your client that in addition to the fact that the trial date is some months into the future there is the possible problem of an appeal, should there be judicial error, and that this will delay recovery for possibly a year or more. With these facts before him the client may well agree that a settlement now is in his best interest.

Third, you must mention the routine hazards of every trial—the low verdict and the defense verdict. It is no reflection on yourself to bring up this subject and you are duty bound to tell the client that it is a potential reality. It is in every case. Most clients don't like to face up to this reality just as they prefer to ignore all of life's unpleasant aspects. The "it can't happen to me" syndrome is strong in all of us. But someone has to be the devil's advocate and that someone is the attorney.

If the client is made aware of, and thoroughly understands, the normal risks of a trial and still wants to proceed, then all is well, but he must never be placed in the position of authorizing you to try the case when he has no definite knowledge of the risks involved. Each of us would go after a doctor quickly if he failed to advise his patient of the risks, hazards and dangers of an operation—and I don't mean the obvious danger of dying. There are many hazards in an operation that a patient does not know as a matter of ordinary experience or common sense and these must be explained to him by the physician. The doctrine of "Informed Consent" applies as much to us as it does to the medical profession.

Another reason that we must go into this matter is so that we can avoid, or diminish, the severe disappointment and, sometimes, bitter recriminations that follow a poor verdict. It is at times like this that we re-learn the fact that our clients are very human. They will blithely reject an offer, take their case to trial in the cheerful expectation that they will secure much more in a verdict and then, when they end up with nothing, will display ill will and resentment that sometimes approaches malevolence toward the lawyer. You must face the incontrovertible fact that the vast majority of the people of this world will not accept responsibility for their own actions and decisions.

So, protect yourself. Prepare a short statement that will set forth the fact that you and the client have discussed the case in detail, that a settlement offer has been made by the defendant, that its acceptance has been recommended by you, that the client rejects the offer with full awareness of the fact that a trial may result in less than the offer, or a defense verdict, and that you are directed to proceed with the trial. Something along this line will adequately safeguard your interests if a client is unhappy with the results of a trial.

## RECOMMEND A SETTLEMENT RANGE

Under the best of circumstances it is difficult to evaluate a case, but why compound the problem by putting a precise figure on a claim when you are discussing it with your client? If you tell him that his case is worth $13,500.00 and an offer of $11,750.00 is made, the first reaction of the client is to reject it for no other reason than that it is less than you told him the case was worth. As a result of your specificity the client has thought of, hoped for, and dreamed of receiving exactly $13,500.00. He might reluctantly acknowledge that a variation of a few hundred dollars was contemplated by him but at no time did he consider a diminution of $1,750.00. Most likely the client will reject this offer no matter how strongly you argue in favor of it.

In addition to creating problems of this kind there is no particular value in putting a definite figure on a case. You know that settlement is a negotiating process, that it is a subjective matter to a great extent, that there are numerous variables involved in appraising the case, and that it is impossible to put a value on a lawsuit as one might put a price on a can of beans. There is a little more involved than computing the cost of materials, of production, of transportation and then adding a fixed percentage for the profit margin. You simply cannot go through your files, attach a money label to each of them, and then go out and sell them to the defendants—this one for $7,754.95, another for $47,899.99 and a third for an equally definite amount. It can't be done. Spare yourself this difficulty by avoiding the absolute monetary figure and speak, instead, of a settlement range.

When you appraise a case as having a value of "about $15,000—$17,500" you accomplish two things vis - a -vis your client: first, you make him aware that the whole matter is judgmental, non-specific, and subject to adjustment via the negotiating process; second, although you are giving him a pretty definite idea of the value of the case, you are not binding either him or yourself to some exact, and unattainable, goal.

As a result of this kind of approach the client is psychologically attuned to the fact that any offer in the settlement range is acceptable, though, naturally, you will strive to go above it. At the same time, in my hypothetical example, neither you nor he will be inclined to reject an offer of $14,750.00. By talking and thinking in terms of a "value range" the necessary flexibility is built into your dealings with your client and your negotiations with the defendant. This flexibility will save you untold frustrations and both ulcers and headaches.

## GET YOUR CLIENT'S CONSENT—AND WRITE IT DOWN

Once you have arrived at a settlement range that is satisfactory to your client, call in your secretary, dictate a brief memo, and have your client sign it. When he leaves your office you are going to begin negotiations with the defense attorney or the insurance personnel and you must do so with the firm belief that your client will stand by your agreement. Unfortunately that is not always true.

When your client leaves your office he is still thinking about your conversation and the settlement range you have agreed upon. As the days go by he will continue to think upon this subject—now feeling that the range is too low; then changing his mind, deciding that it is acceptable. Sometimes he will decide that he made a mistake. Then the fun begins—especially if you are just about to conclude the settlement. The client wants more money, but the insurance company wants to hold you to your demand or the negotiated figure. This can be embarrassing. It doesn't help much to argue with your client that you and he agreed upon a settlement range and that you then proceeded to negotiate on the assumption that he would stand by that agreement. The client will deny that he committed himself, will claim that he did not understand, and will use every tactic and technique that he knows of to get out of the settlement.

That is when your memo, with his signature affixed, becomes important. When you show it to him most of his arguments will evaporate and he will become much more tractable. The average layman is afraid of a written document that contains his signature. The result will be that you can get him settled down, go back over the case with him, convince him that his original decision was a good one, and then get the matter concluded.

With regard to that latter point — concluding the matter — since you are aware that trouble is brewing when the client calls to renege on your agreement, try to have a release available when he comes to your office to discuss the subject. After he agrees that his original decision was sound, make him sign the release then and there. In that way there will be no repetition of the previous conduct.

## THE OBSTINATE CLIENT

From time to time we all have a client who insists on an impossible settlement figure, irrespective of our advice, and will not budge from that preconceived and misconceived evaluation despite all of our reasoning, exhortation and threats. What is to be done with him? You could withdraw from the case. That may assuage your anger but someone else will still have to handle the client. You could just go ahead and try the case, but that may cost you a great deal in time and expenses that you cannot afford. You could also just let the file sit in a drawer and do nothing and that leads to malpractice actions—against you. Don't do any of these things. There is a short prayer which I have seen on the walls of many harassed public officials, judges, doctors and attorneys which is apropos here:

> "God, grant me the serenity to accept
> the things I cannot change;
> the Courage to change the things I can;
> and the Wisdom to know the difference."

This type of client falls in the category of "things that you can change" if you have the courage. Look upon such clients as presenting you with a fine challenge to your abilities as a lawyer, to your patience (which may be short, and thus needs to be occasionally challenged), and to your duty to a person who needs help. These clients do need help—all that you can give. Don't abandon them, don't try their lawsuits with an "I don't care" attitude, but don't spend a lot of money on their cases. Work with them.

Take a moment to consider the clients and their point of view. Usually they are persons of modest means; nearly always they are inexperienced and unsophisticated in complicated business matters; frequently they are relatively uneducated; and always they believe that this case represents their one big chance to get a substantial amount of money. Here is a recurring example:

A case has a settlement value of about $25,000.00 to $30,000.00 and will ultimately settle for that amount. Yet, you are forced to go to a pretrial conciliation and, with a straight face, make a demand of $65,000.00. The client may also caution you not to vary from that figure! Probably the offer will be low and the client will return home somewhat chastened and sobered by this turn of events. It's reasonably certain that the defense attorneys, who may know you well, sensed what was happening and they simply closed the door on settlement, gently but firmly, at this time.

Prior to the pretrial, you have conferred on three occasions with this client to try to get him to face reality. At each meeting, your arguments are rebutted by the client. He produces newspaper clippings about high verdicts, cites television news stories concerning giant settlements and tells you stories of various persons he knew whose damages were less than his and whose awards were higher than his demand.

Have you been through this?

There is nothing to do but to bite your tongue, be patient and constantly reason with the client. Sometimes the offer, as in this case, will have a sobering effect. In another case it will be helpful to compute your expenses to date and the anticipated costs of trial, ask the client to pay the current expenses now and to begin promptly to make arrangements to get the money needed to cover the future expenses. The realization of the amount of money that they will have to pay will be a shock to most clients and will make them revise their attitude toward settlement. But in every case you have to call the client back to your office time after time, show medical reports and witnesses' statements, explain the law, and constantly chip away at his adamant attitude. If your conduct justifies the title "Advocate," you will be successful.

## DISCUSSION AND PATIENCE ARE THE
## KEYS TO SETTLEMENT

These are the best tools you have when trying to work out a settlement range with your client. He will come to your office with vague ideas about the value of his case and with the hope that he may strike the pot of gold at the end of the rainbow. You must be sympathetic and explain the realities of the situation to him. With some tact and patience you can help both him and his spouse to understand the basis for your settlement recommendation and to accept it. There is no other way, and it is hard work.

# CHAPTER 16

# When to Settle and at What Figure

The key to settlement lies in the answer to these two, seemingly innocuous, questions: When should I undertake settlement negotiations? What is my settlement figure?

Neither question lends itself to a simple answer. The only solution lies in a good analysis of the case, awareness of community standards in this field, willingness to keep pressure on the claims personnel of the insurance company—a matter of stamina, really—and your acumen at the "give and take" of bargaining.

Experience certainly plays a role in this process, but curiously it can be a hindrance to settlement in certain respects. Experience comes with age, but I've also found that older, experienced attorneys tend to become a little jaded, somewhat weary of the time involved, and sometimes rather irascible. As a result of their reliance on their experience, they are inclined to appraise a case quickly and submit a demand on a "take it or leave it" basis. That's a good way to ruin settlement negotiations. As an amusing corollary to this situation you may have noticed how the older lawyer will turn the case over to a younger man with explicit instructions (erroneous) to try it unless the insurance company pays the demand (unrealistic) which he previously submitted. This frequently happens, much to the chagrin of the younger attorney who is now responsible for a case he cannot settle and really hates to try.

On the supposition that you want to settle some of your cases and are willing to take the time to do whatever is necessary to achieve that goal, the following pages contain some general guidelines that will help.

## THERE IS A RIGHT TIME FOR SETTLEMENT

The "right time" to commence settlement negotiations is that day when you can honestly say that your file is complete and that you know your case. It will be the date on which you have completed your investigation, concluded all of the discovery you intend to invoke, have received final medical reports on your client's condition and have documentary support for your damages and losses. Then you are in a position to analyze, evaluate and talk.

Until that time, you will be unprepared to enter into settlement negotiations except in rare instances.

For example, if the insurance company is willing to concede liability for settlement purposes, then you might begin negotiations without completing investigation and discovery. However, if they raise even one liability issue, you had better resolve that point rather than let it linger like the proverbial thorn in your side. Its existence as an area of dispute will constantly confront you during the settlement talks.

Another illustration would be the case in which the defendant company concedes both liability and damages. They are rare, but they do happen—where you have a death case as a result of an airplane crash, for example, caused by obvious pilot error, and the damages are pretty well fixed; or where a building collapses and it becomes quickly apparent that the poured concrete had a lot of sand in it but very little cement. In these cases your argument revolves around the sole question of "how much," and your settlement negotiations can begin as soon as you can dial the insurance company and make contact with the man who is handling the claim.

In the main, however, you are going to have to do all of the preparatory work just as though the case was going to go to trial. A good settlement is the result of hard work—not a way around it. When the preliminary work is done well—then, on that date, it is time to talk settlement.

### Make Sure Your File Is Complete

You must have a complete file in order to conduct effective settlement negotiations. The defendant is going to want documentary proof of every aspect of your claim. Accordingly, you might as well have it all together and make copies for the insurance company before you begin to talk with them. This will normally include hospital and doctor bills and reports; income tax returns or a letter from the employer regarding employment, job classification, rate of pay and time lost; car repair and rental bills, if any; and other similar items of proof of loss or damage. It may be that as the negotiations proceed they will want to see photographs, witnesses' statements, physical evidence, and the like. You will have to decide, as you go along, on the merits of giving them these things, but certainly they should be available if needed. I think that the reason so many cases are settled at the time of Pretrial is because of the fact that it is the earliest date at which all parties finally have a complete file. Up to that point their respective files are very much incomplete. Accordingly, if you are trying to secure a prompt settlement, make certain that you have everything that you—and the insurance company—are going to need to be able to talk about the case intelligently.

### Know Your Case Thoroughly

It stands to reason that if you are going to argue successfully with a claims man, you must know your case thoroughly, both its strengths and weaknesses. Insurance people have usually been around for some time; they have a large caseload, and they are negotiating with someone nearly every day. Ordinarily, you are not in that position, so that the insurance adjustor or supervisor begins the process one step ahead of you in terms of experience. He can detect bluff, puffing, exaggeration, and uncertainty rather quickly. He won't be taken in by the former and he will take advantage of the latter. It is far better for you to know your case so well that you can deal with him with an attitude of confidence, an attitude founded on clear and definite knowledge of your case. You may well find that it is he who has failed to do his homework, and that he cannot disparage or reasonably challenge your position, with the result that you force him to go back to his file to re-examine it and make a decided re-evaluation of your case.

For example, in a medical malpractice case I changed my theory of liability, but the claims manager would not take me seriously. When we arrived at the Pretrial I explained my theory of liability to him (again) and the judge, showed them my documentary proof, and resubmitted my demand. I was told by the claims manager's assistant that when he returned to his office he called out "Get the Home Office on the phone, we have a new lawsuit on our hands." It was a new lawsuit because the claims manager refused to take the time to review and study the information I had previously given him. When you hear your adversary begin to make statements like "I didn't know that," or "Will you send me proof of that fact," then you know that you have him on the run and are forcing him to an "agonizing reappraisal" which can only inure to your benefit. That is not going to happen unless you know your case and are prepared to challenge his statements and to back up your own with proof.

Just as your case has its strengths so it also has its weaknesses. Those weaknesses will have to be studied, evaluated, and be reflected in the demand you make. There is no point in making a demand based on a theory of clear liability when, in point of fact, liability is very clouded. You won't be able to judge this matter unless you have reviewed your case carefully and extensively, know the facts, and then analyze the areas in which you are going to have problems and the extent of those problems.

To repeat, thorough understanding of your case is essential to settlement negotiations.

## IN YOUR COMMUNITY, WHAT IS THE VERDICT RANGE

## FOR THIS TYPE OF CASE?

Verdicts are the standards by which settlements are measured. In general, the highest verdict for a particular type of case in your area will be the maximum you can expect as a settlement. Of course you have to be careful that the verdict is not some kind of aberration, that the case was similar to yours, and that conditions in your community are about the same as they were at the time of the verdict. If the verdict was returned five years ago, it hardly represents a current standard and can be disregarded. It behooves you, therefore, to make inquiry of court personnel or to search the records to find a representative case that will act as a guide to you in your settlement negotiations.

If court sources are unavailing, you must turn to your fellow lawyers to gain their knowledge regarding verdicts in your type of case and their experience with regard to settlement. Be sure to talk to several of them to get an idea of a settlement area because any one or two of them may have a distorted view—either too high or too low—depending on the number of times they have handled the type of case you have and their own ability. From this kind of a study you can get a fair idea of the verdict range for the case and the settlement values which seem to be representative in your area.

### Look at Texts Dealing with Settlements

Where you have a novel case, where there have been no verdicts in similar cases in your area, and where your lawyer friends turn out to have little help to offer, do not proceed on a "hit and miss" basis. Instead, go to the library and look up some of the numerous texts, periodicals and services which deal with the subject. There are several of them that will give you some basis for arriving at a settlement figure. The monthly News Letter of the Association of Trial Lawyers of America always lists some verdicts and settlements—though usually these are extraordinary awards for very serious cases. Nonetheless, they are a help. Another service which can be helpful is the Personal Injury Valuation Handbooks published by Jury Verdict Research Inc., Caxton Building, Cleveland, Ohio 44115. This is a multi-volume set which categorizes cases in every way possible, gives you an estimate of your chances of success, and provides settlement figures and verdict awards. These and other books will provide you with some information, which is far better than working in complete ignorance. They do have their drawbacks in that they usually contain data from all over the United States which really doesn't help a great deal for your problem in your community; second, the ranges they give are often so broad as to have little specific value (it is of some help, but not much, to know that a settlement range is $6,000 to $20,000); and finally the details of liability and injury are so brief that it is difficult to compare cases. Nonetheless, these valuations do give you a documented and definite place to start. I encourage their use for that reason.

### Try One of the "Gadgets" Available

If you have been to any lawyers' convention, especially one of the American Trial Lawyers Association groups, you will have seen numerous devices on display in the nature of discs, modified slide rules, and other similar objects, designed to help you arrive at a settlement figure. The merit of these gadgets is that they force you to organize your thoughts by compiling a list of damages and losses, itemizing your injuries, reviewing Life Expectancy Tables, and thinking about pain and suffering, the value of a partial disability, or a loss of consortium.

These devices lose some of their practical value, however, because invariably they require you to insert your own figure for an intangible such as pain and suffering, partial disability, or a loss of consortium. No mathematical equation exists to help you with these matters. As a result, I don't see any real merit in using these objects and regard them as more of a nuisance than a help. Nevertheless, if they help you, by all means, use them. Use any tool that will help you to itemize in detail all of your damages and losses and that will assist you in evaluating them. I would recommend that you take three or four cases to an experienced friend of yours, get an appraisal from him, and then try out your settlement device to see how close it comes to that figure. If it works for you, keep using it.

### The Multiplication Approach

Many attorneys—and a few insurance companies—will add up all of the items of loss and then, using some arbitrary multiplicand (usually 3, 5 or 7) will arrive at a settlement figure. (I am curious why the multiplicand is always an odd number. It must have some psychological significance.) If your specials amount to $1,500, the settlement figure is $4,500 and so forth. "Five times specials" is commonly heard in my area. At the very least, it is a way to begin. This is what I refer to as a "street figure"—the kind you give to someone when you are rushing from your office to the courthouse and he stops you to ask for a quick evaluation of his case. It certainly has little validity. Three simple examples will illustrate the foolishness of multiplying specials:

1. Clear liability, a simple fracture of the arm, closed reduction, good recovery, medical specials of $150. This case is worth a great deal more than $450 or $750 (multiplication of 3 or 5).

2. Same case except the injured party earns $3,000 per month and loses one month's wages. Total specials $3,150. Do you think for one minute, one second, that any claims manager in his right mind, would authorize $9,450 or $15,750 to settle that case? Yet, the multiplication is the same in both cases.

3. Consider a good liability case with a severe cervical sprain in which the doctor orders physical therapy, a cervical collar, and medication, but finally tells the plaintiff to suffer with the pain, using the collar and medication as needed. The injury lingers for eighteen months with only check-up visits to the doctor. It finally clears up. Specials: doctor—$65; physical therapy—$250; collar—$25; medicine—$25. Total: $365. You may have a $5,000 case on your hands, but the multiplication technique says it's worth only $1,095 or $1,825.

Don't use this simplistic approach. In some cases it may be all right as a place of beginning, as a very general rule of thumb. Actually, it's worth next to nothing. If a good lawyer uses this method to appraise your case, he is trying to tell you in a nice way that he is too busy to really help you.

## ANALYZE THE LIABILITY

Perhaps the first question to ask yourself is whether you can win the case and what your chances are. Look at the case objectively. How strong are your witnesses? Will your plaintiff make a good appearance? Is there photographic or documentary support for their testimony? As you think about these things you should assign your case some kind of value based on 100-percent perfect. If you must deduct 30 percent because of liability problems, then if your case would be worth $10,000 with clear liability you might begin with a figure of $7,000 because of your particular liability, and so forth. This will give you one figure to work with. Naturally, you must go on and consider other matters.

Suppose, in this hypothetical case, your medical testimony will be very strong. That, in itself, would be just cause for increasing the settlement amount to $8,000. Other matters come into play here—whether the accident was a dramatic one; whether the plaintiff is a child or an 80-year-old man. If you will just analyze the case and keep making adjustments in your evaluation, you can come to a definite conclusion, arriving at a settlement figure that you can sell to the insurance company with a good deal of vigor. Your argument will be sound because you have taken into consideration the "pluses and minuses" of your case.

In going through this process you might pause for a moment to give some thought to your own personality. How objective can you be? If you are naturally exuberant and overly optimistic, you might realistically reduce your figures a little to take that fact into consideration; at the same time, advise your pessimistic brother not to cut so deeply.

There is another aspect of this analysis which requires a little thought: Suppose you have a serious case in which, realistically, you have only a 50-50 chance of a successful verdict. You have enough evidence to get past a non-suit, barely. However, the verdict range should be around $75,000 if you win. You might say that the settlement range is around $37,500. That is not necessarily true. The insurance company might well be convinced to pay you $45,000 to $50,000 to avoid the 50-50 chance that they will pay very much more in a verdict. They look upon that extra $25,000 or $30,000 as a great deal of money and don't want to take a chance on losing it. Their fear is that once you get to the jury, even with a weak case, that jury is likely to award full value in their verdict. Rather than take that risk, the insurance company will pay more than the case is theoretically worth.

Just the opposite psychology applies in the smaller case. If you have an offer of $3,500 in a case worth about $5,000, and the same chances of winning it, what is the point in not accepting the offer? If you do not, you and your client will be spending three days in trial, incurring non-reimburseable expenses for witnesses, and time lost from work for your plaintiff, and all this for a small, gross gain of $1,500. By the time the costs of trial are deducted you and your client will have lost money.

It's important to look carefully at the issue of liability and to let the possibilities of winning or losing the case have an effect upon your settlement range.

## CONSIDER THE DAMAGES

I think we would all be better off if we spent less time on liability and more time on damages. For settlement purposes, making a list of your client's financial losses is barely a beginning. You must also itemize the injuries in the case, which are frequently multiple. Each injury may have existed for a different period of time and required different treatment. For example, it often occurs in a rear-end collision that the injured plaintiff sustains a cervical sprain, a concussion, and a fracture of the arm, or clavicle. The effects of the concussion may last for a few weeks, the fracture may heal in a few months but the sprain may linger for a year. Each injury could be treated by a different doctor, an orthopedist for one and a neurologist for the other, and each may have its unique effect upon your plaintiff. Study these things carefully before you talk to any insurance man about them. Give some thought to pain and suffering and reflect on the extent of any disability that exists.

I think it would be worthwhile to make up a simple chart that would itemize the following:

1. Injuries:
   (a) Type
   (b) Severity
   (c) Length of treatment

2. Medical Expenses:
   (a) Hospital
   (b) Doctors
   (c) Medicines
   (d) Prosthetic Devices

3. Lost Wages

4. Future Expenses and Losses

5.    Degree of Disability

     (a)   Temporary
     (b)   Permanent

6.    Life Expectancy

7.    Pain and Suffering

8.    Effect on Spouse and Children
     (Loss of Consortium or Nurture)

By itemizing these various aspects of injury and loss you can get a clearer idea of the difficulties that your client went through, and thus arrive at a fairer evaluation of your case. In addition it is helpful to have all of this information before you on one sheet of paper when you are arguing with the claims man. You will know what you are talking about. The chances are that he will not make up a list like this and will not know what he is talking about. This is when you will gain a distinct advantage over him which will result in his discussing a much higher sum for settlement than he intended to. Unless stubbornness intervenes, he has no alternative.

### Some Illustrative Settlement Problems

To demonstrate further the problem of pulling together liability, damages, and other matters in the determination of a settlement figure, let us consider three examples of persons with the same injury—a simple fracture of the arm which requires a closed reduction, with casting that lasts for one month, followed by a six-week recuperative and follow-up period. Look at three persons:

1.    A ten-year-old child injured in the early summer.

2.    A college student injured in February, who cannot write because of the cast, and who thus loses an entire semester from college, and tuition of $2,000.

3.    A steelworker, earning $1,500 per month, who loses ten weeks of work amounting to $3,750.

In each instance the medical expenses amount to $150.

Each of these cases has a substantially different value: the child, $2,000; the college student, $5,000; and the steelworker, $7,500.

Now look at the liability:

1.    The child was injured when it "darted out" onto a roadway.

2.  The college student was injured in a rear-end collision.

3.  The steelworker was injured in an intersection collision.

This changes the picture dramatically:

1.  You may have to settle the child's case for $750.

2.  The college student should get $5,000 in a settlement.

3.  The steelworker's case will probably go to trial unless you would consider a low settlement of about $4,000. (If you would, your client probably would not.)

But we're not through. The insurance company has a few ideas:

1.  It sympathizes with the child, but won't pay more than nuisance value.

2.  It can prove the college student had a record of absenteeism in the fall semester, failed two courses, and was on the verge of dropping out in that spring semester.

3.  The steelworker, at an annual physical examination during his recuperative period, was approved for work by the mill doctor eight weeks after the accident, but his family doctor felt, as a matter of caution, that he ought to stay off work two more weeks.

In looking over these cases, it would appear that you must settle the child's case. The contributory negligence is so clear that there is no point in trying it.

The college student poses a good test of your settlement ability. It should settle despite the insurance company's argument, because in point of fact that young person was in college, had begun the second semester and for the short time involved was performing satisfactorily. Hold fast to your demand. To show good faith you might give up a few dollars, but there is no point in going below $4,500. This is a time to argue strenuously, pointing out the clear facts of liability, the unquestionable injury, the definite bills and losses. Nothing but the unique stubborness of an adjuster or supervisor will avoid settlement of this case. This is one of those cases in which all he can do is to "chip away" at your figure until you insist that you can go no further.

The steelworker's case is one in which you have to look at other facts to see if it will settle for a good figure. It might. Much will depend on the depositions of the parties, the manner of their appearance and the conviction with which they speak. What do the photographs show about the point of impact of the cars? Are there any witnesses to support one side or the other? Is there any physical evidence at the scene which helps to locate, at the intersection, where the impact took place? Based on these factors, you may have a very good case that the insurance company will want to settle, but you are going to have to argue at great length about each one of these matters. This is where time, effort and patience are involved. If you stay with it, you may be able to destroy the defenses, one by one, until the insurance company has to concede it is liable.

Then there is the matter of the lost time. Based on the testimony of the mill doctor, you have eight weeks lost time; the family doctor's opinion is ten weeks. If settlement ultimately depends on this issue, the time has come for you to give a little to get a little. Reduce your demand to take into consideration that a jury may believe the mill doctor or that the family doctor may waver a little in justifying his opinion. By adjusting your demand and continuing to argue you may well be able to settle that case for $6,500 to $7,000, which would be acceptable.

As you can see there are many significant matters that enter into the settlement process. Your job is to recognize the vital factors, analyze them and then bargain with the insurance company with a willingness to push hard on the basis of your strengths and to be flexible in your demand because of your weaknesses.

### Work on a Settlement Range

Despite the fact that I have frequently used single figures in my discussions in this chapter, this was done solely as a matter of convenience.

There is no one settlement figure for any case and it is a mistake to get into your head the idea that "only" $17,000 will settle one case or $42,000 another. Instead of dealing in impractical specifics, try to determine a range that will satisfy you and your client. In that way you are not going to get involved in a lot of needless arguments with your client or unnecessary worries yourself. It is amazing how tenaciously clients will cling to a specific figure if you present one to them. If you tell them that a case is worth $13,500, they will promptly and casually reject an offer of $12,750. Give them a range of $11,000 to $14,000, however, and show them that it is a valid settlement area, and they will happily accept $12,750.

You also begin to deceive yourself when you talk about a single figure. It tends to become a fixation and if you are an obdurate type of person, you become wedded to that figure. Its precision leaves you no room for flexibility in dealing with the other side, and instead of negotiating you find yourself issuing ultimatums and then becoming offended when the claims man says "No."

On the other hand, if you work with a settlement range, you know that your demand is negotiable and you can proceed to argue your case with more freedom than you would otherwise have. Submit your demand of $15,000, having in mind that you will accept $12,000, and possibly you can get the case settled for $14,000. But you know in advance that you are not going to turn down $12,250. This makes the settlement discussion much easier for all concerned and leads to a successful conclusion of the case at that time.

The lurking danger that you must beware of is the tendency to aim for the lower figure. You must avoid that. If you have decided on a settlement range, try to look on the high figure as the one you really want and the lower figure as something you accept with reluctance. Remember that there is no rush and that you do not have to keep decreasing your demand to the lowest acceptable level. Keep negotiating in the higher portion of the settlement range and reserve to the very last moment your acceptance of the lesser amount.

In this matter, as in so many others, the question arises whether you have the intellectual stamina to stand by a high demand and force the other side upward rather than allow them to force you down to your lowest figure. If the latter occurs, the frequent cause is that at some point you have allowed yourself to become tired of the negotiations and abruptly agreed to the low figure just to get the case closed. This represents a poor attitude, an acknowledgment of failure to a certain degree, and if you do it persistently the insurance companies will begin to take advantage of you. In addition, your partners or associates might become a little unhappy. I do not mention the client in this context because I assume he had previously agreed to the lesser amount.

### Have a Clear Idea of What You Are After

At first glance this is a trite statement. Unfortunately, too many lawyers do not have a clear and definite goal in settlement negotiations. Even after they have gone through the various steps that I have outlined they will still come up with a vague idea of settlement value. There is no need for this and it is a reflection on the ability of the attorney to make up his mind. After you have carefully analyzed your case and have arrived at a settlement range, you have to believe firmly that the figures do represent a justifiable, reasonable compromise area and that you are going to settle this case in that area. With this attitude you can go to the insurance company with a firm attitude and either get the case settled or prepare for trial. You have defeated your purpose if you decide on a range of $12,000-$15,000, submit a demand of $15,000, come down to $12,500, and settle for $10,000. Such a settlement makes the whole procedure an exercise in futility. Anyone can do as well. Your demand should have been $18,000, you should have reduced it to $16,500 after lengthy discussion, and you might be able to settle it for $14,750.

You must have a clear concept of the settlement goal and set out to achieve it with determination.

# CHAPTER 17

# Expediting the Negotiations

## KNOW THE INSURANCE COMPANY

Every insurance company has a personality of its own and the differences can be dramatic. In my area two of the largest national companies have diametrically opposite policies toward settlement—the one believes in moving its cases by settling them fairly and quickly; the other adamantly refuses any kind of a reasonable settlement until the very last minute—usually after the jury is selected and maybe even after the first day or two of trial. Yet both are obviously successful and apparently profitable. It is beyond my knowledge, and the scope of this book, as to why this is so. For settlement purposes we must accept the fact that the attitudes are real and you have to know of them and adapt yourself to them.

The companies in your area will each have a different approach to settlement and it is your job to know these companies and to know what their policies are. Sometimes they will want to settle one type of case but try another. They may have a "hang-up" about motorcycle cases for example, but are more than willing to talk in automobile cases. Many will seem quite affable about settling a "homeowners" case where the mailman falls on your sidewalk or your dog bites a neighbor, but will not settle a medical malpractice case. There are only three ways to learn these peculiarities of the individual company:

1. You can have enough cases so that merely by experience you learn the companies who will or will not settle and the kinds of

cases that are most likely to settle. Most of us don't have the large number of cases to learn this way.

2. You can mix and mingle with the claims personnel as much as possible, becoming friends or good acquaintances of theirs, and in normal conversation pick up the details of the manner in which their company functions. This is a grand way to learn since these men are always good company, but I have found that the senior men are reluctant to associate too closely with plaintiffs' attorneys for obvious reasons.

3. You can bring up the subject as often as possible whenever you gather with other plaintiffs' attorneys and gain the advantage of their experience. This is probably the most practical way of learning since you will normally socialize with these men and, between and among you, you will have handled enough cases of different kinds that you can learn the pattern of the insurance companies in your area.

It matters little what means you use to learn about the attitudes of the companies in your community; the important fact is that you must know them.

## COMPANY POLICY REGARDING SETTLEMENT

Every company has a settlement policy but it is a general thing which, I sometimes think, reflects the attitude of the personnel more than a written directive in a manual. For example, I'm sure that no company has a written rule to the effect that substantial settlements are to be discouraged prior to trial. At the same time the senior officers of the company may have this attitude and it becomes then a matter of company policy. Certainly the amount of monetary authority given to the claims adjuster, supervisor or manager is a matter of written policy and if that authority is relatively small, so that most matters have to be referred to the Home Office and thus to a person who has little direct contact with the case and the people who are involved in it, then settlements will be inhibited.

In like manner, if a company, as a matter of policy, tried to affix a value nationally or on a regional basis for all similar cases, settlement is going to be effectively blocked because case evaluation is too local a matter to be governed by activities in another city some distance away. No lawyer in New York or California where verdicts (and therefore settlements) are very high would want to be subject to settlements made in Pennsylvania where the verdicts are much lower.

Another illustration of company policy which is a direct blow to settlement negotiations is either the application of a formula to arrive at a settlement figure or the use of a committee system to evaluate cases. There is a company locally which used such a complicated formula that I simply had to laugh as the insurance adjuster tried to fit together and assign values to the number of hospital days, days lost from work, days required to be at rest at home, and so many other factors that he soon became hopelessly enmeshed and entangled in his calculations. When he finished his complicated arithmetic he had finally arrived at a figure that was completely unrealistic and the case did not settle.

The committee system is just as bad. In this instance a committee meets, reviews a large number of files, assigns a value to them, and every one who deals with a particular case is limited to this value. Occasionally a small variation of 10 percent or so is permitted. There is no flexibility allowed for negotiations. Should plaintiff's counsel submit a new demand the matter has to be referred back to the committee and frequently they will not consider it unless some new facts have also been developed. This is cumbersome, dogmatic and unrealistic. It cannot do other than hinder effective settlement negotiations. Apparently the companies involved don't care. At trial time, however, they do abandon this system and permit the defense attorney, or their adjuster at the scene, to engage in direct negotiations with plaintiff's counsel.

## THE ATTITUDE OF THE LOCAL CLAIMS MANAGER

I once asked an experienced defense attorney which was more important in terms of settlement—company policy or the attitude of the local claims manager. Without hesitation he cited the latter as having the greatest influence, provided the company allowed the claims manager some discretion. A claims manager in a substantial city is a man of great responsibility who supervises a large case-load, many employees, and usually a good-sized physical plant. He has the opportunity to set the tone of his office, especially if his personal authority to settle cases is high. He will play a very active role in the operation of his office, supervising the adjusters, keeping track of the cases at trial or coming to trial, selecting the defense attorneys and getting to know the plaintiffs' attorneys and the judges. If he is a believer in reasonable settlements, the cases will move; if he is reluctant to spend money whether because of a lack of self-confidence, inexperience, or his firm belief in the "wait to the last minute" approach then you can forget about settlement with his company.

I saw this happen recently in a company which specializes in medical insurance. Hitherto, the cases could be settled after a lot of hard work and argument. Recently a new claims manager entered the picture and all settlement negotiations have collapsed. There is not even any conversation anymore. When this happens a very heavy burden is placed on the plaintiff's attorney. He has been given a direct challenge—you will either take these cases to trial, consistently win them, and thus force the company to reappraise its attitude or you will never settle with them except on their terms.

The power of the local claims manager is aptly illustrated when you meet with plaintiffs' attorneys from different cities. Just ask them whether a particular company is as hard to deal with as you find it to be. How often do you get a response that this is not true in their area, but that it is another company which gives them trouble—one which, surprisingly, you have no difficulty with at all. The answer to the paradox has to be that the companies allow their claims managers great discretion and that what we are seeing is the reflection of the personal attitude of the individual claims managers.

It is of the utmost importance, therefore, that you get to know your local claims manager as well as possible. Naturally, he is not going to get involved in very small lawsuits or claims, but when your case assumes a value of $12,000—$15,000 and above, you enter his immediate sphere of influence. This is a good opportunity to find out what kind of a man he is. Aside from that, you must be observant, and even when working on the small cases, try to pick up some clues as to the kind of office he runs. Your knowledge of these facts will go a long way in helping you to decide whether your case can be settled and how to handle the negotiations.

## SEASONAL FLUCTUATIONS IN POLICY

Strange as it may sound the time of the year can affect settlement possibilities. How often near the end of the year, in November and early December, I have received calls from insurance people asking me if I would like to settle some cases. Apparently there is a good deal of pressure to "clear the books" before the New Year begins. I have found that this factor alone can vary settlement value by as much as 10 percent—25 percent.

Another curiosity is the pressure that comes before vacation time, usually early June. The reason is essentially the same—to try to get some cases moving before everyone leaves for vacations. Certainly July and August rival December as the worst months for settlement. You simply can't find anyone to talk to. The adjuster is gone and the supervisor hates to get involved, or the adjuster is willing to recommend your figure to the claims manager but that fine person is on vacation. If by some chance you find them all at work then it turns out that they want to talk to the defense attorney and he is not available.

As far as December is concerned, between Christmas parties (in and out of the office), hangovers, and holiday shopping, you might as well forget about settlement between December 15 and January 2. It is hard to realize that the time of year has such an effect on these things but it certainly is true.

## OTHER FACTORS AFFECTING SETTLEMENT

The volume of business, the state of the stock market, the profit and loss picture, changes in personnel, to name a few, are some of the factors which affect the possibility of your settling a case. I have had insurance people tell me straight out that the company was temporarily in a financial bind and that there would be no settlements. On another occasion I had a claims manager tell me that there was no change in his position, that I was to proceed with the lawsuit, but to check back in a few months because "by then we may have a back-log built up and we may get orders to start moving cases." These are things over which you have absolutely no control, but they affect your work.

Other factors that will upset things would be a fight in your state legislature over a change in the law (no-fault automobile insurance, a proposal to change strict contributory negligence to comparative negligence), or a strike by doctors over their insurance rates. These events will either cause the companies to come running to your door or will cause them to back away when it comes to settlement. Bear these factors in mind when you begin to think about the subject.

### Limitations on Authority

You have to realize that everyone you speak with in a claims department has a limit placed by the company on the amount he can spend to settle a claim. For the average insurance adjuster the limit seems to vary between $500.00 and $1,500.00; the supervisor usually has authority to about $5,000.00, and the claims manager normally can settle a case in an area between $10,000 to $25,000. The variation is due to the differing arbitrary limits set by the individual companies. The significance of this fact for you is that there is hardly any point in talking to an adjuster if your case has a reasonable value of $5,000. He will be simply a pipeline—a messenger boy—in such instances. You might just as well find out who the supervisor is and deal directly with him. He will be making the decisions anyway.

In like manner if your case has a value of $35,000, recognize the fact that while the word of the claims manager will have great influence, the ultimate decisions in your case will be made by the Home Office.

Recognition of these facts will help you to decide with whom you should speak so that you do not waste time trying to convince a man who simply cannot help you.

### The Insurance Adjuster or Supervisor— The Man in Between

I certainly sympathize with the average insurance adjuster or supervisor. They are truly overworked and underpaid. At the same time they are caught in a vise in which they are subject, constantly, to criticism from you (and sometimes the courts) for offering too little, and, on the other hand, the very real threat of displeasure and sanctions from their company for paying too much. No wonder they are "gun-shy" about paying out money and will do anything to pass the responsibility on to someone else.

You can tell pretty quickly whether the man you are dealing with is willing to exercise whatever authority he has to settle your case. When he becomes inflexible, when he engages in "nit-picking" to justify his refusal to adjust his offer, and when he squarely refuses to face the reality of the incontrovertible facts, then it is time for you to stop. There is no point in dealing with this person any longer. [At this stage your options narrow down to a demand to speak to his superior (which is always a good idea), an acceptance of the offer (which is probably foolish) or a continuation of the lawsuit].

A confident, experienced claims man will treat settlement negotiations as just what they are—a matter of give and take, a lively discussion of the issues, a good knowledge of the statements of the witnesses, and some knowledge of the treating or examining doctors. He is also reasonable and eminently practical. If you adopt the same attitude, and have the same knowledge and the same strong feelings, your case will settle.

A phenomenon of recent days is the appearance on the scene of the female adjuster. Hitherto it has been pretty much a man's world. My recent contact with such persons has been universally poor—not only are they even more inflexible than a man but the discussions degenerate into arguments and they tend to become quite personally involved. At the moment I attribute this to inexperience and an overwhelming desire to establish a good record. It remains to be seen whether experience will develop that degree of self-confidence which will lead to a more flexible approach in negotiations and, inevitably, to more settlements.

A matter to be scrupulously avoided is the insertion of personalitites and emotions into the negotiations. It is foolish to get angry because a claims man will not pay you what you want; it is unforgivable to take it out on him personally. The man has the job of paying as little as possible commensurate with the facts of the case and he has a right to analyze those facts differently from you. Just as you and your client have a right to file a lawsuit so do he and his company have a right to take the case to a jury rather than pay you the settlement figure that you demand. You have to get along with defense attorneys with whom you engage in very spirited contest in the courtroom; just so, and to the same extent, you have to get along with claims people with whom you engage in argument in your office or on the phone. And don't forget one vital difference—you may have no one to answer to; .the adjuster always has a superior or that lurking menace—the Home Office—looking over his shoulder.

## FEED THEM THE DATA—ALL OF IT

It has always struck me as the height of absurdity to hear an attorney brag about the fact that he refused to give an insurance company copies of his bills, a list of his specials, or a doctor's report. By what strange reasoning does he think that they are literally going to buy a "pig in a poke"? Insurance companies are willing to pay, but only when they have the facts. Why should they take your word as to the amount of the wage loss? They want proof not words.

Send them what they need, whether it be a statement from the employer as to the amount of time your plaintiff has lost, his earnings, and the total loss in dollars, or a tax return or a letter from the doctor discussing the injuries. If the claims man has doubts about pain and suffering, pull the nurses' notes from the hospital records, which state the fact that your client was crying with pain, and mail them off. If they want a written projection from an economist concerning the potential increase in your client's earnings had he been able to work, get it for them. What is the purpose of hiding anything? You want to settle this case and you cannot do it if the company lacks essential data. In any event, if your court has an effective pretrial system, they are going to get the information at that time.

I grant that, on occasion, the demands of the insurance company seem insatiable, but if they feel that the data is necessary before they will settle the case what is the point in your arguing? They control the purse strings and if they are not satisfied with the information you give them, they can simply close the purse and bid you adieu until the time of trial. There is no point in hiding necessary information from the company with whom you are dealing. They need the facts to evaluate the case; if you have those facts give them to the company.

## CONVINCE THE COMPANY—WRITE A BRIEF

It isn't often that you are going to have a case which is so novel that the insurance personnel have not had experience with it, but it does happen from time to time. When it does, when the problems are peculiar or the law rarely utilized, write a brief for the company explaining why they are liable. You are safe in assuming that the claims people are too busy and too harassed to give detailed attention to the intricacies of your case— especially if, in monetary value, it is an ordinary lawsuit. (They will mark it for special attention if its potential value begins to run to $50,000, $100,000 or above.)

Where your case rests on an exception to the Hearsay Rule, an aberration of the Dead Man's Rule or a Guest Statute, or involves some little used Federal statute, you might as well explain it to them in writing or they simply won't know what you are talking about and will set up a minimal reserve. It doesn't do any good to expect the defense attorney to advise them because they may take their time in asking for his opinion, and, if it is an unusual problem, he won't know the answer quickly and may take more time doing the very research which you have already completed. Since you know your position and your theory well, since you have done the research and know that you are correct, then go ahead and write a brief or memorandum to the company so that they can learn that your position is correct, that they are liable, and should pay. Understanding is essential to all human relationships and yours, vis-a-vis the claims man, is no exception. If you can convince the company in this easy manner, you will have gone a long way toward effecting a settlement.

## BE FRANK AND DEFINITE—THIS IS
## NO TIME FOR IDLE TALK

In the normal course of negotiations there are going to be many, many minutes, sometimes hours, of serious talk. At times it will seem to go on forever. Therefore, this is no time to engage in idle, haphazard statements about the facts. The process becomes interminable and almost hopeless unless you are both frank and definite about your position with regard to the facts and the law. You might convince an adjuster or supervisor to pay more money than he really wants to, but you are not going to be able to bluster your way to that goal. The chances are that due to his high volume of cases, in comparison to yours, he has been through this process much more often than you have, and he will be quick to recognize any phony attempts on your part to change the facts—to underplay the bad and overplay the good. This approach is fatuous from the beginning.

You have the same rights in this matter as does the claims man. When he begins to tell you stories about the testimony of witnesses, challenge him immediately and offer to exchange his statement of the witness for your statement. If he begs off for some reason (company policy, the statement is on a tape which is unavailable, or the handwriting is undecipherable except to the writer who's on vacation), you know that he is kidding you and you can tell him so. If he has dreamed up some anomaly at the scene of the accident, offer to send him your photographs so that he can see for himself that his belief isn't true. Force him to be candid with you by challenging his statements and daring him to submit proof of his contentions or to accept your proof that he is wrong. If the man is honest, he will (reluctantly) come around to your way of thinking; if he is not honest, stop dealing with him.

## ALWAYS START HIGH—IT'S EXPECTED

Settlement negotiations are like the proverbial horse trading—the defendants will never believe that your first demand is serious and will never make a firm first offer. You can complain about this system all you want—in all of my years of practice it has never changed. In fact, as I have learned from older lawyers, in the years of practice of men who have gone before me it has not changed and I see no sign that it is changing now. It's simply in the category of "Games People Play" and, I believe, a matter of human nature. In this instance don't even try to be "fair" because no one will believe you, and "fairness" has nothing to do with the matter. Rather than thinking in terms of that word it would be better to use the word "reasonable." The insurance company expects a high demand from you so give it to them. Be sure, however, to avoid the absurd. Your job is to arrive at, and present, a figure that is what I will call the "high side of reasonableness." A local judge of our Federal Court will be remembered for beginning every settlement conference by turning to Plaintiff's Counsel and asking

1.  What is your demand?
     (And after he secured a figure)

2.  What will you settle for?
     (And thereafter)

3.  Now, what do you really want?

Invariably he got three separate figures.

The insurance people do the same thing. They will huff and puff that $7,500 is their top offer when you and they really know that the case will settle for about $11,000. In fact it has reached the stage where I can tell from the first offer whether there is any serious intent on the part of the insurance company to settle the case, and I suppose they can tell almost the same thing from my demand.

Many lawyers don't like this part of settlement negotiations. They feel that it is below their dignity and that it partakes of the aspect of haggling in an Oriental bazaar. I sympathize with them, but until they find a way to change the system we have to work this way. Call it "negotiations," "bargaining," "give and take," whatever you will, this is the way—and the only way—that cases are settled.

## BE FLEXIBLE

Once you accept the fact that settlement is a negotiation process, you can appreciate this admonition to be flexible. Granted that at some point you are going to have to say "thus far and no further," still that point is at the end of the bargaining, not at the beginning. Since you began with a demand that was deliberately high, you must be willing to adjust that demand downward to reflect your acceptance of some of the arguments of the other side. In this connection I suggest that you make haste slowly. There is no need to reduce your demand near to your final figure in the early stages of negotiations. Make the claims man aware of the strong facts that lie in your favor and point out to him that while your original demand may be a little high, and you are willing to reduce it, you certainly can see no justification for reducing it by more than a small amount. If your case really is as strong as you would have him believe, he will become aware of it quickly and his problem will be whether he can get you to go any lower, and if so, how much lower. In other words about all that he can do is to chip away at your figure and you can accommodate him by reducing it in small amounts until he realizes that you have gone as far as you intend to go. At that point the case should settle.

On the other hand if your case is a poor one or one that will be bitterly contested, then you may have to adopt a different approach. In the initial phases of the negotiations you will, as usual, move in small degrees from your original demand. As the argument proceeds it may become apparent that you will have to make a substantial adjustment in your demand. If you sense that such an adjustment will lead to a settlement, and if you want to settle the case, then have no hesitancy in sharply reducing the demand. This signals to the insurance adjuster the two facts that you recognize the serious problems you face and that you genuinely want to settle the case. The burden shifts to him. If he wants a settlement, he may have to pay a little more than he wants to, but if he forces you to trial, the potential verdict, if all goes well for you, may be greatly in excess of your present demand. It's a real dilemma for him. The key to placing him in this position is your flexibility in being willing to adjust your demand to the realities of the case.

## KEEP THE NEGOTIATIONS MOVING

It would be a small-scale miracle if you could settle a case on one phone call or at one meeting. Things just don't work that way. While you may have complete authority from your client, the man you're dealing with rarely has that power. He always has to talk to someone else. This causes delays. In addition he may be working on so many cases that when he hangs up the phone, or leaves your office, your case is temporarily shelved. The burden of keeping the negotiations moving is on you. If ten days or two weeks have passed with no response from your adjuster, it's time to get on the phone and prod him for a response to your last conversation. More times than not he has sent the file to a supervisor or the claims manager and simply hasn't heard from them. Your call will force him to get in touch with them and get a response. Then there will be additional phone calls, more arguments and, perhaps, another referral to his superiors. This takes time. Keep after the man. Don't let him forget your case or procrastinate too long in giving you an answer. Some claims people will dodge the responsibility of a firm commitment for a long time if you let them. It is only because of your courteous but constant pressure that a decision will be made.

## THE CONTRIBUTION OF THE DEFENSE ATTORNEY

If the case is in suit and a defense attorney is involved, don't hesitate to use him to help you get a settlement. Sometimes as a matter of policy he will not get involved, but when you know that he is being consulted then try to confer with him. Insurance people often get a mental block because of a misunderstanding or misapplication of legal principles. They do know a great deal about tort law, but they are not lawyers. When the insurance agent simply cannot accept the validity of your theory of liability, use the defense attorney to convince him. That man has an interest in doing so since he is going to have to meet you in court and if your theory is sound, there is no point in his trying the case just because the claims man misunderstands the law. Many times he will be willing to talk to the insurance personnel after you have explained what you are about.

Another area in which he can be of help is the instance in which the insurance company has grossly undervalued your claim. This sometimes happens when an inexperienced person is handling the case or when the Home Office—out of touch with the realities of the local situation—has set too low a figure on the case. At your request, the defense attorney may talk to them to make them realize that they are not dealing realistically with your case.

Your utilization of a defense attorney is useful only when you are dealing with a confident, skilled lawyer who has a close rapport with his company. If the attorney is unsure of himself, he will not want to get involved; if he is not completely trusted and respected by his company, his suggestions will be ignored. As a result there is no point in trying to secure the help of opposing counsel unless you are sure that he can be of help. That, in turn, depends on your knowledge of, and close association with, the defense attorneys in your area.

## FORCE THEM TO GIVE YOU A FIGURE— AND TO JUSTIFY IT

There is nothing more wearying than constant argument over values that bear no relation to reality. There is no point in even talking with an adjuster who refuses to look at the facts of your case. If you honestly appraise the case as having a value of approximately $12,500 and the adjuster makes an offer of $1,000, it is obvious that one of you is very much in error. If you re-examine your case and are satisfied of the correctness of your position, then it is appropriate to sharply challenge the adjuster. Demand that he justify his figure. As you listen to him it will become obvious that he either does not know the case, or is simply and deliberately ignoring some essential aspect of it, thereby wasting his time and yours. In the latter instance either close the file and set it aside for trial or go over his head and deal with his superiors. If his problem is simply one of ignorance, then you can at least try to educate him on the provable facts of the case.

I find that ignorance, misunderstanding, and a refusal to accept the facts as they are constitute the principal obstacles to settlement. Until you force the claims man to justify his position you will not know in what areas he may be in error. When you do learn the basis for his offer, then you are in a position to correct his misconception. This is a far better process than merely arguing over figures.

Speaking of amounts, one approach of the experienced adjuster is to avoid making an offer, while constantly arguing about your demand. If he is successful, you will find that you have come down and down and that never once has he committed himself to a definite offer. I have seen this happen and I have to congratulate the claims people who have done it with such skill. Don't fall into this trap. Soon after the negotiations are under way you should demand a firm offer which you can use as a basis—a foundation—for further negotiations. If settlement is a two-way street, make certain that the other man is moving up that street as you move down, and that he is not parked at the farther end waiting for you to move to him.

## GET HELP FROM THE COURT

A judge is a great help in settlement negotiations. He can be objective and he can cut through the rhetoric. His objectivity permits him to appreciate quickly where one party or the other has refused to face the realities of the situation, and when there have been too many offers and demands, he can promptly arrive at a figure that represents a reasonable compromise. So often the negotiations have proceeded to the point that the parties get mired down in nothing but talk. The presence of the judge as a third party, and having the benefit of his suggestions, makes each side realize that a settlement is within reach if they will only stop talking and move. The judge can see through personality conflicts that may have arisen, matters of pride or just plain stubbornness.

The problem is how to get the judge involved. He certainly will not get involved unless a case is at suit. At the other extreme it is his duty to discuss settlement at the time of a Pretrial or immediately before testimony begins at trial. In between these stages it becomes a matter of your knowing your Court and taking the initiative to get the judge into the negotiations. This can sometimes be accomplished by agreement of counsel or by your asking for a special Pretrial or a Conciliation Hearing, advising the Court that settlement negotiations have been going on and that settlement is reasonably close, but that the parties are stymied by one or two particular problems. Your motion may get a favorable response if there are numerous parties involved or if the judge believes that a meeting in his presence will readily effect a settlement.

Judges are very anxious to move cases along, especially where there are numerous parties, to avoid a lengthy trial. This is a tactic that should be used more often. It requires, however, that all preliminary negotiations will have been concluded, that the parties understand their case well, that all pertinent data have already been secured and interchanged, and that all that is left is for some neutral party to take a look at the facts, at the current position of the parties, and suggest a resolution of the dilemma.

A good example of the efficacy of this procedure is where the parties agree that a case has a particular value if the plaintiff can get his case to the jury—i.e., avoid a non-suit. It's a great help to appear before a judge, explain the problem, perhaps do some quick research in his chambers, and then let him tell the insurance adjuster and defense attorney that he would have to let the case go to the jury. With this opinion before them, and if the defense people can call their superiors from chambers and explain it, the case stands a good chance of settling right then and there.

By all means, use the Court in your negotiations if you can find some practical way to get a judge involved.

## THE "HOME OFFICE" PROBLEM

If you have any kind of a substantial case, then sooner or later you will begin to hear references to the "Home Office." A more insubstantial, unknowing and unknowable entity never existed. Like a mirage it is real enough, but forever unreachable. If you want a pleasant evening, gather around some defense attorneys and claims managers as they regale one another with stories—sometimes bitter, always sardonic—about the Home Office. You will learn that that organization demands the right to make the decisions, never makes right ones, and never takes the responsibility for the wrong ones.

Aside from the amusing aspects of the situation, the Home Office does exist and does get involved in the bigger cases. You will rarely, if ever, have direct contact with the nameless beings in Chicago, New York, Hartford or Fort Wayne who make the final decisions in your case. They rely on the contents of their file and the recommendations of the claims manager and defense attorney. The struggle that sometimes develops is the classic one of the differing attitudes of the men on the scene and their distant superiors. There is no practical way you can deal with these men. They will demand, through the local people, that you submit documentation of your claim and possibly a letter outlining your theory of liability, but they are not interested in any verbal expression of your position nor any argument. The best that you can do will be to present your views to the defense attorney or the claims manager and hope that he adequately conveys them to his superior.

When you get before a judge, however, the situation can change if he is the least bit aggressive. As the possibilities of settlement grow more likely, and it appears that the approval of the Home Office is needed to increase the offer, many judges will require the defense attorney to call that office from his chambers (absent the presence of Plaintiff's counsel) and get an immediate answer. This occurs often enough in my area that it could be called a matter of routine. It is very effective. I have known of instances in which a judge has participated in the conversation explaining why the case has been undervalued and what change must be made to achieve a settlement. If your judges are not prone to do this sort of thing, you should try to encourage them. When the average judge is induced to try it, and realizes the effect of his presence or his words, he will become inclined to use this device more often—to your great advantage.

Beyond that there isn't much you can do. The Home Office is simply beyond your reach. If you have given them all of the material that they have asked for, if you have written, or verbally apprised them of your position via the claims manager, and they still refuse to make a reasonable offer, you have no alternative but to prepare for trial.

It is appropriate to mention one important difference in dealing with the Home Office rather than the local claims personnel—that is, in the offers made during trial. If the Home Office has been making the decisions, you may find an abrupt and substantial increase in their offer during trial. This will be the result of the fact that your witnesses have done better than they expected and your case has gone in more smoothly than they anticipated. Then they will change their offer very quickly. That doesn't happen very often when you deal with a local claims manager or supervisor. He knows you, your case, the judge and the jurors too well to be surprised. The file is not a mass of papers to him—it assumes "flesh and blood" proportions. His offer will be based on certain intangibles that aren't in the file. As a result he will not have any need to increase the offer very markedly during the trial.

## CONCLUDING THE SETTLEMENT

After the figure has been agreed upon, there remain only administrative details to consummate the settlement. A release will be prepared and submitted to you for your client's signature. I suggest you read it carefully. Occasionally you will find the release inaccurate in that you are releasing more than you intended (as in a Joint Tortfeasor's Release, for example), or there is a poorly drafted "hold harmless" clause, or the release would be broad enough to release parties in another claim occurring after the instant accident but before this settlement.

Beware of the archaic release (which is still sometimes in use) that releases the defendants and "any and all other persons, companies, corporations, entities, and things whatsoever from any claim existing from the Beginning Of The World to the date of these presents." That's rather all-encompassing and while at first glance, and considering the intent of the parties, it should not bar a later claim against different defendants, nonetheless if your client signs it, don't be surprised at the other defense attorney trying to take advantage of it. At the least, you may have a Motion and Argument on your hands, when a simple caution at the time you read the release would have avoided it.

# Index

# INDEX

## J